Survey of Contents

THIS CONTRIBUTION HAS BEEN FINANCIALLY SPONSORED
BY THE STIFTUNG VOLKSWAGENWERK IN HANNOVER (GERMANY)

Chapter 6

CREATION OF RELATIONSHIPS OF KINSHIP

Harry D. Krause

I. INTRODUCTION*

1. Kinship relations are the basic glue that holds society together. The same facts – nature, instinct and *faits accomplis* – underlie kinship relations everywhere. What a seemingly ideal subject for legal comparison! And so it would be if *Rudolf von Ihering*'s view to the effect that "law is the sum of the conditions of social life in the widest sense of the term, as secured by the power of the state through means of external compulsion" were true in the kinship context.[1] Unfortunately, too much law describes kinship relations inaccurately, for several reasons. In some instances, alien legal systems were superimposed on indigenous cultures, sometimes by voluntary reception, more often by conquest. In many cases, ancient postulates remain law although they have been rendered obsolete by passage of time and social change. In still other cases, cultural revolutions, whether Christian, French, or communist, have sought to remodel life by imposing a deliberately inaccurate, idealistic conception of what kinship behavior ought to be. In short, much of the law of kinship relations is but a dull mirror of social reality.

A. HISTORICAL FACTORS

2. *General.* – Since time immemorial, blood ties have been the principal determinant of kinship and resulting legal rights. Human sophistication, in response to more or less clearly perceived needs of different societies, complicated the matter early. Tests of "legitimacy" were superimposed on the test of blood relationships and different legal relationship were prescribed for blood relatives within and without the compass of the legitimacy test. At least in part, this was the result of the natural truth expressed in the adage that "maternity is a matter of fact, whereas paternity is a matter of opinion". However, differentiation between legitimate and irregular offspring has also been based on the social preference – often expressed in religious terms – for permanent man-woman relationships over temporary liaisons. Both factors have tended toward classification of children on the basis of whether or not they were born to parents who complied with prevailing social and legal norms applicable to sexual unions.

Based on these considerations and on society's wish to assure that children would be born within institutional structures capable of raising them – stable families – a preference for the child of legitimate birth may be found in early law[2] and most cultures.[3] Organized religions have reinforced these attitudes on a spiritual level. The Christian church, for example, insisted on monogamy as the "only form of marriage under cover of which blameless intercourse could be had, with the consequence that all progeny not so begotten were deemed unlawful."[4] "Sins of the flesh" were discouraged, and illegitimates came to be viewed as sin turned into flesh – *irregulares ex defectu.* With flawless logic, this led to classifica-

* During the long period of gestation of this paper, many research assistants and informants have contributed their time and work. Only a few can be mentioned here. Special thanks are due *Nancy* and *Robert Carter, Jürgen Frisinger, Rainer Frank, Robert Hallock, Jochen Meinecke, Hubert Steinkemper, Jean Massé, Arlette Mayer-Pareyn, Ole Waerenskjold, Ulrich Magnus* and *Dieter Martiny.* Without the excellent and patient work of *Jean Samet,* my secretary, this paper could not have been done. For the generous hospitality and help they extended at their institutions, appreciation goes to Lic. *Hector Fix Zamudio,* Director of the Instituto de Investigaciones Jurídicas at the National University of Mexico, Lic. *Elsa Bieler* and their colleagues, as well as to Professor *Crisolito Pasqual,* Director, University of the Philippines Law Center, and his colleagues, and The Honorable *Corazón J. Agrava,* Presiding Judge, Juvenile and Domestic Relations Court, Manila. Acknowledgment also must be made of the untiring effort of Professor *Ulrich Drobnig* in the final stages of manuscript preparation. Finally, I am most grateful to my friend *Max Rheinstein,* the Editor-in-Chief of this volume when this paper was written, for his continuing encouragement and for his many constructive and knowledgeable suggestions, and to my wife, for her patience and good humor.

1 *von Ihering,* Der Zweck im Recht I (ed. 6-8 Leipzig 1923) 399.

2 See *H. J. Wolff,* The Background of the Postclassical Legislation on Illegitimacy: 3 Seminar 21-45, 22 (1945); *Ayer,* Legitimacy and Marriage: 16 Harv.L. Rev. 22 (1902).

3 See *Goode,* Illegitimacy in the Caribbean Social Structure: *Roberts,* The Unwed Mother (New York 1966) 42-60.

4 *Hooper* 3; *Friedmann,* Law in a Changing Society (ed. 1 New York 1959) 251. Biblical aversion to the bastard antedates the Christian church: "A bastard shall not enter into the congregation of the Lord; even to his tenth generation shall he not enter into the congregation of the Lord" (Deuteronomy 23.2).

tions that distinguished between illegitimates on the basis of the degree of sinfulness of their parents' misconduct. For example, children born in "concubinage" (a stable, semi-approved union giving rise to some legal consequences) came to be preferred over offspring of casual unions. The latter, in turn, were better off than "adulterous" or "incestuous bastards".[5] An unfortunate variant adopted by AMERICAN law was the "miscegenous bastard".[6]

Most systems now have abandoned discrimination among subclasses of illegitimates. The latest to give up the distinction was FRANCE in 1972. Until then, FRANCE had continued substantial preferences for the "natural child" (whose parents could have married) and disadvantages for the incestuous or adulterous child (whose parents could not have married). FRANCE's change of heart, however, could not affect the many systems to which FRANCE had given her law and some of which continue these discriminations to this day.

3. *Medieval Europe.* – However widely spread, discrimination against the illegitimate did not take the same form at all places and all times. ROMAN law which had come to recognize the child's relation to his mother, although denying a relationship with the father[7] contrasts sharply with attitudes held in CENTRAL EUROPE during the Middle Ages.[8] There and then, the bastard in many places had scant, if any legal relationship to either parent, was barred from public office and from appearing as a party or witness in court, his estate escheated to his lord unless he left his own legitimate descendants, penalties for his murder had been reduced to farcical levels and burial was denied him; instead, his body might escheat to a medical school upon his death.[9] The thirteenth century restatement of SAXON law, the *Sachsenspiegel*, placed the bastard on the rightless level of fighters, robbers, thieves, and actors.[10] Frequent infanticide resulted.[11] CANON law did not help.[12]

4. *The old Common Law.* – In the COMMON LAW, the illegitimate was *filius nullius*, no one's son – no more, but no less. One consequence of this logic was that the illegitimate child of bondfolk was free.[13] Another was that he could not inherit. Beyond that, illegitimacy seems to have had no serious legal consequences. Of course, as a consequence of fact – then as now – it usually consigned its victims to the "poor".[14] *Pollock and Maitland* speculated that "the divergence of English from continental laws [may be] due to no deeper cause than the subjection of England to kings who proudly traced their descent from a mighty bastard."[15] *William the Bastard* – the Conqueror of England – liked to refer to himself as such.[16] Two centuries ago, *William Blackstone* sharply criticized discriminatory CONTINENTAL law and maintained that[17]: "any other distinction but that of not inheriting, which civil policy renders necessary, would, with regard to the

[5] Inventively taking still other variations into account, the law of *Alfonso the Wise of Castile and León* distinguished between illegitimates born of "live-in" concubines, those born as a result of the man's adultery or of his relationship with a female relative or with a nun, and those born to prostitutes, concubines kept outside of the home or as the result of a wife's adultery.

Las Siete Partidas III 4 tit. 15 ley 1 (1348). Similar classifications existed in ROMAN law. See *Kaser*, Roman Private Law (ed. 2 London 1968) 249, 265.

[6] See LOUISIANA CC art. 920, 1488. Such discrimination now is unconstitutional. *Weber v. Aetna Cas. & Sur. Co.*, 406 U.S. 164 (1972); *Loving v. Virginia*, 388 U.S. 1 (1967).

[7] ROMAN law, of course, spanned many centuries and attitudes changed. See *Kaser* (*supra* n. 5) 265-266.

[8] *Hübner*, Grundzüge des deutschen Privatrechts (ed. 5 Leipzig 1930) 711; *Robbins and Deák*, The Familial Property Rights of Illegitimate Children – A Comparative Study: 30 Colum.L.Rev. 308, 315 (1930).

[9] *Bückling*, Die Rechtsstellung der unehelichen Kinder im Mittelalter und in der heutigen Reformbewegung (Breslau 1920) 75-89. *Cf. Rexroth* 633, 634.

[10] *Eike von Repgow*, Sachsenspiegel, Landrecht. Book I art. XXXVIII (ca. 1220).

[11] *Foote, Levy and Sander*, Cases and Materials on Family Law (Boston and Toronto 1966) 13 ss.; *Hankins*, Illegitimacy, Social Aspects: 7 Enc.Soc. Sc. (1932) 579, 580-581. In 1777 *Frederick the Great* wrote to *Voltaire* that the largest number of the executions occurring in GERMANY were of girls who had killed their infants ... Widespread infanticide led the church in the sixth century to establish in ITALY the first foundling asylum and in the twelfth century to utilize the *tour*, or turn box, to receive the child without revealing the mother's identity (*cf. Foote, Levy and Sander* (*supra*) 15). See also *Werner* 24-27.

[12] See *Herrmann*, Die Stellung unehelicher Kinder nach kanonischem Recht (Amsterdam 1971), reviewed by *Neuhaus*, Archiv für katholisches Kirchenrecht 1971, 307. Today, of course, the clerical position has changed substantially. See, *e.g.*, Vorschläge des Katholischen Arbeitskreises für die Reform des Unehelichenrechts: FamRZ 1967, 1-10.

[13] *Pollock and Maitland*, History of English Law II (ed. 2 Cambridge 1968) 397; *Adams*, Nullius Filius – A Study of the Exception of Bastardy in the Law Courts of Medieval England: 6 U.Tor.L.J. 361, 378-383 (1946).

[14] *Cf. Hooper* 29.

[15] *Pollock and Maitland* (*supra* n. 13) II 397.

[16] *Hooper* 5.

[17] *Blackstone* (*-Kerr*), Commentaries on the Laws of England I (London 1857) 485-486.

innocent offspring of his parents' crimes, be odious, unjust, and cruel to the last degree." On the other hand, in the "Rechtsvergleichendes Handwörterbuch", which was the first serious attempt to present a global treatment of comparative law, *Rexroth* contradicted *Blackstone*, maintaining: "*Am ungünstigsten war die Stellung des unehelichen Kindes von jeher im angelsächsischen Recht.*"[18]

B. TOPICAL COVERAGE

5. *Parent and child.* – This chapter will be concerned with the relationship upon which all other kinship relations are based – that of parent and child. Normally, biological parenthood creates that relationship, but it may come into existence also by legal *fiat*, through the presumption that a child born to a married woman is that of her husband or through adoption. As has already been implied, an important concern of this chapter will be with the child whose parents' relationship did not measure up – fully or partially – to prevailing social norms, *i.e.*, with the child born out of wedlock. This will require careful review of rules that have defined legitimacy and, consequently, illegitimacy. A principal question will be what recognition, if any, the law has afforded the illegitimate child in terms of a legal relationship with his blood parents and kin. After dealing with legitimacy and illegitimacy, this chapter will concern itself with adoption – the creation of partial and full kinship relations by agreement and law instead of blood – and will briefly review legal aspects of the modern practice of artificial insemination.

6. *Other kinship relations.* – There are other types of kinship relations.[19] For example, some Christian cultures continue to take the godparent quite seriously. Latins put stock in "*compadrazgo*".[20] "Affinity" relationships created by marriage remain the subject of legislation in many places.[21] Many other forms of quasi-kinship relationships exist and some have found recognition in law. Many of these relationships are local or too loosely defined to fit with the discussion in this chapter of specific *legal* and, more or less, universal relationships.[22] Although all but universal, the relatively new form of "semi-legitimate" child-parent relationships created by divorce has not yet been carefully considered on its own facts. While the law has paid lip service to the principle that the children of divorced parents are the legal equals of legitimate children in going families, obvious differences in their factual situations have generally been ignored. Law reform in this area is a pressing and pervasive need. Beyond the uncertain status of the "child of divorce", of interest are the ties that continue to bind divorced ex-spouses and even ex-in-laws and the new ties that are developed between the child and a divorced and remarried custodial parent's new spouse. These often amount to *de facto* adoption and may have *some* legal consequences, but usually result in a full legal relationship only when they have culminated in formal adoption. Whether the connecting link be a support decree, visitation rights, interest relating to children or grandchildren, or marriage to a person having children of a previous alliance, a new, quasi-kinship structure is developing.[23]

C. CAVEAT – BOOK LAW V. PRACTICE

7. *General.* – Trite as it sounds, the comparative lawyer must constantly remind himself that social conditions and living habits vary widely from country to country and that comparative evaluation of abstract law is not a very useful exercise if it is taken out of the context in which it lives. The book law should be related to its practice – its

[18] "Since time immemorial, the position of the illegitimate child has been least favorable in the anglo-saxon law" (*Rexroth* 635).

[19] *Pitt-Rivers*, Pseudo-Kinship: 8 Int.Enc.Soc.Sc. 408-413 (1968).

[20] Coparenthood, derived from the Christian notion of spiritual kinship and involving ties between godparent and godchild and between godparent and natural parent; see *Pitt-Rivers* (*supra* n. 19) 390, 410.

[21] Especially in terms of marriage prohibitions. For AMERICAN law, see *Clark* 34, 72, 119. Generally, see *Dölle* I 104-111.

[22] Generally, see *Eggan, Goody and Pitt-Rivers*, Kinship: 8 Int.Enc.Soc.Sc. 390-413 (1968); *Weinstein*, Adoption: 1 Int.Enc.Soc.Sc. 96-100 (1968); *Josselin De Jong*, Lévi-Strauss's Theory on Kinship and Marriage (Leyden 1952).

[23] *Cf. Mead*, Anomalies in American Postdivorce Relationships: *Bohannon*, Divorce and After (Garden City, N.Y. 1970) 97, 108-112. The law has been slow to give legal recognition to the step-child. In the UNITED STATES, uncertain movement in this direction is discernible in connection with welfare situations in which some states have sought to burden stepfathers with support obligations which otherwise would have had to be borne by the public fisc. *E.g.*, *Application of Slochowsky*, 342 N.Y.S.2d 525 (S.Ct. Nassau Co. 1973). See generally, *Boehmer*, Die Rechtsstellung des Stiefkindes nach heutigem und künftigem Recht (Munich and Berlin 1941).

practice not only in the courts but also in "extra-judicial", custom-oriented life. This "caveat" operates at many levels.

8. *Modern trends.* – For example, aside from change in kinship structures wrought by divorce, even traditional family relationships have undergone decisive changes with little reflection in law, especially in industrializing countries. Thus, as an economic and social unit, the extended farm family of parents, children, grandparents and collaterals[24] has given ground to the nuclear, urban family consisting simply of parents and minor children. Awareness of social and financial responsibility for ascendants and collaterals has decreased in line with mounting government (or self-insurance) support of the aged. This has been reflected dimly in changed or atrophied "relative responsibility" laws. Relaxed enforcement practices have been closer to social realities. In some modern societies, even the child-rearing function, long the exclusive province of the family, has been partially or wholly delegated to communal systems. With the rapidly accelerating, world-wide trend toward an equal *role* (not just equal rights) for women, communal child rearing will seriously modify the family of the future, if it has not already changed the family of the present.

In many "developed" countries, kinship developments have outstripped the progress of the law – the law is behind actuality. The reverse is true in some of the newer countries, where the actuality of kinship practice has not reached – and indeed may never reach – the law that was put on the books, often under the influence of colonial conquerors. For example, to what extent does a family law derived from SPAIN actually describe the life of the people of MEXICO and the PHILIPPINES out of whose customs it did not grow?[25] How is that ill-fitting book law enforced in the courts? Who has access to the courts? Indeed, are courts generally available? Unfortunately, reliable data are difficult to obtain. There are no statistics on many points of interest. Worse, the difficulty is not limited to sociological data. On the law itself, detailed and specific information can sometimes not be found. In MEXICO, the Civil Codes leave many gaps which are not filled in satisfactorily by reported cases or commentaries of MEXICAN jurists. Of course, the very absence of a reasonable degree of book law certainty on vital questions is in itself a telling commentary on the relative unimportance of book law in life.

If PHILIPPINE book law seems better developed than that of MEXICO, the diversity of its people is even greater. MEXICO's rural Indian-oriented culture differs significantly from the FRENCH-SPANISH "city law", but in the PHILIPPINES, the contrasts go even further. The same PHILIPPINE law purports to deal with Stone Age tribes, some only recently discovered, and modern man of widely different religions. An impression of that diversity may be gained from the preamble of a bill (H. No. 342) proposed in 1968 to the 7th Congress, 1st Session, Republic of the Philippines by Congressman *Anni*:

> "The Muslims and other non-Christian tribes in non-Christian provinces are not yet completely assimilated or integrated into the mainstream of the Philippine body politic. Considering this situation coupled with the present high rate of illiteracy in these areas and the fact that these groups of people are still practising their customs, traditions and rites with respect to marriages between them, since their customs are deeply rooted, enough time should be given so as to enable them to fully grasp and understand the policies of our government particularly on the application of laws substantially affecting their customs which were in observance since time immemorial. An extension therefore of another twenty years with respect to the applicability of the Civil Code of the Philippines on the formalities of marriage between Muslims and other non-christians residing in non-christian provinces is most appropriate and necessary".

9. *Description v. comparison.* – So much for the difficulty of sensible *description*. Sensible *comparison* involves further pitfalls. In MEXICO, for example, the law on the books does not provide a support remedy to the unacknowledged illegitimate. However, since many of these illegitimates live in *de facto* families with their fathers, they actually do obtain paternal support. In most of the UNITED STATES, on the other hand, the illegitimate child *has* a legal right of support against his father. Court proceedings, however, result in only a small portion of illegitimates actually being provided with paternal support. In short, the laws and living customs of MEXICO and the UNITED STATES differ diametrically on this issue – to opposite ends. A similar illustration of the divergence of book law and practice is furnished in many

24 There may be some question whether this idyll ever existed on a grand scale. When the "extended family" is supposed to have held sway, drastically lower life expectancies coupled with (or caused by) virtual absence of medical care (because of lack of treatment capability) reduced the problem of the elderly to much lesser dimensions than we now face.

25 See *Borah and Cook*, Marriage and Legitimacy in Mexican Culture – Mexico and California: 54 Calif.L. Rev. 946 (1966).

countries where constitutions expressly provide the illegitimate with legal equality – prevalent in LATIN AMERICA – but little or nothing is done to implement that mandate. WEST GERMANY fell into that category until 1970.

Another factor is that, in a meaningful comparison, the relative importance of laws on illegitimacy must be weighed in a particular system. For example, if a country has a relatively low rate of illegitimacy (take WEST GERMANY at approximately 5 per cent), and a large percentage of children born illegitimately are legitimated by the subsequent marriage of their parents or find "legitimate" parents by adoption, the law of illegitimacy operates on a very limited scale. It does not nearly have the social impact and importance there that it has in a system in which the percentage of illegitimate births is higher and the adoption rate is lower. Thus, MEXICO, with an illegitimacy rate in excess of 20 per cent and little relief through adoption, should take its illegitimacy laws more seriously than need WEST GERMANY. Of course, experience has proved the opposite.

Explainable? Probably only in terms of deeper cultural differences, although it should be noted that even the statistics on illegitimacy may be suspect. Thus, indigenous Indian populations in MEXICO have never fully accepted the SPANISH-derived family law imposed upon them and the MEXICAN statistics on illegitimacy count many perfectly stable unions as illegitimate merely because of a failure to comply with formalities of civil ceremony and registration. Haphazard official efforts are sometimes made to remedy this difficulty. To illustrate:

"Ester Zuño de Echeverría, wife of President Luis Echeverría, will officiate September 24 at the mass wedding of 1,300 couples who have lived together for years under common law.

The Mexican government will pay legal fees and host the brides, bridegrooms and, in many cases, their children and grandchildren at a fiesta after the ceremony."[26]

A similar illustration may be derived from the UNITED STATES where approximately 30 per cent of the black children are illegitimate as compared with a "white rate" of about 5 per cent. A game played with statistics demonstrates a startlingly different social significance of the AMERICAN law of illegitimacy: If adoption rates (white adoptions: 70 per cent; non-white adoptions: 4 per cent) are applied to AMERICA's 1968 illegitimacy figures (155 000 white, 184 000 black) it may be estimated that only 46 500 white children, but 176 640 black children remained unadopted. This means that approximately 80 per cent of all children disadvantaged by the operation of the AMERICAN illegitimacy laws are black. In short, although the AMERICAN illegitimacy laws originally had nothing to do with racial discrimination, they actually now have that effect.[27]

D. PRINCIPAL APPROACHES TO LEGITIMACY AND ILLEGITIMACY

10. *Introductory.* – To this day, illegitimacy everywhere remains an unsolved problem – "a problem as old and unsolved as human existence itself."[28] There are no perfect solutions, and the law has merely made attempts to deal with illegitimacy. Perplexingly, illegitimacy seems to defy solution so long as there is marriage:

"Now bastardy and marriage in this world are quite complementary – you cannot have one without the other. In another world, you may indeed separate the two institutions and eliminate one of them, either by having marriage so perfect – in various senses – that no one will ever commit fornication or adultery, or by having fornication so perfect that no one will ever commit marriage."[29]

11. *Legitimacy.* – Approaches to legitimacy range from narrow, puristic laws which reserve legitimate status to children conceived and born in marriage to liberal legislation which throws the cloak of legitimacy around potential illegitimates, such as children not conceived but born in marriage or even those born of void or voidable marriages. Quite typically, once the law has recognized a child as legitimate, it has protected that status. All but universally, a legal presumption of legitimacy, once created, is difficult to overcome. Generally, however, the protection of legitimacy is tempered with realism and the child becomes illegitimate if the mother's husband can definitely prove his non-paternity. Protection of legitimacy has been provided also by limiting the groups of persons permitted to challenge legitimacy. Thus, many systems allow an attack on legitimacy to be made only by a person directly concerned, such as the husband or the child, precluding, for example, a collateral attack by competing heirs. In short, while the presumption of legitimacy produces some incidental – even accidental – recog-

[26] Chicago Sun Times, 14 Sept. 1971, p. 5 (UPI).
[27] See *Krause* 257-260.
[28] *Davis*, Illegitimacy and the Social Structure: 45 Am.J.Sociology 215 (1939).
[29] *Brinton*, French Revolutionary Legislation on Illegitimacy 1789-1804 (Cambridge 1936) 82-83.

nition of the "social paternity" that is created by the birth of a child to a man's wife, *biological* paternity typically has been viewed as the controlling value. This insight is of crucial importance in assessing the law of illegitimacy.

12. *Illegitimacy.* – At the extremes, legal approaches to illegitimacy have ranged from rightlessness *vis-à-vis* his parents – as expressed by the doctrine of *filius nullius* – to that measure of equality the law can furnish when the facts are inherently unequal. Most systems, however, have furnished the illegitimate child more than none and less than all of the incidents of legitimate status, perhaps granting a right of support during minority, but refusing a right of succession upon the parent's death. Many systems have provided full equality to the child in his legal relationship to his mother, probably on the ground that illegitimate maternity, as distinguished from paternity, typically *is* as certain as legitimate maternity. Some systems, however, to this day, require a specific acknowledgment by the mother of her illegitimate child before their *legal* relationship is recognized.

Why one system has chosen this approach and another that, is not clear. Historical accident has played a larger role than it should have. For example, FRANCE had briefly pioneered legal equality in the wake of the Revolution of 1789. But FRANCE soon retreated from that extreme and postulated: "*La recherche de la paternité est interdite.*"[30] Soon, *Napoleon*'s Code was exported through war as well as its inherent quality and, today, FRANCE's restrictive law on illegitimacy lives on in many parts of the world, although, in FRANCE itself, equality is now again the rule!

Ideology, religion, or systematic differences often have played important roles in the approach a particular system has adopted to these vexing problems. However, identical results have been achieved on different premises and different results have followed from the same premises. For example, seeking to protect marriage, Christianity achieved a long period of most un-Christian treatment of the illegitimate. Early, anti-Christian SOVIET law, in its distrust of the bourgeois family, provided the bastard with equality. Since then, SOVIET RUSSIA's attitude on illegitimacy has changed several times until, today, it resembles that of MEXICO! To round off, some, but not all, WESTERN style democracies have lately felt an urge to translate into practice egalitarian notions long held on paper – and have found illegitimacy an inviting target. That ideology is of little help in illuminating the "why" of kinship law is illustrated further by the SOCIALIST countries of EASTERN EUROPE which have gone separate ways on illegitimacy.

13. *Comparative evaluation,* as distinguished from descriptive comparison, is fraught with special difficulty in this area. It is possible (and often fruitful) to compare aspects of the law of contracts and arrive at a logically supportable conclusion as to which system of contract law provides the most rational, result-oriented method. Systems of kinship relations, on the other hand, cannot be evaluated on a simple criterion of pragmatic efficiency.

True, one could define reasonable social objectives with some clarity. For example, "stability of the family" is a worthy goal that has been accepted widely. Even if some now think it antiquated that sexual relationships are regulated, support and inheritance relationships must be fixed by law between husband, wife and children to avoid social chaos (and to relieve society of potential welfare cases). Even more significantly, most systems continue to delegate the task of socializing children to the family, although with increasing state assistance in terms of schooling or even communal child care arrangements or state-directed youth activities. But if there is agreement that the stable family remains a basic social objective, it is disputed hotly how that objective may best be achieved. It is a point of faith whether the family can be protected only if the illegitimate child is stigmatized or whether, quite to the contrary, illegitimacy is encouraged and regular relationships are discouraged if the law burdens only *married* fathers with a support obligation. Empirical evidence makes it seem unlikely that there is a cause and effect relationship between liberal laws on illegitimacy and the incidence of illegitimacy.[31] To use just one example, the SCANDINAVIAN countries are relatively similar in history, population, values and in many other ways. For unknown reasons, their laws on illegitimacy have ranged in the last two generations from full equality in NORWAY to less liberal laws in DENMARK to more restrictive laws in SWEDEN. Yet, the rate of illegitimacy in NORWAY now stands at about 5 per cent, in DENMARK at 10 per cent and in SWEDEN at 20 per cent. These figures seem to show that there is no positive correlation between laws

[30] CC 5 March 1803 art. 340: "The investigation of paternity is prohibited".

[31] See, generally, *Goode*, Illegitimacy, Anomie, and Cultural Penetration: 26 Am. Soc.Rev. 910–925 (1961); *Hartley*, The Amazing Rise of Illegitimacy in Great Britain: 44 Social Forces 533–545 (1965).

discriminating against illegitimate children and the incidence of illegitimacy and may even mean that there is a negative correlation.[32]

However that may be, much or most of the argument over the merits, in terms of family protection, of laws that discriminate against the illegitimate child is not relevant to the child. Whether or not such laws have a beneficial or detrimental effect on the family, the illegitimate child has a substantial interest in a legal relationship with his father. Romantics have long conceded this and much literary ink deploring the illegitimate's lot has been spilled.[33]

14. *The (il)logic of discrimination.* – In the UNITED STATES, the rationality of discrimination against the illegitimate child has lately come under *logical* scrutiny. Getting away from emotional value judgments which – for better or for worse – have governed the legal lot of the illegitimate child throughout history, an attempt has been made to derive a mandate from the general equality clause of the Federal Constitution. In brief (and therefore incomplete) summary, that clause requires to be treated as legally equal what is in fact equal, what is not distinguishable in terms of reasonable legislative objectives. Supposed grounds for discriminatory legislation on this subject were analyzed and found wanting.[34]

One rational argument against the illegitimate's demand for legal rights traditionally has been the difficulty of ascertaining illegitimate paternity. Today, however, that concern may be largely satisfied by advanced methods of blood typing and other safeguards which have transformed the ascertainment of illegitimate paternity from an abstract demand into a realistic goal. (This point is so crucial that it will later be discussed at some length.) To sum up, if uncertainty of illegitimate paternity is the sole *rational* obstacle to legal equality of legitimate and illegitimate children, those systems that have provided legal equality for the child of ascertained parents win the evaluative comparison.

15. *The room for choice.* – So much for a value judgment on the basis of "fairness" as perceived in the light of abstract goals of equality. On a more pragmatic plane, whatever philosophical position one may hold on illegitimacy, it may be argued that the law has a choice on this issue only so long as the rate of illegitimacy remains small. Only in that situation can a system afford to sacrifice the legal position of these children for the goal of family protection (regardless of the amazing illogic of supposing that men will be deterred from illicit relationships by *not* imposing a financial and legal responsibility on them for their children.) Quickly this option passes. Humanitarian notions increasingly demand that the state step in where the parent has failed. If the illegitimacy rate reaches a certain level, public funds will be inadequate to provide for them.

The AMERICAN states now have to carry a serious financial burden largely because of a fatherless child population that is a small fraction of the total child population. While support is provided only at or below desirable subsistence levels, AMERICA, traditionally the land of individual liberty coupled with individual responsibility, continues to view illegitimacy as a problem that must be solved primarily by public welfare. So far, no serious effort to find the illegitimate father is made, although legislation enacted in 1975 (P.L. 93-647), when implemented, will give the federal government an active role in child support enforcement. One might predict that, if the illegitimacy rate reached 20 per cent, the current AMERICAN welfare system would break down. At that point, individual support obligations would have to be looked to unless the whole system were changed to provide for state support of *all* children. Any other model might find more and more parents refusing to marry for unwilling-

[32] Reasonably recent illegitimacy statistics are collected in *Saario* 216-224 and in *Council of Europe*, The Social and Legal Protection of Unmarried Mothers and Their Children (SOC (70)1, 49-60) (Strasbourg 1970). See, generally, *Goode* (*supra* n. 31) 910, discussing the relationship between rates of illegitimacy and cultural conditions; *Christensen*, Cultural Relativism and Premarital Sex Norms: *Roberts*, The Unwed Mother (New York 1966) 61-77, comparing sex norms in UTAH, INDIANA and DENMARK. A thorough and intriguing study of the cause and effect relationship between law and social practice (in the field of divorce) is described and analyzed in detail by *Rheinstein*, Marriage Breakdown in Ticino and Comasco: Festschrift Hans G. Ficker (Frankfurt and Berlin 1967) 385.

[33] See, *e.g.*, *DeFord*, Love-Children – A Book of Illustrious Illegitimates (New York 1931); *Hawthorne*, The Scarlet Letter (Boston 1850); *Sir Walter Scott*, Heart of Midlothian (1818); *Kleist*, Käthchen von Heilbronn (1807); *Goethe*, Faust I; generally, *Werner*, *passim*.

[34] *Krause* 59-104; *Weber v. Aetna Cas. & Sur. Co.*, *supra* n. 6; *Stanley v. Illinois*, 405 U.S. 645 (1972); *Gomez v. Perez*, 409 U.S. 535 (1973). An earlier attempt to make the procreation of illegitimate children a tort failed: *Zepeda v. Zepeda*, 41 Ill.App.2d 240, 190 N.E.2d 849 (1963). See *Rheinstein*, Rechtswidrige Erzeugung menschlichen Lebens – Ein neuer Grund deliktischer Haftung?: Festschrift Fritz von Hippel (Tübingen 1967) 373.

ness or even simple inability to take care of their own children after paying the taxes that would be needed to support an ever increasing number of fatherless children. Therefore, the question whether the illegitimate child should have equal legal rights against his father ultimately may turn into the question of whether the family is to remain "the basic unit of society".

SWEDEN now stands at this crossroad. SWEDEN has reached an illegitimacy rate of about 20 per cent of all births along with a significant drop in its marriage rate. So far, Socialist SWEDEN has chosen to stay with individual, parental responsibility for child support, regardless of legitimacy status, and efficient procedures find fathers for some 95 per cent of illegitimate children. Since SWEDEN's tax rates are already among the world's highest and necessary to finance its comprehensive social services, no other course seems open, although it should be noted that the alternative – state support for *all* children – is being implemented in a limited way with relatively small payments to all children, regardless of legitimacy, status or need, as well as free health care and education.

16. *Social welfare laws relating to illegitimacy.* – This is no idle digression. The next point to be made is that the social impact of laws on illegitimacy can be assessed meaningfully only in the context of a system's social welfare laws. Clearly, the law's failure to ask a parent to provide financial support for his child is quite a different matter if support is provided by the state than when the child is left destitute. It is a further and equally significant point that the very conditions which welfare laws attack may at least in part be encouraged by these laws.[35] If governmental assistance is limited to children of unwed parents it may constitute an incentive to irregular relationships and thus aggravate the very problem it seeks to alleviate.

17. *"New lifestyles".* – Aside from the cost problem, there arises the question of what regulatory stance the law should take *vis-à-vis* new life styles that seem to be developing in many WESTERN countries. In SWEDEN, as previously noted, the formal marriage rate has dropped substantially in recent years with an attendant increase in the illegitimacy rate to 20 per cent. Respect for individual liberties may dictate that the system tolerate the adult choices involved in these matters, but can the law stand by and allow parents to choose, in effect, that their children shall have only one legal parent? Arguably, society owes the child a moral duty to adapt its law to changing social circumstances.

18. *Summary.* – In short, the variables are all but infinite. The problem is so complex that it seems to defy intelligent comparison. Of course, this is an encyclopedia of law, not one of sociology. Accordingly, the comparison that follows deals with legal rules – what is asked here is only that sociological caveats be kept in mind throughout. Comparison of laws is simpler than comparison of life. But this is not all bad. Simplification can point out trends, can show up the forest instead of just the trees. For example, comparison of laws shows quickly that the modern ethos, for varying reasons and regardless of specific ideology, looks askance at discrimination against the illegitimate.

19. *World-wide trend toward equality.* – Throughout the world, the illegitimate's demand for a measure of equality increasingly is being recognized as a basic human right. In January 1967, a subcommission of the Commission on Human Rights of the United Nations adopted a statement on "General Principles of Equality and Non-Discrimination in Respect of Persons Born out of Wedlock" which demands that "every person, once his filiation has been established, shall have the same legal status as a person born in wedlock."[36] The Council of Europe is currently involved in a comparative study of the subject and completed in 1970 a comparative study of "The Social and Legal Protection of Unmarried Mothers and Their Children."[37] The 7th International Congress of Comparative Law considered the subject in 1966,[38] and the 9th Congress reconsidered the matter in 1974.[39] These supranational efforts reflect active and extensive movements towards reform of the law of illegitimacy that are under way in many countries.[40]

For example, the SCANDINAVIAN countries have long granted substantially equal rights to the illegitimate. In 1915, NORWEGIAN law set the pace by establishing substantial equality for the illegitimate child in his legal relationship to his mother and father.[41] The early statute was superseded by the NORWEGIAN Law of 21 Dec. 1956, which

[35] See *Krause* 267-284.

[36] *Saario* 226.

[37] *Council of Europe,* supra n. 32. Letter dated 11 Feb. 1972 to *Harry D. Krause* from *A. Papandreou,* Directorate of Legal Affairs, Council of Europe.

[38] See the general report by *A. Ionasco.*

[39] See the general report by *Gabriel García Cantero.*

[40] See, generally, *Saario.*

[41] *Magnusson,* Norwegian Laws Concerning Illegitimate Children (U.S.Dept. of Labor, Children's Bureau, Leg.Ser. no. 1, Bureau Pub. no. 31) (Washington 1918).

abolished nearly all remaining legal distinctions between legitimate and illegitimate children.[42] The DANISH Law of 18 May 1960, concerning the rights of children, broadly deals with the rights of legitimate and illegitimate children and does not distinguish between them. Among other things, it provides an equal right of support and very effective means to ascertain paternity.[43] Current SWEDISH law has largely equalized the legal position of legitimate and illegitimate children in SWEDEN.[44] The 1949 Constitution of WEST GERMANY demands equality for the illegitimate and this mandate was implemented with detailed legislation in 1969.[45] The AUSTRIAN parliament has enacted a Law in 1970 that gives children substantial equality, with exceptions in the area of inheritance.[46] In SWITZERLAND the report of an official committee has proposed substantially improved means of ascertaining paternity of illegitimates and has offered inheritance rights with respect to the father.[47] FRANCE wholly reformed her antiquated laws on illegitimacy in 1972.

In GREAT BRITAIN, the Family Law Reform Act of 1969 (s. 14) has achieved a broad reform of the illegitimate child's right of inheritance granting a right of intestate succession with regard to the father as well as the mother. In NEW ZEALAND, the position of the illegitimate child has been made largely equivalent to that of the legitimate child.[48]

In the UNITED STATES, the equal protection clause of the Federal Constitution has been employed to strike down several state laws that discriminated between legitimate and illegitimate children, many state legislatures have moved toward equality, and broadly conceived uniform legislation has been proposed by the National Conference of Commissioners on Uniform State Laws and enacted in several states.[49]

Many countries of LATIN AMERICA have provisions for legal equality of legitimate and illegitimate children.[50] For example, the BOLIVIAN Constitution of 1967 provides that „All children, without distinction as to origin, have equal rights and duties in respect of their parents" (art. 195). ECUADOR'S Constitution of 1967 gives the same rights with respect to name, upbringing, education and inheritance to all "Children whether born in or out of wedlock" (art. 29). GUATEMALA'S Constitution of 1965 provides that "All children are equal before the law and have identical rights" and that "The law shall establish the means of proof in investigating paternity" (art. 86 par. 2, 3). PANAMA'S Constitution of 1946, as amended in 1961, provides: "Parents have the same duties with respect to their children born out of wedlock as toward their children born in wedlock. All children are equal before the law and they have the same rights of inheritance in intestate succession" (art. 58). URUGUAYS'S Constitution of 1967 contains the following provision: "Parents have the same duties toward children born outside of wedlock as toward children born within it" (art. 42).

Finally, a number of EASTERN EUROPEAN countries have constitutional[51] and statutory provisions which grant equal or nearly equal rights to the child born out of wedlock.[52] The PEOPLE'S REPUBLIC OF CHINA has had provisions on legal equality for illegitimacy since its early revolutionary legislation,[53] whereas the SOVIET UNION has pur-

[42] *Lov no. 9.* See *Arnholm*, The New Norwegian Legislation Relating to Parents and Children: Scand. Stud. L. 3 (1959) 9, 14-20.

[43] *Lov no. 200; Bitsch*; see *Marcus*, Das neue dänische Kindergesetz: RabelsZ 26 (1961) 51.

[44] *Lind.*

[45] *Nichtehelichengesetz*; see also WEST GERMAN Const. art. 6 par. 5.

[46] *Kralik*, Die Neuordnung der Rechtsstellung des unehelichen Kindes: JBl. 1971, 273; *Meyer*, Das Recht des unehelichen Kindes (Vienna 1971).

[47] Bericht der Studienkommission für die Teilrevision des Familienrechts (Ausserehelichen-, Adoptions- und Ehegüterrecht), erstattet dem Eidgenössischen Justiz- und Polizeidepartement am 13.6.1962 (mimeographed). See *Hegnauer*, Die Revision der Gesetzgebung über das aussereheliche Kindesverhältnis: ZSR 84 (1965) I 35-38; *idem*, Grundgedanken des neuen Kindesrechts: Festschrift Max Guldener (Zürich 1973) 127-150.

[48] *Robson*, New Zealand: *Keeton* (ed.), The British Commonwealth IV (London 1954) 333; *Cameron*, Family Law Reforms in New Zealand: 4 Fam.L.Q. 167, 178 (1970).

[49] *Supra* n. 34; Uniform Parentage Act, adopted in 1975 in HAWAII, MONTANA and NORTH DAKOTA.

[50] The following provisions are cited according to the translation by *Blaustein and Flanz*, Constitutions of the Countries of the World (Dobbs Ferry, N.Y. 1972).

[51] ALBANIA: Const. of 4 July 1950, art. 19 par. 4; BULGARIA: Const. of 16 May 1971, art. 38 par. 4; POLAND: Const. of 22 July 1952, art. 67 par. 2; YUGOSLAVIA: Const. of 21 Feb. 1974, art. 190 par. 4 (English translations in *Blaustein and Flanz*, *supra* n. 50). Generally, see *Borchers*, Das Recht der Unehelichen in Ost- und Südosteuropa: WGO 6 (1964) 2-22.

[52] See the Family Codes of the EUROPEAN SOCIALIST countries cited in the List of Statutory Materials. For a discussion of the YUGOSLAV statute see *Cigoj*, Die Gleichstellung der ehelichen und unehelichen Kinder im jugoslawischen Recht: RabelsZ 23 (1958) 139. Concerning POLAND, see *Lasok* 139 ss.

[53] Art. 19 of the Marriage Law of the CHINESE SOVIET REPUBLIC of 1934 provided that "children born

sued a changing policy on the issue of illegitimacy.[54] Since 1968, however, the illegitimate child has had full legal equality under SOVIET law, although serious restrictions hamper the ascertainment of paternity.[55]

E. ADOPTION

20. *Purposes.* – The matter of adoption is not nearly as complex as is that of illegitimacy. Indeed, whereas illegitimacy is a "problem", adoption is a "solution". But there are differences in the conception of the problem that is solved by adoption. For example, the cultures of ancient Rome, India and Asia introduced adoption as a device to produce descendants for the purpose of "ancestor worship". More this-world-oriented systems have used adoption to provide male heirs for purposes of transmission of property or of titles. Today, almost everywhere, adoption has come to be viewed as a device to help childless couples to children and parentless children to parents, to fill an emotional need. Beyond that, the view is gaining ground that adoption can help solve the social problem posed by the fatherless welfare child. Considerable advances have recently been made in AMERICA in breaking down social and legal barriers to interracial adoptions. On the international scale, interracial adoption has been employed to provide homes for foreign children orphaned or fathered by war.

Unfortunately, as in the case of illegitimacy, it is the exceptional legal system that has seen its own objectives clearly and has fashioned its law accordingly. It would be a meaningful exercise if AMERICAN laws of adoption were compared with AMERICAN social goals that may be performed by adoption and if the efficiency of AMERICA's laws were measured in terms of how they help to achieve these goals. And an evaluation of the *laws* alone would not suffice. Adoption practice, not least because of the heavy involvement of adoption agencies which apply their own, extra-legal standards, present a *de facto* situation which often differs materially from book law. That, of course, is not the type of comparison attempted in this article. But even the broadbrush, cross-cultural, legal comparison that will be presented here has some value. For instance, FRANCE's recognition that adoption may have different ends and her provision of two legal forms of adoption – complete and limited – may be worth emulating elsewhere.

21. *Historical factors.* – Adoption involves the voluntary assumption of parental obligations by an individual who usually is not the biological parent of the person adopted.[56] While adoption was unavailable under the COMMON LAW and in many CIVIL LAW systems until rather late,[57] it had been developed in ROMAN law. The principal purpose of the *adoptio minus plena* in the law of *Justinian* was the provision of an heir. He had to be at least eighteen years older than the person to be adopted. The adopted person could be either a child or an adult. When adopted, he assumed the family name of the adopter, acquired inheritance rights from the adopter, but nevertheless retained inheritance rights in his natural family.[58] Today adoption is recognized all but universally, but many modern states were late in joining the tide. For example, ENGLAND did not enact an adoption statute until 1926, and the NETHERLANDS and PORTUGAL waited until 1956 and 1966, respectively. In the UNITED STATES, by comparison, the first adoption statute became law in 1851 and, by now, all 50 states have enacted adoption statutes.[59]

F. METHOD OF PRESENTATION AND GEOGRAPHIC COVERAGE

22. Traditional comparative legal method asks that comparison of legal systems be run concurrently, that issue after issue be treated in terms of various legal systems and that a particular con-

out of wedlock shall enjoy all the rights granted to legitimate children by this marriage law". This theme was carried forward in subsequent laws, and ultimately embodied in art. 19 of the Marriage Law of the CHINESE PEOPLE'S REPUBLIC of 13 April 1950: *Meijer* 284, 285, 289, 297, 301. See also, *Müller-Freienfels*, Zur revolutionären Familiengesetzgebung, insbesondere zum Ehegesetz der Volksrepublik China v. 1.5.1950: Festschrift Max Rheinstein. Ius Privatum Gentium II (Tübingen 1969) 843, 903.

54 See *Gorecki*, Kommunistische Familienstruktur – Die Rechtsprechung als Instrument des Wandels: Kölner Zeitschrift für Soziologie und Sozialpsychologie, spec. no. 14 (1970) 490–507.

55 Fundamentals of Family Law art. 4.

56 There are cases in which an illegitimate child may be adopted by his natural parent. Some states have enacted specific provisions for such adoptions, others treat them under their general statute.

57 *U.S. Dept. of Labor, Children's Bureau*, Adoption Laws in the United States 1 (1925); *Dölle* II 564.

58 See *Hall*, Digest of Justinian I (Monroe 1904) 31–39; *Sherman*, Roman Law in the Modern World (3 vol.) (ed. 3 New York 1937) § 496–504.

59 *Clark* 602–671; *Leavy* 1.

tribution made by a particular country be dealt with where it fits substantively without attempting a full representation of any one country's law in the area studied.[60] This approach has the advantage of providing a readily readable account and it can give the illusion of broad, even worldwide coverage. An all too frequent flaw, however, is that issue-centered cross comparison tends to obscure important relationships between the treatment of interdependent issues within one system.

The account that follows seeks a compromise: The topic is divided into relatively broad sub-topics and, in sequence, each of these sub-topics is discussed with respect to one system or several closely related countries. The reader who wishes to gain a coherent picture of any *one* system can do so by selecting the discussion of only that system under each heading. This approach carries a price. To achieve the kind of coverage attempted here, any pretense of completeness in terms of geographic coverage had to be sacrificed. Instead, selections have been made from the world's major legal systems as much in terms of their objective importance as from the standpoint of interesting contributions that a particular system may have made to this subject. On that basis, the choice has fallen on the COMMON LAW which is represented by the law of the 50 UNITED STATES and that of ENGLAND. The FRENCH family of legal systems is represented by FRANCE in terms of a "comparative" discussion of traditional FRENCH law and the 1972 reform of her laws on illegitimacy. NORWEGIAN and WEST-GERMAN law represent one of the early and one of the most recent attempts to provide legal equality for the illegitimate child. The law of the EUROPEAN SOCIALIST countries is represented by SOVIET RUSSIA, EAST GERMANY, POLAND, and CZECHOSLOVAKIA. The greater FRENCH family of law is represented by MEXICAN and PHILIPPINE law, both of which represent SPANISH transplants to distant cultures which show striking parallels to this day.[61] These parallels show up on the books, in terms of their mutual FRENCH ancestry, as well as in terms of liberalizing tendencies that have overcome some of the old-line FRENCH restrictiveness. The PHILIPPINES add a further note of interest in terms of their COMMON LAW heritage, derived from half a century of AMERICAN suzerainty and because of the strong influence of Roman-Catholic ideology.

[60] See *Rexroth; Wahl; Schnitzer*, Vergleichende Rechtslehre (ed. 2 Basle 1961) 532-549, 538-542.

[61] In the case of MEXICO, the Civil Code of the Federal District of 30 Aug. 1928 is used as the primary source. That Code has served as the model for the Civil Codes of the MEXICAN STATES. MEXICO, of course, is not intended to be representative of LATIN AMERICAN legal systems. In some ways, MEXICO may be viewed as rather conservative, especially in respect of the limited circumstances in which paternity may be ascertained and the limited legal consequences resulting from the ascertainment of paternity. This is made quite clear by the excellent and detailed comparative table presented in *Gesche-Müller* 255.

II. LEGITIMACY

A. DEFINITION, PRESUMPTION AND CHALLENGE

i. *Principal Approaches*

23. *General.* – By universal definition, the *legitimate* child is the child who has a *full* legal relationship with both of his parents. What that relationship encompasses varies among legal systems, and, in its details, is the subject of ch. 7 in this volume. A variety of general considerations has already been discussed in this chapter (*supra* s. 10–19). Now to the specifics.

Typically, the legitimate child is a full-fledged member of the family of both parents, has rights and duties of support, stands in a reciprocal inheritance relationship with members of both parents' families, carries the name of his father, and is in the custody of both parents.

Universally, legitimacy is defined primarily by reference to the marital status of the child's parents, although legitimate status may sometimes be obtained without parental marriage. Differences between legal systems may be perceived in terms of the question of "married when?"

The definition of legitimate status automatically provides the definition of illegitimate status.[62] A child who is not legitimate is illegitimate and has a more tenuous, if any, legal link with his parents than is possessed by his legitimate brother. One might suppose that if a legal system – as many now do – granted full legal equality to the illegitimate child, a definition of legitimacy would become unnecessary. But this is not so – even the systems that provide equality find it helpful to distinguish between the factual situation of the child whose parents are married and the child whose parents are not married. Certain inequalities of fact cannot be equalized by law. Moreover, an important role of what used to be the definition of "legitimacy" now is to distinguish cases in which paternity is established "automatically" from cases in which special procedures must be used to ascertain paternity.

24. *Protection of legitimacy – Presumption of legitimacy.* – Once the law has thrown the cloak of legitimacy around a child, it protects what it has given by presuming that a child born by a married woman was produced by her husband. This presumption has its basis in the very nature of the institution of marriage and, if there is one aspect of marriage that is universal, it is that, in contrast to other offspring, the offspring of legitimate marriage has full legal rights *vis-à-vis* both parents as of the time of his birth.

Logically, disproof of the presumption that the child born by a married woman was produced by her husband divides into two steps: First, a contestant may try to show that the mother did not have intercourse with her husband at the probable time of the child's conception. The various legal systems differ as to how that may be proved. ENGLISH law once required proof that intercourse during the critical period was absolutely impossible. Moreover, such absolute impossibility could be shown only by proof that the husband had been "beyond the four seas". Later, proof of other kinds of impossibility was admitted. For instance, it might be shown that the husband had been imprisoned or was impotent. The next step was admission of proof of high improbability of intercourse. Gradually the degree of improbability required for that proof was lowered so that in ENGLAND as well as in most AMERICAN jurisdictions "improbability" now is shown if husband and wife were separated at the probable time of the child's conception under circumstances which make it improbable that they had intercourse at that time. A separate issue is that the law may impose restrictions on the *means* by which the impossibility or improbability of intercourse may be proved. For instance, in those COMMON LAW jurisdictions which still follow "Lord Mansfield's rule", the spouses may not testify in such a manner as to impeach the legitimacy of a child born after their marriage. This includes, of course, testimony as to non-access.

Second, if the presumption of intercourse has not been or cannot be disproved, a contestant may prove that it was *impossible* for the child to have been produced by intercourse between the mother and her husband. However, given cohabitation at

[62] In modern legislative usage, derogatory terms such as "bastard" in COMMON LAW systems, have been supplanted by "illegitimate" or "child born out of wedlock", although many COMMON LAW books still speak of "bastards" without apparent ill will. Of course, the appellation "illegitimate" – unlawful – is hardly an improvement! In the WEST GERMAN reform discussion, it should be noted, the question of nomenclature developed into a major issue. Ultimately, the term "nichtehelich" (non-marital) triumphed over "unehelich" (un-marital). See *Klette*, "Nichtehelich" – nicht "unehelich": FamRZ 1967, 206–207.

the time of the child's probable conception, the standard of proof required is very high. At one extreme, CALIFORNIA provides that "notwithstanding any other provision of law, the issue of a wife cohabiting with her husband, who is not impotent, is conclusively presumed to be legitimate."[63] Elsewhere, the standard of proof is very difficult to meet. Indeed, until the advent of blood typing evidence, the presumption was all but impossible to rebut in many systems.

Another important question goes to the procedure by which the presumption of paternity of the mother's husband may be disproved. Part of this question is *who* may within what period contest a child's legitimacy and between whom a resulting judgment has the effect of *res judicata.* There also is the question whether legitimacy may be challenged in any context or only in a special "status proceeding".

Two final thoughts: First, it should be noted that, to the extent attack on legitimate status is made difficult, the presumption of legitimacy may create a "socially-based" family relationship which may transcend biology. It nevertheless remains clear in all systems that the definition of legitimacy is only secondarily involved with social relationship and that the primary focus remains on biological ties. Second: it seems strange that there is little, if any, meaningful correlation between the importance given to the status of legitimacy in a particular system, the stringency of the definition of the status of legitimacy, and the extent to which the status, once conferred, is protected.

ii. *Illustrations*

25. *Common Law.* – In defining legitimacy, the COMMON LAW is principally concerned with the parents' marital status at the time of the child's birth.[64] Illegitimacy usually involves the fact that the child was *born* out of wedlock and not legitimated, or was born to a married mother in circumstances in which the husband could not have been the father. Some AMERICAN statutes expressly include a reference to the time of conception to cover the child who was conceived before marriage, but most or all imply the same. The parents' divorce or the husband's death prior to the birth of the child normally does not affect the legitimacy of the child if the child is born within a certain period after the termination of the marriage, often set at ten months or 300 days.[65]

In the interest of stabilizing family relationships, the COMMON LAW employs the universal presumption of legitimacy in favor of children born in wedlock. The presumption is rooted in case law but also has found statutory expression.[66] In ENGLAND, the rule colorfully referred to the husband's presence within the "four seas" – if present, a child born to his wife was legitimate unless he could prove impotency.[67]

26. *England.* – Today, ENGLISH law continues to accord a presumption of legitimacy to every child born during the existence of marriage. As a general proposition, the presumption also arises where the child is born after the dissolution of the marriage but within the possible period of gestation.[68]

It has been said that ENGLAND's presumption of legitimacy operates on two levels. It is presumed that the husband and wife had intercourse.[69] Therefore, the presumption arises only if opportunity of access during the relevant period is shown.[70] ENGLAND allows the husband or wife to testify as to access or lack of access, but neither may be compelled to give such evidence.[71] Evidence concerning natural impossibility is also admissible.[72] Even beyond the question of access, however, the ENGLISH presumption of legitimacy is rebuttable by proof meeting the standard required in ordinary civil proceedings.[73] The

[63] CALIFORNIA Evidence Code § 621 (West 1966); *Hess v. Whitsitt*, 257 Cal.App.2d 552, 65 Cal.Rptr. 45 (2 Dist. 1967); but *cf. Jackson v. Jackson*, 67 Cal.2d 241, 430 P.2d 289, 60 Cal.Rptr. 649 (1967); *Hughes v. Hughes*, 125 Cal.App.2d 781, 271 P.2d 172 (1954). *Comment*, California's Tangled Web - Blood Tests and the Conclusive Presumption of Legitimacy: 20 Stan. L.Rev. 754 (1968); *Comment*, Evidence – Presumption of Legitimacy – Blood Grouping Test Insufficient to Prove Non-Paternity Where Statutory Presumption is Conclusive: 16 Rutgers L.Rev. 767 (1962).

[64] For AMERICAN sources see *Krause* 15-17.

[65] See *e.g.* CALIFORNIA Evidence Code (*supra* n. 63); MONTANA Rev. Codes Ann. § 61-102 (1962).

[66] See generally *Clark* 156, 172, 492.

[67] *Madden* 338-343; *Nicolas* 10-14.

[68] *Bromley* 230.

[69] *Idem* 231.

[70] *Hargrave v. Hargrave* (1846), 9 Beav. 552, 50 E.R. 457 (S.C.); *R. v. Mansfield Inhabitants* (1841), 1 Q.B. 444, 113 E.R. 1203; *Ettenfield v. Ettenfield*, [1940] P. 96, 105-106, [1940] 1 All E.R. 293, 298-299 (C.A.); *Bowen v. Norman*, [1938] 2 All E.R. 776 (K.B.).

[71] Matrimonial Causes Act 1965, s. 43. *Russell v. Russell*, [1924] A.C. 687 (H.L.) had disallowed evidence of a husband or wife which would bastardize a child.

[72] *Halsbury* (-*Whiteside*), Bastardy § 143-144.

[73] Family Law Reform Act 1969, s. 26; *Bromley* 231.

former rule was that the presumption could be rebutted only by evidence which was "strong and satisfactory."[74]

27. *United States.* – While all AMERICAN states admit proof of improbability or at least impossibility of access, some states still render it next to impossible to prove that the child is not the offspring of actual or presumed intercourse between the mother and her husband.[75] As recently as 1967, a CALIFORNIA court held that a part-Negro child born to a white woman was the legitimate child of the mother's white husband.[76] Even those states that have a rebuttable presumption typically make a rebuttal difficult.[77] In many of these states, actual impossibility of the husband's paternity often turns out to be the only basis for bastardizing a child born in wedlock. To show impossibility, conclusive proof of non-paternity by blood test exclusions may suffice, and so may proof of non-access by the husband during the relevant period, or proof of the husband's sterility or impotency. In AMERICA, in contrast to ENGLAND, the presumption of legitimacy continues to be supported further by rules of evidence which restrict a spouse's ability to testify to non-access.[78] It is notable (because not altogether sensible) that the same presumption of legitimacy has been applied with nearly equal force to a child conceived prior to marriage and born in wedlock, and to a child conceived during marriage and born after a divorce.

In most COMMON LAW jurisdictions, paternity of the mother's husband may be attacked collaterally by anyone, at any time, and in any context in which the question of paternity is relevant. In addition, a judicial determination made upon such a collateral attack will have *res judicata* effect only between the parties and their privies. However, some AMERICAN statutes provide that only the husband may question the legitimacy of a child born to his wife, others limit the action to the husband and wife and their descendants.

In the future, more COMMON LAW jurisdictions may tend to limit the contestants as well as the time for contest. A recent AMERICAN example is contained in s. 6 of the "Uniform Parentage Act" approved in 1973 by the National Conference of Commissioners on Uniform State Laws.[79]

28. FRANCE premises her presumption of legitimacy on *conception* in wedlock (CC art. 312). Conception is presumed to have taken place within the period from the 300th to the 180th day before birth (CC art. 311 par. 1). Prior law made the presumption very strong, but the 1972 reform has weakened it. Previously, the child could be disavowed only in limited circumstances, but now a child may be "bastardized" by simple proof that the mother's husband is not the father.[80] While prior law granted legitimacy to the child born later than 300 days after the termination of the marriage, at least until disavowed specifically, current law does not. In doubtful cases, the time limits are adhered to strictly. The time starts running as soon as there is legal or *de facto* separation or divorce (CC art. 315). On the other hand, a child born in wedlock prior to the 180th day after marriage remains legitimate until disavowed.[81] To accomplish the disavowal, current law gives the husband six months after the birth (or after his return, if he was absent, or after his discovery of the birth, if the birth was hidden from him), instead of the two months provided by earlier law.[82] After the husband's death, his heirs may bring an action within the same period.[83] Given certain circumstances, the child may bring the action at any time (CC art. 325). The child's mother may dispute her husband's paternity only if and when the marries the child's actual father (CC art. 318).

29. In WEST GERMANY, a child is legitimate if born during his parents' marriage or within 302 days of its termination (CC § 1593). If the child was born later than 180 days after the celebration and not more than 302 days after the dissolution of his parents' marriage, a strong presumption of legitimacy applies.[84] The presumption may be rebutted by proof that the husband had no possibility of access to his wife at the relevant time (CC § 1591 par. 1) or if a conclusion other than that the child is illegitimate would be "obviously

74 *Bromley, ibidem.*

75 AMERICAN sources in *Krause* 16–17.

76 *Hess. v. Whitsitt, supra* n. 63.

77 *E.g.* NORTH DAKOTA Cent. Code § 14-09-03 (1960).

78 See *Clark* 169, 398.

79 See *Krause*, The Uniform Parentage Act: 8 Fam. L.Q. 1-25 (1974).

80 CC art. 312, 313 (former version); CC art. 311 par. 3, 312 par. 2 (as revised 1972).

81 CC art. 314; *Carbonnier* 490. Disavowal is made more difficult if the mother's husband knew of the pregnancy or if, after the child's birth, he behaved as if he were the father (*cf.* CC art. 314 par. 3).

82 CC art. 316, 316-2, 326.

83 CC art. 327, as revised.

84 CC § 1591, 1592 presume legitimacy if married parents had intercourse within the period from 302 to 180 days before the child's birth and that married parents did have intercourse within that time. *Cf. Dölle* II 45 ss.

impossible" (CC § 1591 par. 2). Legitimacy must be contested formally (CC § 1593) and within a certain time of the child's birth (CC § 1594). It may be contested only by the husband or, in the case of the husband's death, by his parents (CC § 1595 a) or, under certain circumstances, by the child (CC § 1596). To illustrate, the child of a marriage terminated by divorce or annulment is entitled to contest his legitimacy (CC § 1596 par. 1 no. 2) within two years after obtaining knowledge of the possibility that he may be illegitimate (CC § 596 par. 2).

30. In EAST GERMANY, also, a child is legitimate if born during his parents' marriage or within 302 days of its termination (FC § 54 par. 5).[85] The child's legitimacy may be disputed by the mother or her husband within one year of the child's birth. The state's attorney, on the other hand, may challenge the child's legitimacy in the child's interest at any time.[86] EAST GERMANY differs from WEST GERMANY insofar as no formal presumptions determine legitimacy, such as, for instance, the WEST GERMAN presumption that the husband actually had intercourse with his wife during the legally recognized period of conception.

31. In NORWAY, a child born to a married mother is legitimate, unless her husband has been judicially declared not to be the child's father or another man has been held to be the child's illegitimate father. A child born after the dissolution of the marriage who could have been conceived during the marriage, is the former husband's legitimate child, unless the mother is married to someone else at the time of his birth, in which case the child is the legitimate child of the mother's new husband. No definite dates define the period of gestation and limit with precision the period during which the presumption operates.[88] The presumption may be rebutted by the husband, within three years of obtaining knowledge of the child's birth. To succeed, the husband must show either that another man has had sexual relations with the mother and it is probable that he is the child's father or that it is certain that the husband is not the child's father. Special rules apply to a challenge of a child's legitimacy after the death of the mother's husband.[89]

32. The SOVIET UNION is conspicuous in its de-emphasis of the status of legitimacy.[90] A child is called legitimate if he is descended from parents who are married to each other. Entry of a birth in the birth registry is made upon application of one or both of the parents and a false entry of parentage may be attacked within one year. A child may prove his descent from the marriage by showing the marriage registration of his parents. Registration as the child of his parents' marriage also is extended to a child born within ten months after a divorce or an annulment of the marriage or after the death of the mother's husband.[91]

33. CZECHOSLOVAKIA and POLAND, on the other hand, continue to express a traditional presumption that a child born during a marriage or within 300 days of its termination is the legitimate child of the mother's husband, unless the mother has remarried in which case the child is presumed to be the legitimate child of her new husband.[92] A challenge must be made within six months of obtaining knowledge of the birth, and proof of actual impossibility of paternity is required if the child was born later than 180 days of the marriage and earlier than 300 days after its termination.[93]

34. MEXICO and the PHILIPPINES presume that children born at least 180 days after marriage or within 300 days of its termination are legitimate. In both countries, this nearly conclusive presumption may be overcome *solely* by proving that the husband could not possibly have had intercourse with his wife during the first 120 of the 300 days immediately preceding the child's birth.[94]

Technically, a MEXICAN child born more than 300 days after the judicial separation of the spouses incident to divorce or annulment proceedings remains legitimate until he has been disavowed by the mother's husband who continues to be the husband until the final decree is rendered. The husband's disavowal of his wife's child may be contested by the mother, the child or its guardian, on the basis of proof showing that sexual relations between mother and husband continued even after a judicial separation.[95] After the dissolution of the marriage, the child's legitimacy may be attacked by any other person who is disadvantaged by the child's legitimate status (CC art. 329).

[85] In its language, the EAST GERMAN Family Code does not distinguish between legitimate and illegitimate birth; instead, the distinction is made between children whose parents are married or unmarried.

[86] FC § 61, 62.

[87] *Lov no. 9* § 5; *Arnholm* 35.

[88] *Lov no. 9* § 1 par. 2; *Arnholm* 34.

[89] *Lov no. 9* § 3 par. 2, 3.

[90] *Cf. Drobnig*, Ideologie, Recht und Wirklichkeit der Familie in der DDR: JbOstR 8 (1967) II 157, 175–177; *Stone* 392, 423.

[91] RSFSR FC art. 47, 49, 149 par. 3, 4.

[92] CZECHOSLOVAKIA: FC § 51; POLAND: FC art. 62.

[93] CZECHOSLOVAKIA: FC § 57, 58; POLAND: FC art. 63, 64, 67.

[94] MEXICO: CC art. 324, 325; PHILIPPINES: CC art. 255.

[95] CC art. 327; *Rojina Villegas* 433, 444.

PHILIPPINE law, on the other hand, provides expressly that no presumption of legitimacy or illegitimacy applies to a child born more than 300 days after separation or annulment (divorce not being permitted under PHILIPPINE law) and the legitimacy or illegitimacy of such a child must be proved affirmatively (CC art. 261).

In MEXICO (CC art. 328) and the PHILIPPINES (CC art. 258), a child born *within* 180 days of the marriage is conclusively presumed legitimate, if the husband knew of his wife's pregnancy prior to the marriage, or if he was present at the certification of the child's birth and signed the birth certificate, or, in the PHILIPPINES, if, being present, he consented to having his surname put on the record of birth of the child, or if he expressly or tacitly recognized the child as his own. In MEXICO, the child born within 180 days of marriage also is presumed legitimate if the mother's husband has expressly and formally recognized the child as his or if the child is stillborn (CC art. 328). Finally, PHILIPPINE law raises a *prima facie* presumption of legitimacy of children born within 180 days of the marriage who are unable to fulfill the requirements of the conclusive presumption (CC art. 258).

Although both systems specifically prohibit the remarriage of the woman within 300 days of the dissolution of her prior marriage,[96] specific provision is made to govern the status of a child born within this period to a woman who has remarried in violation of the prohibition. Thus, a child born within 300 days of the dissolution of the earlier marriage is attributed to that marriage, unless his birth comes 180 or more days after the later marriage in which case he is deemed to be the child of the later marriage.[97] In both countries, these presumptions are rebuttable. Also note that MEXICAN law specifically deems a child illegitimate if he is born within 180 days of the later marriage, but more than 300 days after the dissolution of the earlier marriage (CC art. 334), whereas PHILIPPINE law, under these circumstances, would employ a rebuttable presumption of legitimacy.[98]

In MEXICO (CC art. 345) and the PHILIPPINES (CC art. 256) so long as the husband lives, only he may dispute the legitimacy of a child conceived by his wife during the marriage and even the mother's testimony cannot serve to impeach the legitimacy of a child born in wedlock. In MEXICO, the husband must dispute the legitimacy of a child born to his wife within 60 days reckoned from the child's birth, if the husband was present (CC art. 330). The comparable period allowed by PHILIPPINE law is one year (CC art. 263). If the birth was kept secret from the husband, the MEXICAN 60 day period and the PHILIPPINE one year period are reckoned from the time he gained knowledge of the birth. If the husband was absent at the time of the child's birth, MEXICAN law reckons its 60 day period from the time of his return, whereas PHILIPPINE law imposes a flat period of eighteen months in the case of a husband resident in the PHILIPPINES and two years in the case of a non-resident.[99] MEXICO provides specifically that a mentally incompetent husband may be represented by his guardian, but if his right of challenge is not exercised, the husband may himself exercise it within 60 days of regaining legal capacity. If the husband dies without having regained legal capacity, the right may be exercised by his heirs.[100] The heirs of a deceased husband, however, may not question the legitimacy of a child born to his wife within 180 days of the marriage, unless the husband had himself started the disavowal proceedings (CC art. 333). In the PHILIPPINES, the heirs of the husband may impugn the legitimacy of the child only if the husband has died before the expiration of the period fixed for bringing his action, if he has died after filing the complaint, or if the child was born after his death (CC art. 262).

MEXICO provides that the disavowal of a child by the husband or his heirs must be accomplished by judicial proceeding. Any other form of disavowal is ineffective (CC art. 335). The mother and the child (or his guardian, if the child is a minor) must be heard (CC art. 336). Only a final judgment may result in loss of legitimate status. Effective legal protections, including injunctive relief, apply to the enjoyment of filial rights.[101] A disavowal proceeding may be instituted only if a child was legally "born", which requires that he has lived separately from the mother for at least 24 hours or was shown alive to an officer of the civil register (CC art. 337).

Settlements or compromises concerning the child's *status* are not allowed under MEXICAN law (CC art. 338). Settlements *are* permissible, however, if they merely concern *financial* claims that relate to legitimate descent. For example, the father's agreement to allow his illegitimate child to use his name would be invalid, because it would deal with a non-financial aspect of status.[102]

[96] MEXICO: CC art. 158; PHILIPPINES: CC art. 84, PC art. 351.

[97] MEXICO: CC art. 334; PHILIPPINES: CC art. 259.

[98] CC art. 258, 261.

[99] MEXICO: CC art. 330; PHILIPPINES: CC art. 263.

[100] CC art. 331, 332.

[101] CC art. 353; CCProc. art. 24.

[102] CC art. 339; *Rojina Villegas* 466, 467.

iii. *Comparative Summary*

35. *Applicability of presumption of legitimacy.* – The comparative study of legitimacy shows that two issues are universal: biological paternity, a question of fact, and legitimacy, a question of law. Both issues usually are resolved by the presumption that the husband of a married mother is the child's father. Normally, this accords with the facts. With respect to the child born to a married mother, the issue of biological paternity arises only if the presumption of the husband's paternity, and with it the child's legitimacy, is rebutted.

The general presumption that the husband is the father of a child born to his wife often consists of a chain of special presumptions, such as the presumption of intercourse, the presumption that the child was conceived by the intercourse, and presumptions relating to the period of gestation. The father-child relationship that is thus established is universally described by the concept of legitimacy which represents a social-legal status.

Although uniformly based on the marriage of the child's mother, time periods covered by presumptions at both the inception and the termination of a marriage vary remarkably. For children conceived before marriage, there are three positions. The strict rule holds that the presumption of legitimacy does not apply to children born within 180 days after marriage (MEXICO, PHILIPPINES and further, SPAIN[103]), and within 200 days in JAPAN.[104] The stringency of the rule is mitigated somewhat by extending legitimacy to those children who, in form (MEXICO) or in effect (MEXICO, PHILIPPINES and SPAIN[105]), are recognized by the father. A second approach includes all children born after marriage within the presumption, but allows the husband to contest paternity if the birth took place within 180 days after marriage (FRANCE, ITALY, GREECE, SWITZERLAND and ARGENTINA[106]). Only certain circumstances, such as the husband's knowledge of the wife's premarital pregnancy,[107] may preclude his right to contest the child's legitimacy.[108] A third approach is most liberal and most frequently employed today. No more than birth after the celebration of marriage is required in order to apply the presumption of legitimacy (UNITED STATES, ENGLAND, WEST GERMANY, NORWAY, EUROPEAN SOCIALIST countries, and, further, SWEDEN, NETHERLANDS and AUSTRIA[109]).

After termination of marriage, the presumption of paternity usually applies if conception could have occurred during wedlock.[110] Many systems fix a precise period, such as 300 days (states in the UNITED STATES, FRANCE, CZECHOSLOVAKIA, POLAND, the PHILIPPINES, and, among others, JAPAN, ARGENTINA, BELGIUM and GREECE[112]) or 302 days (WEST and EAST GERMANY) or ten months (states in the UNITED STATES, and SOVIET UNION). A few countries, however, are more flexible and refer to the biological period of gestation (states in the UNITED STATES, ENGLAND, NORWAY and SWEDEN[113]). This, of course, is more difficult to ascertain. Some laws extend the presumption to children born more than 300 days after dissolution of the marriage, but permit contest of their legitimacy by simple declaration.[114]

If the wife remarries shortly after dissolution of a prior marriage and gives birth to a child during the period covered by presumptions in favor of both prior and present husbands, the presumption in favor of the latter usually prevails (NORWAY, CZECHOSLOVAKIA, POLAND, and, further, BELGIUM, NETHERLANDS and AUSTRIA[115]). Other countries (MEXICO, PHILIPPINES, and, among others, ARGENTINA, PORTUGAL and GREECE[116]) establish a rebut-

[103] SPAIN: CC art. 110.

[104] CC art. 772 par. 2; but the Supreme Court (23 Jan. 1940, Minshū 19, 54) has decided that a child conceived in "*naien*" (a non-registered marriage-like union) is legitimate if born after formal registration of the marriage.

[105] SPAIN: CC art. 110.

[106] FRANCE: CC art. 314 (even by simple declaration); ITALY: CC art. 233; GREECE: CC art. 1466, 1468; SWITZERLAND: CC art. 255; similarly ARGENTINA: CC art. 246, 253.

[107] See FRENCH CC art. 314; GREEK CC art. 1469; ITALIAN CC art. 233 par. 2.

[108] The limited scope of the presumption of paternity is enlarged by permitting the child to rely on a status of "apparent legitimacy" (*possession d'état*) if legitimacy cannot be proved otherwise; *e.g.* SPAIN: CC art. 117; FRANCE: CC art. 319 ss.

[109] SWEDEN: *Föräldrabalk* ch. 1 § 1; NETHERLANDS: New CC art. 197; AUSTRIA: CC § 138.

[110] With the exception of some FRENCH-based laws, *infra* n. 114.

[111] According to FRENCH CC art. 313 a divorce or separation suit may set in motion the 300-day-limit, given certain circumstances.

[112] JAPAN: CC art. 772; ARGENTINA: CC art. 240; BELGIUM: CC art. 315 (with certain limitations); GREECE: CC art. 1446.

[113] *Föräldrabalk* ch. 1 § 1.

[114] ITALY: CC art. 234; SPAIN: CC art. 111; formerly also in FRANCE.

[115] BELGIUM: CC art. 315; NETHERLANDS: New CC art. 197; AUSTRIA: CC § 138 par. 2.

[116] ARGENTINA: CC art. 241, 242; PORTUGAL: CC art. 1806; GREECE: CC art. 1467.

table presumption to the same effect only if the birth occurred at least 180 days after the inception of the new marriage. In JAPAN, neither presumption is given preference, and the court must decide who the father is.[117]

36. *Rebuttal of presumption of legitimacy.* – Generally, the presumption of the husband's paternity may be rebutted. Certain circumstances (such as knowledge of the wife's premarital pregnancy or recognition of the child[118]) may preclude the husband from contesting legitimacy.

The traditional tendency to set extremely high standards for rebuttal has been relaxed. This may be due as much to changing sex *mores* in many of the countries under study as to the increasing accuracy of scientific methods of determining paternity. However, the extent to which the laws rely on these tests differs. Certain links in the chain of presumptions constituting the presumption of legitimacy may remain irrebuttable either by express command or in practical result (*e.g.*, the presumption of conception due to intercourse in some states in the UNITED STATES). In other systems, certain methods of contest or disproof are restricted by procedural means or may be precluded altogether (states in the UNITED STATES limit testimony as to non-access; in MEXICO, the PHILIPPINES and elsewhere, the mother cannot testify against her husband's paternity).

Great variation exists as to who may challenge legitimacy during what period and by what procedure. The COMMON LAW and CIVIL LAW take opposing views. The COMMON LAW allows contest by anyone, at any time, in any procedure, generally limiting the *res judicata* effect to the parties to the proceeding. The CIVIL LAW differs on all four points. The group of persons who may attack legitimacy and the period during which contest is allowed are limited. A specific "status proceeding" is prescribed which has binding effect *erga omnes*. Recent AMERICAN legislative efforts to limit the circle of persons who may contest and the period for contests may indicate some future convergence between the two approaches.[119]

Although they all follow the general scheme outlined above, the CIVIL LAW systems are far from uniform. Those allowed to contest paternity are, first of course, the husband himself and after his death his parents (WEST GERMANY) or, more frequently, his heirs (under varying conditions, FRANCE, MEXICO, the PHILIPPINES, and, further, BELGIUM, GREECE, SWEDEN, SWITZERLAND and SPAIN[120]). Although these laws do not normally permit others to contest paternity, the modern trend may be to widen the circle of potential contesters. NORWAY and SWEDEN and, to a limited extent, FRANCE and WEST GERMANY, allow the child to bring suit. The mother is always eligible to contest paternity in EAST GERMANY and, exceptionally, in FRANCE. EAST GERMANY and AUSTRIA[121] also give standing to the public prosecutor.

The period for bringing the action ranges from one month after birth in BELGIUM[122] to three years in NORWAY. Rather short periods (of six months to a year) seem to be favored by most laws.[123] No time limits at all apply to the child in FRANCE or to the public prosecutor in EAST GERMANY. The length of the period in which paternity may be contested seems to correlate to the degree of disfavor with which the system views the contest of paternity. Those systems which limit the presumption of paternity strictly generally seem to prefer short periods for contest. Conversely, the further the presumption is extended, the longer it may be rebutted.

The two most important grounds of contest are lack of access by the husband and, if there was access, natural impossibility of procreation. NORWAY and the EUROPEAN SOCIALIST countries do not recognize lack of access as a separate category. Other countries, such as MEXICO and the PHILIPPINES, preclude impotence as a basis for contest.

37. *Conclusion.* – While the scope of the presumption has generally remained unchanged, rebuttal of the presumption has been facilitated

[117] JAPAN: CC art. 773. The decision depends on the balance of probabilities.

[118] NETHERLANDS: Knowledge of premarital pregnancy: New CC art. 201 par. 2 (also if the husband "admitted an act that could have led to conception of the child", New CC art. 201 par. 1). Recognition of child by the husband: SWEDISH *Föräldrabalk* ch. 2 § 1 par. 2.

[119] Uniform Parentage Act § 4, 6. Concerning the "status" effect of divorce decrees in the UNITED STATES, *cf.* Restatement of Judgments (1942) § 74.

[120] BELGIUM: CC art. 316, 317; GREECE: CC art. 1468, 1472, 1474, but see also art. 1470; SWEDEN: *Föräldrabalk* ch. 2 § 2; SWITZERLAND: CC art. 253; SPAIN: CC art. 112.

[121] AUSTRIA: CC § 158; SWITZERLAND: CC art. 256 par. 2, in case of premarital conception, permits contest also by the cantonal authorities.

[122] BELGIUM: CC art. 316. Similar brief periods are imposed by MEXICO; SPAIN: two months (CC art. 113 par. 1, but see also art. 113 par. 2); ITALY: three months (CC art. 244, but see CC art. 248 par. 2); SWITZERLAND: three months (CC art. 253).

[123] Six months: CZECHOSLOVAKIA, POLAND, NETHERLANDS (New CC art. 203 par. 1); one year: EAST GERMANY, PHILIPPINES, also GREECE (CC art. 1474, but see also art. 1468) and AUSTRIA (CC § 156 par. 1).

in favor of the determination of the true father. Nevertheless, biological paternity is not the only factor considered in the determination of legitimacy. Paramount consideration no longer goes to the legal stability of the legitimate family nor to the husband's interest in dissolving his legal relationship to a child that is not his. Rather, the interests of the child are gaining increasing recognition (*e.g.*, the child's established membership in a social setting is receiving attention,[124] as is his right to contest that membership by challenging his mother's husband's paternity).

B. LEGITIMATION THROUGH INVALID MARRIAGE

i. *Principal Approaches*

38. A child who, because of a defect in his parents' marital status, fails to meet the strict definition of legitimacy discussed previously has another chance in most legal systems. Implicitly recognizing that the principal reason behind the reference to marital status is identification of paternity, not morality or even legality, it often is provided that the child of an invalid marriage obtains legitimate status as to both parents.

It is generally agreed that a voidable marriage, especially where the defect is formal only, confers full legitimate status regardless of a later annulment of the marriage.

The void marriage has presented more difficulty. Some systems have been concerned with the reason for the voidness of the marriage. For example, a marriage void by reason of incest or bigamy may be ineffective to confer legitimate status on a resulting child whereas a marriage void by reason of a partner's insanity may be allowed to confer legitimacy. Without convincing logic, but following the historical tradition of the doctrine of putative marriage, some systems base the legitimacy of the offspring of a void marriage on the good faith of the parents and confer legitimacy only as to the parent who was unaware of the impediment.

ii. *Illustrations*

39. *United States.* – Under the COMMON LAW, a void or voidable marriage was declared invalid with *ab initio* effect and any offspring of such a marriage was illegitimate.[125] Today, several AMERICAN states give legitimate status to the child of almost any alliance that resembles a formal marriage, often without distinguishing between a void and a voidable marriage.[126]

Children are covered whose parents' marriage did not meet the test of legality because of failure to comply with formal details, or because of legal disabilities of a parent, such as a continuing prior marriage (bigamy), consanguinity (incest), nonage, idiocy or insanity, and the like. Not all states, however, have been as generous. Apparently no state legitimates the offspring of an invalid, informal (common law) marriage. In some jurisdictions the impediments of prior marriage or consanguinity have given pause, and only children of unions invalid by reason of "lesser" impediments, such as nonage, idiocy, or insanity of one or both partners are legitimated. Under some statutes, the good faith of the parties may play a decisive role. Still others restrict the child's legitimate status to the would-be spouse who was not under an impediment. It is of historical interest that some statutes prohibiting racial inter-marriage and declaring such marriages void specifically excluded (or were judicially interpreted to exclude) the issue of such unions from a general legitimation statute.[127].

40. Until 1959, ENGLAND did not alter the COMMON LAW rule that children of a *void marriage* are illegitimate. Children of void marriages now are deemed legitimate if the father was domiciled in England at the time of the birth and both or either of the parties reasonably believed their marriage to be valid either at the time of conception of the child or at the time of the celebration of the marriage, whichever is later. The provision applies retroactively but not so as to defeat any interests in property created or dispositions made prior to the legislation.[128]

ENGLAND's children of *voidable marriages* are

[124] *Cf.* esp. NETHERLANDS: New CC art. 201 (see *supra* n. 118).

[125] For AMERICAN sources, see *Krause* 11; *Clark* 132–135.

[126] *E.g.* ILLINOIS Rev.Stat. ch. 89 § 17a (1969); MARYLAND Ann.Code art. 16 § 27 and art. 93 § 151 (1957); TEXAS Probate Code Ann. § 42 (1956): "The issue also of marriages deemed null in law shall nevertheless be legitimate." – For further sources see *Clark* 132–135.

[127] For all of s. 39 see *supra* n. 125.

[128] Legitimacy Act, 1959, s. 2. *Hawkins v. A. G.*, [1966] 1 All E.R. 392 (P.); *cf. Philp's Trustees v. Beaton*, 1938 S.C. 733.

legitimated by a separate Act which legitimates children of marriages annulled because, at the time of the marriage, either party was insane, suffering from a mental disorder, subject to recurrent attacks of epilepsy, or suffering from a communicable venereal disease.[129]

41. In FRANCE, a void or voidable marriage produces full legitimacy for the child as to both parents. Earlier law required at least one of the spouses to have acted in good faith,[130] but this requirement has now been dropped.[131]

42. *West Germany and Socialist countries.* – WEST GERMANY deems the child of a void[132] or voidable[133] marriage legitimate regardless of the good or bad faith of one or both of the spouses.[134] CZECHOSLOVAKIA (FC § 17 par. 2), EAST GERMANY (FC § 36 par. 1), and POLAND (FC art. 21) follow this view. SOVIET law provides expressly that "the annulment of a marriage has no effect on the rights of the children born to such a marriage."[135]

43. *Mexico, Philippines.* – In MEXICO, regardless of the spouses' good or bad faith, the declaration that a marriage is invalid does not affect the legitimacy of children born in the invalidated marriage (CC art. 344). In the PHILIPPINES, children conceived or born of marriages void from the beginning (such as an incestuous marriage between brother and sister) have "the same status, rights and obligations as acknowledged natural children, and are called natural children by legal fiction" (CC art. 89). The same protection applies to children conceived even after the final decree of annulment in a marriage voidable, for instance, by reason of fraud or duress, whereas children conceived before the decree are considered to be legitimate (CC art. 89).

iii. *Comparative Summary*

44. Marriage to the child's mother is the universal condition to the husband's presumed paternity and the child's legitimacy. Although the probability of intercourse between the "spouses" would seem to be the same whether or not the marriage suffers from a substantive defect, most laws formerly predicated presumptions of paternity and legitimacy on the validity of the marriage. Today, this rule has been almost universally reversed for the children of voidable marriages who are considered legitimate (but not, for instance, in IRELAND and ITALY).[136] An increasing number of countries also considers the children of void marriages legitimate.[137] Legal systems which retain the traditional rule regarding children of void marriages rarely do so without exception. The majority denies legitimacy only in the presence of additional factors (such as serious marital defects, *e.g.*, bigamy or incest[138] or bad faith of the parents as to the validity of the marriage[139]). Occasionally, the child is given a sort of one-sided or incomplete legitimacy, *i.e.*, he may be legitimate as to only one parent[140] or may have status as an acknowledged "natural" child.[141]

C. EFFECT OF INFORMAL MARRIAGE

i. *Principal Approaches*

45. In all of the world's legal systems, modern trends would abolish "common law" or informal marriage. In many areas, especially in CONTINENTAL EUROPE, this has been accomplished. In other areas, especially DEVELOPING countries and some COMMON LAW jurisdictions, that trend is ongoing. But it may be speculated that "informal marriage" may yet have a new day. Pragmatic modern law will have to come to terms with disuse of "formal" marriage by segments of the population which, among intellectuals in SCANDINAVIA and in

[129] Matrimonial Causes Act 1965, s. 9 (b-d), 11.

[130] CC art. 201, 202. The good faith of one spouse sufficed to produce legitimacy as to both spouses: Cass. civ. 5 Jan. 1910, D.P. 1911.1.338. *Cf.* the "putative spouse doctrine" which had its origin in CANON law and which still is recognized in the law of a number of SOUTHERN and SOUTHWESTERN states of the UNITED STATES: *Foote, Levy and Sander* (*supra* n. 11) 282-285.

[131] CC art. 202, as revised.

[132] *Ehegesetz* § 16-22; CC § 1591.

[133] *Ehegesetz* § 30-34 and 39.

[134] *Palandt* (*-Lauterbach*) § 1591 no. 2.

[135] Fundamentals of Family Law art. 15 par. 2.

[136] Concerning the COMMON LAW *cf. Bromley* 65 and 299-300. IRELAND follows the COMMON LAW rule. ITALY: CC art. 128.

[137] FRANCE, WEST GERMANY, EAST GERMANY, CZECHOSLOVAKIA, POLAND, SOVIET UNION; SPAIN: CC art. 69; NETHERLANDS: New CC art. 77 par. 2 *lit.* a; SWEDEN: *Giftermålsbalk* ch. 10 § 4; SWITZERLAND: CC art. 133; YUGOSLAVIA: Fundamental Act on Marriage art. 49; states of the UNITED STATES.

[138] Some states of the UNITED STATES; also GREECE: CC art. 1382; similarly AUSTRIA: *Ehegesetz* § 29 if the marriage was entered into only to confer name or nationality to the other part.

[139] ENGLAND, some states of the UNITED STATES; *cf.* further *e.g.*, ITALY: CC art. 128; BELGIUM: CC art. 201, 202; ARGENTINA: CC art. 87 ss.

[140] Some states of the UNITED STATES; also ITALY: CC art. 128 par. 3.

[141] PHILIPPINES; but this is also the position of the child in ITALY, BELGIUM, ARGENTINA (*supra* n. 139) if good faith is lacking.

the Black population of the UNITED STATES, for example, has reached impressive proportions.

One crucial effect of the law's failure to recognize informal marriage, of course, is that *de jure* illegitimacy is created where *de facto* families exist. That may be bad policy. It also may be that internal economic relations of longer-run "informal" partnerships ultimately will need regulation by law to reduce over-reaching. In the meantime, however, it must be recognized that many jurisdictions feel that formal marriage should be the sole or prime route to legal rights for spouse and offspring.

ii. *Illustrations*

46. *United States, England.* – ENGLAND abolished common law marriage in 1753 by *Lord Hardwicke*'s Act. In the UNITED STATES, on the other hand, common law marriage has retained some vitality.[142] About one-third of the states still recognize the institution which, in one of its forms, views a union as a valid marriage if the intending spouses have presently consented to be husband and wife, if the marriage has been consummated, and if the spouses have publicly held out each other as such. Where valid, such a union produces legitimate offspring. Where it is not valid, resulting children are illegitimate.

Interestingly, even in jurisdictions where common law marriages are not recognized, the parents' cohabitation may effectively confer legitimacy on their child. Although a valid marriage has not been made out clearly, the COMMON LAW, in certain factual situations, will presume that a valid marriage exists. COMMON LAW courts presume "morality, and not immorality; marriage, and not concubinage; legitimacy, and not bastardy." Optimistically, *Clark* adds to this that "there is the additional basis of probability for these presumptions" (p. 67). Proof that persons have cohabited as man and wife raises a presumption of marriage and the person attacking that presumption bears the burden of proof. Mere absence of a marriage record does not establish the invalidity of a marriage. Conversely, the presence of a marriage record raises a presumption that the marriage has continued. If two marriages are documented, most AMERICAN courts will, in the absence of contrary evidence, presume the validity of the later marriage which means that they will presume that the earlier marriage was effectively dissolved. Indeed, they may apply that presumption even if the first marriage is documented and the second rests on no more than evidence of cohabitation and holding out as husband and wife.[143]

Where applicable, the presumptions in the abstract may operate to provide legitimacy to a child who might otherwise be illegitimate. The matter goes deeper, however. The court's very decision concerning the applicability of a presumption of marriage may be influenced or even determined by the presence of offspring. This means that the presumption can serve as a nearly discretionary device which allows the court to achieve the result it wishes. Some courts come right out and say that the presumption of validity of a marriage is stronger if issue may be bastardized by a contrary holding. In NEW YORK, the presumption of legitimacy of the issue of an earlier common law marriage was held strong enough to overcome the countervailing presumption of the validity of a later ceremonial marriage. Another NEW YORK court held valid a second common law marriage because it had produced offspring, even though there was no showing of the dissolution of the widow's first marriage.[145] Conversely, in the absence of offspring, a TEXAS court refused to find a common law marriage between a man and woman who cohabited for seven months.[146]

It is important to note that ENGLISH law, though not recognizing informal marriages, in fact operates with quite similar presumptions and thus also may establish a marriage and legitimacy, where none may be.[147]

47. Although FRANCE similarly requires formal marriage,[148] she will not have children bastardized for the sole reason that they cannot produce a certificate of legitimate birth. In its absence, possession of status as a legitimate child suffices to prove legitimate descent (CC art. 320). Possession of status (*possession d'état*) is carefully defined.[149] Generally speaking, it exists if the child has been treated continually as a legitimate child by his parents, society at large and public authorities. In addition, FRENCH law admits the possibility of legitimating a child whose *deceased* parents have

[142] For AMERICAN sources, see *Krause* 17.

[143] *Clark* 67-70.

[144] *E.g., Anderson v. Anderson,* 235 Ind. 113, 131 N.E.2d 301 (1956); *Schaffer v. Richardson's Estate,* 125 Md. 88, 93 A. 391 (1915).

[145] *Matter of Meehan,* 150 A.D. 681, 135 N.Y.S. 723 (1912); *In re Cassidy's Estate,* 109 Misc. 202, 178 N.Y.S. 366 (Sur.Ct.N.Y. 1919).

[146] *Lopez v. Mo., K. & T. Ry. Co.,* 222 S.W. 695, 698 (Tex.Civ.App. 1920).

[147] *Bromley* 52-55.

[148] CC art. 194, 195; *cf. Mazeaud,* Leçons no. 813.

[149] CC art. 311-1, 311-2.

lived together as if they were married, if the child's birth certificate does not contradict his reputation as his parents' legitimate child (CC art. 197).

48. *West Germany and Socialist countries.* – In addition to their absolute rigor in requiring formality of marriage, EAST[150] and WEST GERMANY[151] require that a marriage be *proved* by formal documents. This involves a showing of the officially registered marriage records. Absent this required documentary proof, a child is illegitimate. Lost documents may be replaced by appropriate judicial procedures. Similarly, CZECHOSLOVAKIA, POLAND, and the SOVIET UNION require a formal marriage ceremony before state authorities and refuse effect to informal arrangements.[152]

49. MEXICO, on the other hand, is an example of a civil law jurisdiction which formally follows the rule against informal marriage, but clandestinely allows legitimate status to the offspring of many legally doubtful unions. The Civil Code states expressly that the illegitimate child's descent from his father may be established *only* through the father's voluntary recognition or through a paternity judgment (CC art. 360). The Code steers clear of actually legitimating the child of a legally ineffective *de facto* marriage. However, by facilitating proof of legitimacy and making proof of illegitimacy difficult, MEXICAN law provides legitimate status to many children of what may be little more than *de facto* marriages.

The MEXICAN Code provides that the legitimacy of a child born within a marriage is proved by means of his birth certificate and the marriage certificate of his parents (CC art. 340). However, if documents are not available or if those that are available are damaged, incomplete or incorrect, legitimacy is established by the fact of *continued possession of legitimate status.*[153] Failing that, all legal means of proof are admissible; although the testimony of witnesses is admitted only if corroborated by at least a beginning of written proof or other facts.[154]

Moreover, much as in FRANCE, the legitimacy of a child descended from parents who have publicly lived together as man and wife may not be disputed solely on the ground that the child cannot produce a marriage certificate relating to his parents, if (1) the parents are deceased or the place of their marriage cannot be ascertained by reason of their death or absence and (2) the child has possessed *de facto* legitimate status or (3) his descent can be proved by legally permissible means and such proof does not contradict the child's birth certificate.[155]

Further, if through a series of uninterrupted acts a child has been recognized continuously as legitimate by the family of the husband and in society, his legitimate status is proved thereby if, in addition, there exists *one* of the following circumstances: (1) the child has continuously used the father's name with the latter's consent, (2) the father has actually treated the child as legitimate in terms of support, education and other attention, or (3) the putative father, at the time of the child's birth, was of the age required for marriage, which is the prerequisite age for the voluntary recognition of an out-of-wedlock child.[156]

50. PHILIPPINE law resembles MEXICAN law in some respects. In the first instance, it asks that legitimate status be proved by documentation, specifically the record of birth in the civil register, by authentic document, or by a final judgment (CC art. 265). In the absence of any of these, filiation may be proved by continuous possession of status as a legitimate child (CC art. 266). This includes the child's use of the parents' surname, their constant attendance to his support and education and their public recognition of the child as legitimate.[157] In the absence of documents of status, the PHILIPPINE Code provides that "legitimate filiation may be proved by any other means allowed by the rules of court and special laws" (CC art. 267). This would include an act or declaration or family reputation concerning descent or a judicial admission, an admission by a party or possibly even silence.[158]

iii. *Comparative Summary*

51. A small and decreasing number of countries (some states in the UNITED STATES and some DEVELOPING countries[159]) recognizes common law marriages as valid and confers legitimacy on the children born to such marriages. Most countries, however, give no effect to informal marriages and deny their offspring legitimacy. But this prin-

150 *Personenstandsgesetz* § 4.

151 *Personenstandsgesetz* § 60, 66.

152 CZECHOSLOVAKIA: FC § 3; POLAND: FC art. 1, 2 ss.; SOVIET UNION: Fundamentals of Family Law art. 9.

153 *Rojina Villegas* 464.

154 CCProc. art. 289; CC art. 341; *Rojina Villegas* 460-462.

155 CC art. 341, 342.

156 CC art. 344, 361.

157 *Adriano v. De Jesus*, 23 Phil. 350 (1912).

158 *Nolledo* sec. 2 (rule 129), 22, 23, 33, 35 (rule 130).

159 See, *e.g.*, GUATEMALA: CC of 1963 art. 173 ss. (which contain a detailed regulation of a special kind of *de facto* union (*unión de hecho*)). Concerning customary laws, *cf. infra* this volume ch. 11.

ciple is realized with varying degree of success.

Some countries which have nearly achieved legal equality for illegitimate and legitimate children nevertheless deny formal legitimacy if the marriage of the child's parents cannot be proved by formal documents (EAST and WEST GERMANY, POLAND and CZECHOSLOVAKIA).[160] Another group which normally requires proof of a formal marriage will nevertheless presume such a marriage where the parents have lived together as husband and wife (ENGLAND, many of the UNITED STATES, and, among others, NETHERLANDS, ECUADOR, IVORY COAST and ITALY).[161] A related approach bases legitimacy on proof that the child was treated as legitimate by his parents (FRANCE, MEXICO, PHILIPPINES, and, further, ITALY, PORTUGAL and SPAIN).[162] Many countries, although theoretically opposed to informal marriages, thus in fact confer legitimacy on children of invalid marriages.

D. LEGITIMATION THROUGH MARRIAGE AFTER THE CHILD'S BIRTH

i. *Principal Approaches*

52. "Better late than never". Most systems permit an illegitimate child to be legitimated after birth by the subsequent marriage of his parents. Even the CANON law took this view. Until well into this century, the principal exception was represented by ENGLAND which, at least since 1234, had held "once a bastard, always a bastard".[163]

Among modern legal systems, variations principally turn around the question whether an acknowledgment of the child must be made by the father at the time of his marriage to the mother, how such an acknowledgment is made, whether a void or voidable marriage has legitimating effect, and whether all classes of illegitimate children, including *adulterini*, for example, may be legitimated by a subsequent parental marriage. As indicated, while legitimation as such has lost its value in jurisdictions providing for legal equality, a subsequent marriage between the child's parents, coupled with the father's acknowledgment of the child, remains a valuable device to legally fix paternal responsibility.

ii. *Illustrations*

53. *United States.* – In AMERICA, provisions are common which legitimate an illegitimate child when his parents marry.[164] Legitimation may be automatic or may require a specific acknowledgment by the father. The acknowledgment may have to be in writing, by conduct or meet other requirements such as publicity. The effect of a void marriage subsequent to the child's birth is not always clear, although the dual handicap has been overcome where a state had both types of legitimation statutes. Where still recognized, even an informal, common law marriage may effect legitimation.

54. The ENGLISH rule that the subsequent marriage of the parents did not legitimate the child was changed in 1926. As originally enacted, the statute did not legitimate a child born in adultery but since 1959, even a child born in adultery may be legitimated by the subsequent marriage of his parents, if the father was a domiciliary of England or Wales at the time of the celebration of the marriage. However, a person legitimated by the marriage of his parents after his birth remains incapable of succeeding to any dignity or title. If the child dies prior to his parents' marriage which would have legitimated him, the child's spouse, children, and other descendants will succeed to property interests as if the child had been legitimated.[165]

55. The FRENCH illegitimate child is legitimated by the marriage of his parents.[166] A prior or simultaneous acknowledgment is required.[167] In the case of an acknowledgment after the parents' marriage, a judicial order is required (CC art. 331-1). Legitimation provides full legitimate status to the child, but is not retroactive and takes effect at the time of the parents' marriage.[168] Children who are adulterous *a patre* are legitimated by the marriage of their mother and father after the father becomes free to marry. Interestingly, the 1972 law allows the mother of an adulterous child to challenge the paternity of her previous husband so as to legitimate her child upon marriage to the actual father. Note that the mother's challenge of the prior presumption of paternity is permitted only when coupled with remarriage to

[160] Also, *e.g.*, SPAIN: CC art. 115 (generally, but *cf.* art. 116, 117 and *infra* n. 162).

[161] NETHERLANDS: New CC art. 80; ECUADOR: CC art. 349; IVORY COAST: Law no. 64-375 art. 45 ss.; ITALY: CC art. 240; SWISS CC art. 260 allows children of persons who are engaged to be declared legitimate.

[162] ITALY: CC art. 236 par. 2, 237; PORTUGAL: CC art. 1813; SPAIN: CC art. 116.

[163] Statute of Merton, 20 Hen. 3 (1234).

[164] For AMERICAN sources, see *Krause* 13–15.

[165] Legitimacy Act, 1926, s. 1, 5, 10(1).

[166] CC art. 331 to 332-1.

[167] CC art. 329, 331 par. 2.

[168] CC art. 332-1 par. 2. A deceased child's descendants will become fully legitimate as to their grandparents: CC art. 332.

the child's actual father.[169]

56. *West Germany, Norway and Socialist countries.* – In POLAND and CZECHOSLOVAKIA, as well as in EAST and WEST GERMANY and NORWAY, "legitimation" has lost much of its practical importance for the legal father-child relationship in view of the broad rights granted to children born out-of-wedlock.[170] Still, the subsequent marriage of the parents may help ascertain the child's father and it may have significance as to the name of the child[171] and for questions of parental authority.[172] Finally, the inheritance relationship between father and illegitimate child which some of the "equality" systems still limit becomes full fledged.

57. SOVIET law provides full legitimate status only to the child born in marriage or whose parents have been ascertained by common acknowledgment[173] or whose father has been ascertained in a judicial proceeding.[174] The fact of parental marriage has no additional independent significance.[175]

58. MEXICAN[176] and PHILIPPINE[177] law allow the parents' subsequent marriage to legitimate their child born previously, if they jointly or separately expressly recognize the child before, concurrently with, or after the marriage ceremony. In MEXICO, express recognition is not required if the parent's name already shows on the birth certificate (CC art. 356) and, while this appears implied in MEXICAN law, the PHILIPPINES specifically mention also the child whose parentage was established by a paternity judgment (CC art. 271 par. 1). If recognition occurs after the marriage, MEXICAN law retroactively produces all effects of legitimacy as of the time of the marriage (CC art. 357). PHILIPPINE law (while it originally followed the MEXICAN rule)[178] now relates the child's legitimate status back to his birth, regardless of when the legitimation occurred (CC art. 273). Legitimation may also be produced with respect to the descendants of a deceased child.[179] Similarly, the husband's declaration upon marriage that he recognizes his wife's unborn child if she is or might be pregnant serves to confer legitimacy on a child born within 180 days after the marriage.[180]

MEXICO has abandoned the distinction between "natural" and "spurious" illegitimates with which FRENCH law has infected so much of the world. The PHILIPPINES, on the other hand, continue the discrimination and it should be noted that PHILIPPINE law limits the possibility of legitimation to natural children.

iii. *Comparative Summary*

59. Nearly all legal systems permit the legitimation of an illegitimate child by the subsequent marriage of his parents.[181] As more systems provide equal legal treatment for legitimates and illegitimates, this form of legitimation is becoming less important as a means of equalizing the legal positions of legitimates and illegitimates. Some recent reforms (ENGLAND, FRANCE, BELGIUM)[182] reduce or abolish traditional restrictions on the *legitimatio per matrimonium subsequens,* which precluded, for instance, the legitimation of an adulterous child[183] and which required, in addition to marriage, the father's specific acknowledgment of the child.[184] In addition, the legal effect of legitimation has been improved by giving it retroactive effect,[185] although typically not to the extent of affecting vested property interests, and

[169] CC. art. 318 to 318-2.

[170] See *Lasok* 167; *Drobnig* (*supra* n. 90) 175-177.

[171] The child takes the common name of his parents or, absent a common name, the name of either parent, as agreed by them. CZECHOSLOVAKIA: FC § 39 par. 1; EAST GERMANY: FC § 64 par. 2; WEST GERMANY: CC § 1719, 1616; POLAND: FC art. 88 par. 2.

[172] EAST GERMANY: FC § 45, 46; WEST GERMANY: CC § 1719, 1626; POLAND: FC art. 93; *Lasok* 167.

[173] RSFSR FC art. 47 par. 3.

[174] RSFSR FC art. 48 par. 1.

[175] *Bergmann and Ferid, s.v.* UdSSR 34.

[176] CC art. 354, 355.

[177] CC art. 270, 271.

[178] CC art. 123, 602.

[179] MEXICO: CC art. 358; PHILIPPINES: CC art. 274.

[180] MEXICO: CC art. 324, 328, 359. PHILIPPINES: CC art. 258 par. 3; *De Jesus v. Syquia,* 58 Phil. 866 (1933).

[181] In addition to the legislation already referred to, see, *e.g.,* ITALY: CC art. 280 par. 2; GREECE: CC art. 1556; ARGENTINA: CC art. 311; SWEDEN: *Föräldrabalk* ch. 1 § 3; DENMARK: *Lov no. 200* ch. 1 § 1; YUGOSLAVIA: Fundamental Law on the Relations Between Parents and Children art. 23; IRELAND: Legitimacy Act s. 1.

[182] BELGIUM: CC art. 331 (as amended by Law of 10 Feb. 1958, Pasin. 1958, 85).

[183] PHILIPPINES; also ITALY: CC art. 281; ARGENTINA: CC art. 311; SPAIN: CC art. 119; IRELAND: Legitimacy Act s. 1 (2).

[184] Some states in the UNITED STATES, FRANCE, MEXICO, PHILIPPINES, also ITALY: CC art. 283; ARGENTINA: CC art. 317; JAPAN: CC art. 789.

[185] PHILIPPINES (retroactive to date of birth); ENGLAND, WEST GERMANY (retroactive to date of death if the child died before marriage and left descendants), so also, *e.g.,* SPAIN: CC art. 124; ARGENTINA: CC art. 316.

by providing for full equality between children thus legitimated and those born in wedlock.[186]

E. LEGITIMATION BY FATHER

60. For the sake of completeness, it should be indicated that a number of systems also permit the child born out of wedlock to obtain fully legitimate status by the father's formal act of legitimation, without the father's assumption of a marital relationship with the child's mother. As a practical matter, however, such acts of legitimation are rare – for instance, only 255 children were legitimated in this manner in all of WEST GERMANY in 1955.[187] The procedure is mentioned here because this is the logical place, but is discussed in the next subchapter (III A), where it can be put to useful contrast with the more frequent paternal acknowledgment which results in a limited legal relationship between father and child.

[186] In addition to the countries referred to earlier, ITALY: CC art. 283; SPAIN: CC art. 122; GREECE: CC art. 1559; ARGENTINA: CC art. 319; DENMARK, SWEDEN: (*supra* n. 181); NETHERLANDS: New CC art. 217 par. 1. But full equality is denied by, *e.g.*, IRELAND: Legitimacy Act 1931, s. 3 (3).

[187] *Dölle* I 541.

III. ASCERTAINMENT OF PATERNITY (AND MATERNITY)

A. VOLUNTARY ACKNOWLEDGMENT

i. *Principal Approaches*

61. *Acknowledgment by mother.* – The Latin maxim *mater semper certa est* resolves the question of the child's relationship with his mother in most systems. Establishment of the mother-child relationship typically means the legal equivalent of legitimacy. Few jurisdictions continue to impose an inferior status *vis-à-vis* the mother on the illegitimate child although some still limit his right to inherit from maternal relatives.

Only the FRENCH family of law does not consider maternity a matter of course. Thus, the mother must take formal steps to acknowledge her illegitimate child.[188] For FRANCE, the required formalities have been substantially eased by the 1972 legislation. The certificate of birth indicating the mother's name together with the child's possession of status (the child being known as her natural child) amounts to an acknowledgment by the mother (CC art. 337). Several of the systems descended from FRANCE's also have deviated from the originally quite strict requirement of maternal recognition. The MEXICAN Code, for instance, states that the illegitimate child's maternal descent is established by the fact of birth (CC art. 360). Somewhat inconsistently, other MEXICAN provisions refer to recognition of the child by the mother and even to judicial investigation of maternity and appear to confer rights upon the child by virtue of recognition or judgment rather than by virtue of the fact of birth. As a practical matter, the mother usually has been involved in the certification of her child's birth which suffices to produce recognition (CC art. 369). The PHILIPPINES continue to expect acknowledgment by the mother before the mother-child status attaches to a child born out-of wedlock (CC art. 276). Not only do the provisions concerning voluntary acknowledgment apply to father and mother, but the Code expressly requires the mother to recognize her child (by means of a "maternity action", if necessary) in the cases in which the investigation of paternity is permitted and in all other cases in which the birth and identity of the child are clearly proved (CC art. 284). It seems questionable whether, in view of the breadth of the second category, the reference to the paternity action fulfills a sensible purpose, but it is clear that the investigation of maternity is permitted freely.

62. *Acknowledgment by father.* – Acknowledgment is here understood to be the creation of a legal relationship between father and illegitimate child by an act of the father. It is a field beset with variations. In some systems, acknowledgment is permitted only when combined with marriage to the child's mother and it then produces legitimacy for the child. In others, it is available freely, with effects varying from fully legitimate status to limited support duties. Aside from support, acknowledgment may establish an inheritance relationship and thus take on some features of a will. But in contrast to a will, an acknowledgment is usually irrevocable. In some systems descended from FRANCE, acknowledgment may be permissible only with respect to certain classes of "not so very" illegitimate children, often excepting the adulterous or incestuous bastard. Depending on the class of illegitimates involved, acknowledgment may produce different substantive effects. As to formalities, differences are equally wide. Some systems require a formal, notarial document. Elsewhere, an acknowledgment based on any writing or words or conduct may suffice. In GREECE, an acknowledgment may be executed by the paternal grandfather if the father is deceased, insane or missing.[189] In some countries, for instance ECUADOR, an illegitimate child may be recognized by the father before birth (CC art. 293 par. 2).

The relative practical importance of paternal acknowledgment differs among legal systems.[190] In a system with no access or limited access to the courts to establish paternity, acknowledgment may provide the only practical route to a legal father-child relationship. On the other hand, where the judicial paternity action is the principal vehicle to legal paternity, acknowledgment may be rarely used or not even provided for in the law. Paradoxically, acknowledgment has great importance in legal systems which insist that a paternity action be brought in all cases of illegitimate births. In such circumstances, many fathers will "voluntarily" acknowledge their children because

[188] See *Schmidt-Hidding* 39-61.

[189] CC art. 1532, 1533.

[190] *Zweigert and Kötz* I 148-160 present a detailed discussion of the "recognition system" (*Anerkennungssystem*) as a "style-setting trait of the romanic law" (*stilprägendes Merkmal des romanischen Rechts*). Generally, see *Schmidt-Hidding*.

they have nothing to lose but the annoyance and expense of a law suit.

ii. *Illustrations*

63. *United States.* – In AMERICA only some states give the father an opportunity formally to accept responsibility for his illegitimate child by a voluntary acknowledgment procedure.[191] These statutes vary widely in form and operation. They range from procedures resulting in full legitimation, thus providing equality with legitimate children,[192] to arrangements of "partial" legitimation, usually in support and inheritance matters, that sometimes go no further than a judgment in a paternity action. A variation on the legitimation theme is the occasional adoption statute that specifically allows the father to adopt his illegitimate child.[193]

As to form, the father's acknowledgment usually must be in writing, witnessed, and sometimes it must be executed before a notary,[194] other official, or court. Some statutes find that admission of an illegitimate child to the father's family or other acts which show the father's voluntary acceptance of his illegitimate child is sufficient for legitimation.[195]

Some AMERICAN statutes expressly provide that a legitimation after the child's birth is effective retroactively from the date of birth of the child.[196] Such assertions should be viewed with caution. In some instances, as, for example, the issuance of a new birth certificate that eliminates all reference to the child's former illegitimacy, post-birth legitimation may indeed be viewed as retroactive. However, when property interests vested prior to legitimation come in question, retroactive effect is not being given.[197]

64. ENGLAND does *not* provide for voluntary paternal acknowledgment of the illegitimate child.

65. In FRANCE, because of severe restrictions on the paternity action, voluntary parental acknowledgment is the primary method by which illegitimate children may gain status *vis-à-vis* their fathers. To illustrate, in 1963, when there were 51042 illegitimate births, 30700 illegitimates were voluntarily acknowledged by their fathers.[198]

An acknowledgment typically is declared in a public document if it was not accomplished on the birth certificate. The father's acknowledgment is effective as to him only, unless he names the mother, and she has confirmed her relationship to the child expressly or by conduct (CC art. 336).

Since parental acknowledgment merely declares and does not create parentage, FRENCH law views it as retroactive to the birth of the child for all purposes, including inheritance. Accordingly, if the acknowledgment brings the child into an appropriate relationship with a deceased person, estates which have been settled in the interval between the child's birth and the acknowledgment may have to be re-opened.[200]

An acknowledgment may be challenged by any "interested person" who can prove that the author of the acknowledgment is not the child's father (CC art. 339). "Interested persons" are the child, the acknowledging father himself and anyone else who has a significant personal or pecuniary interest, such as another person alleging himself to be the parent. The 1972 law allows the state's attorney to challenge an acknowledgment if there are indications that the acknowledgment does not conform to fact (CC art. 333 par. 2). After an acknowledgment has been supported by possession of status for 10 years or more, only the child himself, his parents or a person who alleges himself to be a parent may challenge the acknowledgment (CC art. 339 par. 3). Regardless of the child's age, his consent to parental acknowledgment is not required.

In addition to acknowledgment, the 1972 reform provides for the possibility of full legitimation of a child whose parents cannot legally marry (CC art. 333-1). Legitimation is accomplished by the decree of a court (CC art. 331-1). It is required that the child "possess status" as a natural child of the person applying for legitimation. If the legitimating person is married to a third party, his spouse must consent to the child's legitimation (CC art. 333-2). When the parents' marriage

[191] See, *e.g.*, CONNECTICUT Gen.Stat.Ann. § 52-4426 (Supp. 1969); for other sources, see *Krause* 19-21.

[192] See, *e.g.*, MICHIGAN Stat.Ann. § 702.83 (1968); MASSACHUSETTS Ann. Laws ch. 190 § 7 (1955).

[193] See, *e.g.*, SOUTH CAROLINA Code Ann. § 10-2587.3(d) (Supp. 1964).

[194] LOUISIANA CC Ann. art. 203 (West 1952); MAINE Rev.Stat.Ann. tit. 18 § 1003 (1965).

[195] See generally, Annotation, 33 A.L.R.2d 705, 732 (1954).

[196] CALIFORNIA CC § 230 (West 1954); IDAHO Code § 16-1510 (Supp. 1967).

[197] Restatement of Conflict of Laws 2d (1971) § 287, notes at 260-261; *Leflar*, American Conflicts Law (Indianapolis 1968) 583-584.

[198] *Savatier* 41 n.4. The acknowledgments do not, of course, necessarily relate only to the births of the same year.

[199] *Acte authentique*, CC art. 335.

[200] See *Carbonnier* 519.

would be unconditionally prohibited, such as in - case of incest for which dispensation cannot be obtained, legitimation of the child may be accoma plished only by *one* of the parents (CC art. 334-10).

Although an acknowledged child now has the same substantive rights as are possessed by a legitimate child, limited circumstances remain, especially in some inheritance situations, where a full legitimation may be advantageous.

66. Past and present WEST GERMAN law allows the father to legitimate his illegitimate child through a formal procedure[201] by which, upon application of the father, the court of guardianship decrees legitimation if that is in the best interest of the child and there are no important opposing reasons. In case of paternal legitimation, the mother will lose her parental authority but she retains her right to have a personal relationship (rights of visitation)with the child.[202] The child's consent is required to be expressed by his guardian if the child is a minor. In that case, the mother's consent is also required. If the child's mother withholds her consent, the child (through his representative) may turn to the court of guardianship which can grant legitimation if a denial would cause undue hardship to the child (CC § 1727). If the father is married, his wife must consent if legitimation is to be accomplished (CC § 1726). The 1969 reform statute brought only minor change in this area. Most importantly, the legal consequences of the father's voluntary legitimation of his child now extend to his relatives. Earlier law had limited the effect of legitimation by the father to him, the child, and the child's descendants (CC § 1737).

An interesting provision of the WEST GERMAN reform statute, borrowed from SWISS law, grants posthumous legitimation to the illegitimate child of a formally engaged couple, if one spouse's death prevented the marriage and if the court of guardianship finds that legitimation would be in the child's best interest.[204] The new statute also declares expressly that an illegitimate child may be adopted by his father or mother.[205]

Short of full legitimation, the father may voluntarily acknowledge his child. This equivalent of a judgment in a paternity action requires the child's consent in the form of a public document. It precludes further proceedings concerning the child's paternity, and is subject to attack on the basis of mistake.[206]

The new WEST GERMAN statute did not repeal a less far-reaching form of acknowledgment under which the father might acknowledge only the child's right of support that had been provided under earlier law.[207] In view of the broad advancement of the child's legal status under the 1969 law, however, it may be expected that the guardian of the child would only rarely (perhaps only in cases of very uncertain paternity) content himself with a limited acknowledgment.

67. *Norway*. – The question of full "legitimation" of the child *vis-à-vis* his father is less important in NORWEGIAN law. In NORWAY, practically no differences remain in the legal status of illegitimate and legitimate children. While "full legitimation" occurs only if the child's parents marry, the only additional right gained by the "legitimate" child is the right to inherit rural property with *odel*.[208] Voluntary acknowledgment of paternity by the father is permissible in a manner quite similar to the WEST GERMAN regulation just described.[209] As a practical matter, this route constitutes the primary route to the father. It should be noted, however, that even if a NORWEGIAN father and mother have reached a settlement and have agreed that the action is to be dismissed, the District Governor may continue formal proceedings by issuing a paternity writ if he believes this necessary for the best interests of the child.[210]

68. In POLAND, CZECHOSLOVAKIA and EAST GERMANY, voluntary recognition of the illegitimate child by his father is officially encouraged[211] with

201 Formerly CC § 1723, 1734; now CC § 1723, as revised.

202 *Gernhuber* 722; but *cf. Dölle* II 558-559.

203 See *Gernhuber* 722.

204 CC § 1740a to 1740g, as revised. *Cf. Simitis*, Die Ehelicherklärung auf Antrag des "Brautkindes" im Referentenentwurf für ein neues Unehelichengesetz: FamRZ 1967, 78; *Grasnick*, Das Problem der Brautkinder bei der Reform des Unehelichenrechts: NJW 1967, 329. For SWISS law, see CC art. 260.

205 CC § 1742a, as revised. See *Jansen and Knöpfel* 337-338.

206 CC § 1600a to 1600m; *cf. Brüggemann*, Die Vaterschaftsfeststellung im Referentenentwurf 1966 zum Unehelichengesetz: FamRZ 1966, 530, 535.

207 *Jansen and Knöpfel* 111; but *cf. Odersky*, Nichtehelichengesetz (ed. 3 Bielefeld 1973) § 1589 no. III 2.

208 "*Odel*" establishes a primary right to rural property in the family of an owner for a period of at least 10 years after the owner's death. See *Lov angaaende odels- og aasetesretten* and NORWEGIAN Const. of 1814 art. 107

209 *Lov no. 10* § 12, 23.

210 *Arnholm* 71.

211 EAST GERMANY: FC-Commentary § 55 no. 1; *Reinwarth*, Zwei bedeutsame Richtlinien des Obersten Gerichts auf dem Gebiet des Familienrechts: NJ 1967, 233; *Halgasch* 78. POLAND: *Gwiazdomorski* 90.

notable results. In EAST GERMANY, for example, more than 80 per cent of illegitimate children were recognized voluntarily in 1963.[212] The legal consequences of recognition differ slightly between the three EASTERN EUROPEAN countries. In POLAND and CZECHOSLOVAKIA, paternal recognition leads to a full father-child relationship involving the same rights and duties as exist between a father and his legitimate child.[213] In EAST GERMANY,[214] on the other hand, the establishment of paternity, whether by recognition or by court action, does not provide fully equal inheritance status to the illegitimate child.

The child is not a formal party to the act of recognition in any of the three countries, although POLAND expressly requires his consent after he has reached majority (FC art. 77 par. 3). In all three countries, the mother's consent is required.[215]

In POLAND and CZECHOSLOVAKIA, the father may recognize his child at any time, even prior to birth.[216] EAST GERMANY allows a recognition only after the child's birth (FC § 55 par. 1). If the child has left descendants, POLAND permits the recognition of a child after his death (FC art. 76). Recognition of paternity and declarations of consent are formal acts which must be performed before a public authority.[217]

In EAST GERMANY, recognition bars the establishment of another man's paternity so long as it remains in effect (FC § 58). A valid recognition may be questioned only by court action and only if previously unknown facts which raise doubt about the child's paternity come to light after the recognition.[218] Only the man who executed the recognition, the mother or the child's public guardian may challenge it, within one year of receiving knowledge of the new facts. After one year, only the state's attorney may challenge the recognition if it is in the best interests of the child (FC § 59 par. 3).

POLAND'S[219] rules are similar as are CZECHOSLOVAKIA'S[220]. The POLISH Family Code of 1950 had not specifically given the child the right to dispute the validity of a recognition, although there was considerable controversy whether the child should have such a right.[221] Under the new POLISH Family Code, the child may bring an action to annul a paternal acknowledgment (FC art. 82 par. 3). If the child was recognized before attaining majority, action must begin within three years after the child attains majority. The challenge must be based on proof of non-paternity (FC art. 81). If the child was recognized after he reached majority (in which case his consent would have been required), his action must begin within one year after recognition and may challenge the validity of his consent.[222]

69. SOVIET law does not permit an acknowledgment of paternity to be limited to the payment of support. A formal acknowledgment by means of a joint application of father and mother or a successful paternity suit inevitably leads to full legal equality of the illegitimate child with legitimate offspring.[223] While prior to 1968, the father could legitimate his child (aside from adoption)[224] only by marrying the mother *and* recognizing his paternity, acknowledgment by joint petition now is available even with respect to children born prior to 1968.[226]

70. *Mexico and Philippines.* – The FRENCH heritage of MEXICAN and PHILIPPINE law restricts the paternity action severely. As a result, voluntary recognition by the father is an important route by which the child may achieve a legal relationship with his father. Both countries permit recognition of an unborn child.[227] MEXICO extends recognition to a deceased child, if he has left descendants (CC art. 364). The PHILIPPINES do so only if recognition is accomplished by marriage.[228] In both countries, a child who has reached the age of majority must consent.[229] MEXICO provides that if the child is not of age, consent must be obtained of his guardian. If he has no guardian, a guardian *ad litem* appointed by the judge may consent (CC art. 375). PHILIPPINE law requires judicial approval for a recognition expressed otherwise than in a record of birth or in a will (CC art. 281).

[212] *Halgasch* 78; FC-Commentary § 55 no. 1.
[213] See *infra* s. 107, 122, 132.
[214] FC § 58, 46, 81; *Einführungsgesetz* § 9.
[215] POLAND: FC art. 77; see also *Lasok* 155; *Gwiazdomorski* 84, 85. EAST GERMANY: FC § 55 par. 1; CZECHOSLOVAKIA: FC § 52 par. 1.
[216] CZECHOSLOVAKIA: FC § 53; POLAND: FC art. 75.
[217] CZECHOSLOVAKIA: FC § 52 par. 2; EAST GERMANY: FC § 55 par. 3; POLAND: FC art. 78, 79.
[218] FC § 59 par. 1; FC-Commentary § 59 no. 2.2; BezG Neubrandenburg 16 June 1969, NJ 1970, 530.
[219] FC art. 80–82; *cf. Lasok* 156, 158; see also *Gwiazdomorski* 87.
[220] FC § 59–62.
[221] *Lasok* 158.
[222] FC art. 80 par. 2, 77 par. 3.
[223] Fundamentals of Family Law art. 16 par. 2, 4; Ratification Law art. 3.
[224] *Kourilsky* 268–269.
[225] Decree of 14 March 1945. *Cf. Bernhard* 226.
[226] Ratification Law art. 3 par. 2, 4.
[227] MEXICO: CC art. 364; PHILIPPINES: *De Jesus v. Syquia, supra* n. 180.
[228] CC art. 274, 611.
[229] MEXICO: CC art. 375; PHILIPPINES: CC art. 281.

A peculiar MEXICAN requirement for recognition of a child born out-of-wedlock is that the recognizing parent must have been of marriageable age at the time of the child's birth.[230] If a minor (CC art. 646), a MEXICAN needs the consent of the person who is exercising parental authority over him, or judicial consent (CC art. 36). PHILIPPINE law requires that the recognizing parent have reached the age at which he could marry without parental consent, unless the recognition is made by a valid will or pursuant to a judicial order, or with parental or a guardian's consent (CC art. 279). A recognition accomplished by a MEXICAN minor may be revoked on proof of fraud, but such disavowal must be accomplished within four years after reaching majority (CC art. 363).

Under MEXICAN law, a married woman or man may recognize a *pre*marital, illegitimate child without the consent of his or her spouse.[231] A husband may recognize an adulterous illegitimate child born during the marriage without his wife's consent (CC art. 373). In either case, however, such a child may be brought into the marital household only if the spouse consents (CC art. 373). The adulterous child of a married woman may not be recognized by his actual father unless her husband has disavowed the child and a final judgment has determined that he is not the husband's child.[232] The actual father may recognize his child, if the married mother is not living with her husband.

In MEXICO, recognition of an out-of-wedlock child must be accomplished either by certification of the child's birth to the officer of the Civil Register, by a special document executed before that official, by a public document, by will, or by express confession in court (CC art. 369). PHILIPPINE law is almost identical (CC art. 278). Parents may recognize their children individually or jointly. Recognition by one parent is legally effective with respect to that parent only.[233] PHILIPPINE law presumes that a child recognized by only one parent is "natural" if the recognizing parent had capacity to marry at the time of the child's conception (CC art. 277).

Both countries provide that if the father and mother recognize the child separately, they may not indicate the name of the other parent in connection with their recognition, nor may they identify circumstances by which the other parent's name may be ascertained.[234] MEXICO specifically provides that words of indication must be rendered illegible. Criminal sanctions are imposed on any executive or judicial official who violates this prohibition (CC art. 371).

MEXICO holds that recognition is irrevocable. For example, if recognition is accomplished by will, a subsequent revocation of the will does not affect the continuing validity of the recognition (CC art. 367). However, recognition may be contested by the state's attorney if it damages the child. Similarly, the natural parent may contest a recognition of the child by another person which would exclude him. Likewise, a third party affected by obligations arising from an illegal recognition may contest it by way of exception. In no case, however, may a recognition be attacked for the purpose of depriving the recognized child of inheritance.[235] If the recognized child was not of age when he was recognized, MEXICAN law allows him to contest it within two years after he reaches majority or learns of the recognition, whichever occurs later.[236] PHILIPPINE law sets a flat four year period from the time of majority (CC art. 281).

Under MEXICAN law, the recognition of a child may also be contested by a woman who has nursed or is nursing that child and who has publicly represented the child as hers and has cared for his support and education. Challenge must be made within 60 days of when she learns of the recognition. In case of contest, the child may not be taken from her without her consent or the final judgment of a court (CC art. 378). If the woman just described contests a recognition accomplished without her consent, it remains ineffective. The question of paternity must be resolved by means of a judicial proceeding (CC art. 379).

The obvious similarities of MEXICAN and PHILIPPINE law related to parental recognition are deceptive. While their methods are similar, their consequences differ greatly. In contrast to MEXICO which grants to *any* recognized child a legal status that is equivalent to legitimacy, PHILIPPINE law distinguishes between fully legitimate children (including legitimat*ed* children), recognized natural children and recognized spurious children, in terms of their legal rights *vis-à-vis* their parents. Only the legitimate child enjoys the full scale of parental rights (CC art. 264). The recognized natural child has lesser rights (CC art. 282) and the recognized spurious child still less (CC art.

[230] 16 for boys and 14 for girls. CC art. 361, 148.

[231] CC art. 372, 373.

[232] CC art. 374; *de Pina* 363.

[233] MEXICO: CC art. 365, 366; PHILIPPINES: CC art. 276, 282.

[234] MEXICO: CC art. 370; PHILIPPINES: CC art. 280.

[235] CC art. 368 par. 4, as amended, D. O. 17 Jan. 1970, 2.

[236] CC art. 376, 377.

287). The unrecognized child born out-of-wedlock has no rights at all in either MEXICO or the PHILIPPINES.

iii. *Comparative Summary*

71. *General.* – Many modern legal systems allow the parent and child relationship to be established by voluntary acknowledgment on the part of one or both parents.[237] Since the mother and child relationship is fully established by the child's birth in most countries, acknowledgment is significant primarily in respect of paternity.[238] Generally, however, an acknowledgment may not interfere with a pre-existing parent and child relationship, whether established by legal presumption or otherwise.[239]

The acknowledgment procedures which depend upon the voluntary act of the parent involved usually are complemented by procedures for the compulsory ascertainment of parentage. There seems to be no convincing reason to explain why one system favors voluntary procedures and allows compulsory procedures only in special, limited circumstances (for instance SOVIET RUSSIA), and another takes quite the opposite view, not permitting the voluntary acknowledgment of paternity and relying wholly on judicial, compulsory procedures (many or most COMMON LAW jurisdictions).

72. *Conditions.* – It may be too obvious to require mention that voluntary acknowledgment must be indicated by the acknowledging parent.[240] Acknowledgment alone usually is not sufficient. A basic and common condition is the consent of the mother.[241] More recent statutes also require the consent of the child or that of his guardian during minority.[242] If the acknowledgment results in full legitimation and the father is married, some countries require the consent of his wife.[243] In addition, many laws of the FRENCH family require that the acknowledging parents of the child must be under no impediment that would have prevented their marriage or, more precisely, that such an impediment would be shown by the aknowledgment.[244]

73. *Form.* – In most countries, acknowledgment must conform to specific formal requirements. In a few jurisdictions, acknowledgment by conduct may create a full-fledged parent and child relationship.[245]

74. *Legal effect.* – The effect of acknowledgment may range from the creation of a support obligation to the establishment of a full parent and child relationship, effective as of birth. Today most countries take an intermediate position, although the tendency in many countries toward equalizing the position of legitimates and illegitimates often has improved the effect of acknowledgment. Some laws provide equality only in specific areas, as support or inheritance,[246] or provide the acknowledged child a special, "intermediate" status.[247] Legitimation generally is held to be effective as of the date of the child's birth,[248] but intervening estate distributions typically may not be voided.[249]

75. *Contest.* – Acknowledgment may be challenged by proof that the acknowledging person is not the child's parent. Wide variations govern the circle of those who may contest the acknowledgment. Normally the child and the acknowledging parent have standing and some countries allow the mother standing as well.[250] In many FRENCH-based legal systems as well as in

237 Otherwise COMMON LAW systems such as ENGLAND, IRELAND, most states in the UNITED STATES.

238 Otherwise some of the FRENCH-based legal systems (*supra* s. 61), which, however, tend to reduce the requirements of maternal acknowledgment (FRANCE, *supra* s. 61).

239 WEST GERMANY: CC § 1600b par. 3; FRANCE: CC art. 334-9.

240 After the father's death or incapacity, some systems pass the right to acknowledge the child to the child's paternal grandfather. *E.g.*, GREECE: CC art. 1532; GUATEMALA: New CC art. 216.

241 BULGARIA: FC art. 35; YUGOSLAVIA: Fundamental Law on the Relations between Parents and Children art. 24; NETHERLANDS: New CC art. 224 par. 1 *lit.* d; SWEDEN: *Föräldrabalk* ch. 3 § 2; *cf.* GUATEMALA: New CC art. 219 and AUSTRIA: CC § 164 par. 1 no. 2.

242 *E.g.*, WEST GERMANY (*supra* s.66); BULGARIA: FC art. 35; NETHERLANDS: New CC art. 224 par. 1 *lit.* e; SWEDEN: *Föräldrabalk* ch. 3 § 2; *cf.* GUATEMALA: New CC art. 214; AUSTRIA: CC § 164 par. 1 no. 2.

243 WEST GERMANY: CC § 1726 par. 1. Similarly GREECE: CC art. 1538, ITALY: CC art. 259, and ECUADOR: CC art. 314, which require the spouse's consent to taking the child into the household.

244 For example ITALY: CC art. 251, 252; NETHERLANDS: New CC art. 224 par. 1 *lit.* a; SWITZERLAND: CC art. 304; more limited: BELGIUM: CC art. 335, 342b.

245 Several of the UNITED STATES (*supra* s. 63); also REPUBLIC OF CHINA: CC § 1065.

246 For example, BELGIUM: CC art. 337.

247 PHILIPPINES (*supra* s. 70); BELGIUM: CC art. 335; SPAIN: CC art. 129 ss.

248 UNITED STATES; but see NETHERLANDS: New CC art. 222.

249 *Cf.* FRANCE (*supra* s. 65).

250 WEST GERMANY: CC § 1600h par. 1; GREECE: CC art. 1535; SWITZERLAND: CC art. 305 par. 1.

those COMMON LAW jurisdictions that provide for acknowledgment, anyone with a legitimate interest is allowed to contest.[251] The period during which an acknowledgment may be challenged commonly ranges from three months[252] to unlimited,[253] with many systems providing a one year period.[254]

76. *Conclusion.* – Today, although there is great variation in detail, voluntary and compulsory procedures for the establishment of the parent and child relationship are often provided as alternatives. Voluntary acknowledgment is increasingly dependent on the consent of all persons directly involved, *i.e.*, the child and his mother.

B. THE PATERNITY ACTION

i. *Principal Approaches*

77. So far, we have defined the circumstances under which a child is born legitimately and how a child born illegitimately can obtain legitimate status or some of the legal incidents of such status through the *voluntary* act of his progenitor. Now we turn to perhaps the most important segment of this chapter, the *involuntary* ascertainment of paternity, the case in which the child, born illegitimately, invokes the aid of the law to find his father. Today, the Napoleonic maxim "*la recherche de la paternité est interdite*" (*Code Napoléon* art. 340) has generally been overcome, and most systems offer the services of their courts to the illegitimate child. Two major categories of the *availability* of paternity actions may be distinguished. First, many FRENCH-based systems and the SOVIET UNION still allow the investigation of paternity only in limited circumstances. Second, most modern systems allow the investigation of paternity freely, on the basis of whatever evidence of paternity may be available. Some of these leave the initiative in private hands, typically in the hands of the mother. However, an increasing minority of jurisdictions, led by the SCANDINAVIANS, forces the investigation of paternity in nearly all cases of illegitimate births in which the father does not step forward voluntarily.

It is not easy to see why some legal systems have restricted access to their courts in matters of paternity. Conditions defined by the FRENCH as well as by the SOVIETS seem to point in several directions at once. On the one hand, there is concern with the danger of frivolous claims. That justification, however, is more historical than valid. Scientific evidence now can cut through most fraudulent paternity claims. On the other hand, there may be an element of "male chauvinism". Limiting access to the courts and emphasizing voluntary acknowledgment by the father delivers the child-father relationship to the grace of the father, but no such choice is made available to the mother. Another important reason for limiting the ascertainment of out-of-wedlock paternity, of course, has been to protect the legitimate family against psychological shock and financial intrusion. Note also that restrictive paternity statutes usually express a social preference for children of *de facto* families over children conceived more casually.

The second category of paternity statutes – allowing the action on whatever evidence of paternity may be available – has produced limited results in practice. Many mothers are reluctant to bring the action because a scandal may result or their own emotions conflict. The child, of course, if no one has acted for him until he can act for himself is likely to lack access to evidence.

The convincing logic of the third position which *requires* a paternity action to be brought for each illegitimate child is that it does the child little, if any, good to have solid or even equal substantive legal rights if no efforts are made to find the father while there is an opportunity. The SCANDINAVIAN countries have been first to recognize this point. Today, in DENMARK, NORWAY and SWEDEN a mandatory paternity action is brought on behalf of each illegitimate child and fathers of illegitimate children are determined (by court decision or voluntary acknowledgment) in about 95 per cent of all cases.

We have two major categories of *results*. Traditionally the paternity action seeks to impose a limited duty of support on the illegitimate father. Increasingly, however, the improvement in the illegitimate child's substantive rights has changed

[251] *Cf.* ARGENTINA: CC art. 335; ECUADOR: CC art. 297; GREECE: CC art. 1535; ITALY: CC art. 263 par. 1; SWITZERLAND: CC art. 306.

[252] *E.g.*, GREECE: CC art. 1536 (three months after obtaining knowledge of the grounds, but not later than two years after acknowledgment); NETHERLANDS: New CC art. 225 par. 3; SWITZERLAND: CC art. 305 par. 1, 306.

[253] *E.g.*, ITALY: CC art. 263 par. 3.

[254] For example, WEST GERMANY: CC § 1600h par. 1 (two years for the child: CC § 1600i). Also *e.g.*, BULGARIA: FC art. 36; AUSTRIA: CC § 164a par. 2; PORTUGAL: CC art. 1837 par. 3, 1838 par. 2. *Cf.* NETHERLANDS: New CC art. 225 par. 4; GUATEMALA: New CC art. 214 par. 3.

the complexion of the action. Today, a limited or full right to inherit and rights to social welfare benefits may follow from the paternity judgment. In the systems which grant full substantive equality to the illegitimate child, full legitimate status automatically follows the paternity judgment.

Procedural variations are legion. A pattern can be detected only in the decreasing use of the *exceptio plurium* and the increasing use of scientific evidence. In too many places, an air of unsavoriness still overhangs the paternity action. Too many actions are inhibited by fear of scandal.

Among other important variables is the question of who is the person in interest. Some modern systems require the paternity action to be brought by or on behalf of the child and, if the state or the mother are involved, they represent the child. Other systems continue to think of the paternity action as the mother's right alone which she may choose to pursue, settle or forfeit as she sees fit. The unwarranted assumption is made that the mother's interests always coincide with those of the child. Under this approach, if the state is involved at all, it is involved only as the keeper of the public purse and seeks to alleviate a welfare burden that it would have to bear if the father were not held responsible.

ii. *Illustrations*

78. *England, United States.* – Judicial means of ascertaining paternity are available in nearly all AMERICAN states in the form of the "bastardy" or "paternity" action.[255] From its inception, the action was designed to help the welfare authorities on whom would fall the burden of supporting the child if the father could not be held responsible. Throughout most of the UNITED STATES, the action is of limited scope. Its primary and usually sole objective is to charge the father with a limited duty to support his illegitimate child. Only a few statutes allow the court to confer legitimate status on the child in the paternity proceeding or award inheritance rights in addition to support. Absent a paternity statute, the COMMON LAW rule of *filius nullius* denies the child any right to be supported by his father. Few courts have undertaken on their own to change this tradition.

In some states the paternity action has not yet evolved from the criminal law.[256] The criminal proceeding in which paternity is determined may still be a prosecution for the crime of bastardy or fornication. In such proceedings, the father's support obligation often is imposed only incidentally, as a condition to a probationary suspension of the criminal penalty. In those states that still view the action as criminal, the safeguards attending a criminal prosecution are applied. Proof must be beyond a reasonable doubt, rules on double jeopardy apply and, among other things, the defendant may have a right to free counsel and a free record on appeal. Another advantage of the criminal process may be the provision of blood tests at public expense, whereas such tests would typically have to be paid for by the parties in a civil action.

More recently, the paternity action which has as its object the support of the illegitimate child has come to be viewed as a civil proceeding. The chief consequence of this is that proof of paternity need measure no higher than a "preponderance of the evidence," and other safeguards of the criminal process do not apply to protect the alleged father. Nevertheless, whatever the form of the action, most states still allow the alleged father a jury trial on the issue of paternity. A number of states employ hybrid proceedings that try to have the best (and sometimes get the worst) of the civil and criminal law. A common approach is to require that proof, in what otherwise remains a civil proceeding, be "clear and convincing"[257] or "to the entire satisfaction of the court",[258] whatever this may mean in practical application.

The declaratory action is an interesting variation in the civil sector. Sometimes it is allowed under a general statute authorizing declaratory judgments. Specific statutes that authorize the declaration of family relationships are rare; although CALIFORNIA has a statute that permits an action to be "brought for the purpose of having declared the existence or non-existence between the parties of the relation of parent and child, by birth or adoption."[259]

One might argue in favor of the criminal law approach because current paternity practice seems so much subject to error that the defendant should be provided with the safeguards that distinguish the criminal from the civil process.[260] To the

[255] TEXAS has no such statute, but see *Gomez v. Perez*, *supra* n. 34. See also *Krause* 105–122, 148, 156–160.

[256] *E.g.* PENNSYLVANIA Stat. title 18 § 4506 (1963); *State v. Robinson*, 245 N.C. 10, 95 S.E.2d 126 (1956).

[257] *Comm'r of Welfare v. Wendtland*, 25 A.D.2d 640, 268 N.Y.S.2d 547 (1966).

[258] *Comm'r of Welfare v. Fields*, 25 A.D.2d 504, 266 N.Y.S.2d 681 (1966); WISCONSIN Stat. § 52.355 (Supp. 1969).

[259] CALIFORNIA CC § 231 (West Supp. 1968).

[260] *Cf.*, *State of Illinois, Family Study Commission*, Report and Recommendations (Springfield, Ill. 1969) 55–56.

extent these safeguards relate to an indigent accused's inability to afford his defense, these protections make sense. However, the social decision to absorb these costs could be implemented with ease in the civil context.

In ENGLAND, "affiliation proceedings", proceedings to establish paternity and impose a maintenance obligation on the father, are "domestic", *i.e.*, civil proceedings. Classification of paternity proceedings as domestic enables cases to be heard *in camera* and restricts reporting in the press.[261]

In AMERICA, the support-oriented paternity action typically is not intended to confer a new "status" on the child. In the great majority of states, the sole function of the action is to impose a support obligation on the alleged father and a family relationship is not declared. A few statutes specifically permit the illegitimate child to be legitimated in the paternity action.[262] In the states in which the concept of illegitimacy has been abolished, a paternity judgment would produce automatically the full range of filial rights against the father.[263] Current developments in constitutional law that are providing an increasing measure of substantive equality to the illegitimate child have been reflected in new paternity statutes in only a few states.

Leaning on its historical origin many AMERICAN states permit the paternity action to be brought by interested public welfare authorities, often with the qualification that the child must be likely to become a public charge or that he was born in a state institution.[264] Generally, the action to establish paternity may also be brought by the mother in her own name, rarely in the name of the child and sometimes in the name of the state.[265] Some states do not allow a married mother to bring such an action, and other states bar the action if the child was still-born. Some statutes allow a paternity suit to be brought by any charitable organization that has an interest in the matter, or by any person having legal custody of the child, or by any interested person, or by any person having knowledge of the facts. Specific clauses sometimes authorize suits to be brought by the father[266] or by the mother's parents.[267] Few courts or statutes recognize the primary interest in the paternity action to be that of the child, although in several states the child or his representative may sue (sometimes only where the mother has died). Many paternity statutes actually have been interpreted to deny the child a right to have his paternity investigated.[268]

In ENGLAND, affiliation proceedings may be commenced by the mother if she was single at the date of the child's birth,[269] or at the date of the application, if the child has not yet been born.[270] Alternatively, the "Supplementary Benefits Commission" may institute affiliation proceedings if it has provided benefits to the child.[271] The Commission may institute such proceedings even if the mother has failed to do so or an order in her favor has been set aside.[272]

Jurisdiction in paternity actions has been extended by the AMERICAN Uniform Reciprocal Enforcement of Support Act which has been adopted in all states.[273] Help has also been derived from the rapidly expanding interpretation of so-called "long arm" statutes. Jurisdiction remains an important issue in the fragmented legal system of the UNITED STATES.

In ENGLAND, the proper venue for the proceeding is the petty sessions area in which the mother resides.[274] Personal jurisdiction of the ENGLISH courts extends to male residents of SCOTLAND and NORTHERN IRELAND if an act of intercourse between the parties, which may have resulted in the birth, occurred in ENGLAND. If the mother is a resident of SCOTLAND or NORTHERN IRELAND and the father a resident of ENGLAND, proceedings may be brought in "a court of summary jurisdiction having jurisdiction in the place in which the person alleged to be the father resides."[275]

A few AMERICAN statutes specifically permit a

261 Legitimacy Act, 1959, s. 5. See also Magistrates' Courts Act, 1952, s. 56–58.

262 ALASKA Stat. § 25.20.050 (1962).

263 NORTH DAKOTA Cent.Code § 56–01–05 (Supp. 1969); OREGON Rev.Stat. § 109.060 (1969); ALASKA Stat. § 25.20.050 (a) (1962).

264 NEBRASKA Rev.Stat. § 13-113 (1962) (suit by attorney general).

265 *E.g.* OKLAHOMA Stat.Ann. tit. 10 § 71 (Supp. 1968).

266 MICHIGAN Stat.Ann. s. 25.494 (f) (1974); Uniform Parentage Act § 6.

267 HAWAII Rev.Laws § 332-1 (1955); WASHINGTON Rev.Code Ann. § 26.24.010 (1958).

268 *E.g., Allen v. Hunnicutt,* 230 N.C. 49, 52 S.E.2d 18 (1949).

269 Legitimacy Act, 1959, s. 4.

270 Affiliation Proceedings Act, 1957, s. 1.

271 National Assistance Act, 1948, s. 44, superseded in part by the Ministry of Social Security Act 1966, s. 24.

272 *Clapham v. National Assistance Board,* [1961] 2 Q.B. 77, [1961] 2 All E. R. 50.

273 See *Brockelbank and Infausto,* Interstate Enforcement of Support (ed. 2 Indianapolis 1971).

274 Affiliation Proceedings Act, 1957, s. 3.

275 Maintenance Orders Act, 1950, s. 3 (2).

suit to be brought during the pregnancy of the mother.[276] The larger number, however, postpone the suit until the mother has given birth to the child. Many states set a specific time limit for the bringing of the suit, typically one, two, or four years after the birth. If the mother is a minor, the applicable statute of limitations may be tolled until she reaches majority. Other statutes set no time limit for the bringing of the action but limit the amount of back support that may be recovered. Still other states apply their general civil or criminal statute of limitations. The father's death usually, but not always, terminates his liability. Once the child has been adopted by others, the mother's right to bring a paternity action – even for her own lying-in expenses – may be forfeited.

In ENGLAND, the mother must institute affiliation proceedings within one year from the child's birth unless the putative father has paid money for the child's support within the year; or, the putative father was outside England, in which case the action must be brought within one year after his return.[277] These limitations do not apply to proceedings instituted by the Supplementary Benefits Commission[278] which are governed by a three year period of limitation measured from the time the first benefits were granted to the child.[279] A special limitation provision applies to the case where there was a marriage void on account of either party being under the age of sixteen years and the putative father had access to the mother during the year before the child's birth. In such cases, the action may be brought at any time.[280]

Some AMERICAN statutes specifically permit the parties to be witnesses, some require them to testify and others provide that they may not be compelled to testify. If the paternity action is a criminal proceeding or if the state views fornication or adultery as a crime, the federal constitutional privilege against self-incrimination is available.

An open admission by the father in court, or a statement from the father under oath is adequate evidence of paternity in many states. In some states, the mother's statement alone may be enough. Other states require corroboration of the mother's testimony. Perhaps leaning on the ancient belief in the relationship between torture and truth, HAWAII permitted accusations made by the mother in time of travail to corroborate her testimony, and CONNECTICUT at one point *required* that the mother "be put to discovery in the time of her travail."[281] In those states that still follow it, "Lord Mansfield's rule" (which denies spouses the right to testify as to the illegitimacy of a child born in their marriage) disallows a married mother's testimony as to the illegitimacy of her child.

Proof that the mother has had sexual relations at the critical time with men other than the putative father is a traditional, world-wide defense to a paternity charge. In many states, the mother's accusation may be discredited by corroborated testimony showing (or the mother's confession concerning) sexual relations between the mother and another man at the critical time. Such evidence generally still bars the action absolutely and no blood tests would be taken to determine whether the other man is excluded as a possible father. This defense should not be confused with evidence of the mother's or the father's unchastity.[282]

The AMERICAN judgment in a paternity suit normally includes an order against the father for the support of the child in accordance with standards to be discussed later (*infra* s. 104). Periodic support payments are the rule, but lump-sum settlements may be permissible. Usually, in addition to the child's support, the cost of the mother's confinement and other expenses incurred by her in connection with her pregnancy are allowed, as are the expenses of prosecuting the paternity action, sometimes including counsel fees.[283]

Similarly, the ENGLISH court may order a weekly payment[284] in an amount to be determined in the court's discretion, reimbursement for expenses incidental to the birth, and, if the child has died, payment of funeral expenses. If the proceedings are instituted within two months subsequent to the child's birth, the weekly payment may be made retroactive to the date of birth. The affiliation order normally runs in favor of the child's mother and she is entitled to payments thereunder until the father's support obligation ceases, or she dies, becomes of unsound mind, or is imprisoned. In the latter circumstances, any two justices of the peace may appoint a guardian who

[276] ILLINOIS Rev.Stat. ch. 106 3/4 § 54 (1967).
[277] Affiliation Proceedings Act, 1957, s. 2(1) (a)-(c).
[278] *National Assistance Board v. Mitchell*, [1956] 1 Q.B. 53, [1955] 3 All E.R. 291.
[279] National Assistance Act, 1948, s. 44.
[280] Affiliation Proceedings Act, 1957, s. 2(2)(a)(b).
[281] *Kotler*, Bastardy Procedure: 11 Conn.B.J. 195 (1937).
[282] See, *e.g.*, *State ex rel. Brown v. Middleton*, 259 Iowa 1140, 147 N.W.2d 40 (1966); *Price v. Simpson*, 205 So.2d 642 (Miss. 1968).
[283] *E.g.*, MARYLAND Ann.Code art. 16 § 66 H (1966).
[284] Maintenance Orders Act 1968, s. 1.

then becomes entitled to the payments under the order.[285] Special provision, including liability for a criminal fine for misapplication of funds, is made for payment to a person, other than the mother, who has custody of the child.[286]

In ENGLAND, the father's support obligation may not be terminated by voluntary agreement of the parties.[287] Moreover, an agreement by the mother to accept a lump sum in discharge of the putative father's liability does not bar an affiliation order.[288]

In AMERICA, on the other hand, the paternity obligation may be the subject of binding settlement. Such a settlement may be a simple contract. However, statutes often require that settlements and compromises be officially approved,[289] either by a court [290] or by the state's attorney,[291] or they prescribe minimum, usually inadequate, terms for a settlement.[292] Typically, the child will be bound by the settlement even though he was not represented. This follows from statutes which allow only the mother to bring the paternity action.[293] Although the requirement of official approval, where applicable, is at least in part intended to compensate for this shortcoming, in practice it has not been an effective safeguard of the child's best interests. On the other hand, where the conflict of interests involves welfare authorities who seek reimbursement from the father for welfare payments made to the mother, a settlement may not stand up.[294] An old MAINE statute expressed this preference by forbidding the mother to settle her claim against the father if the town objected.[295]

A settlement of sorts occurs if the mother and putative father marry, inasmuch as such a marriage will extinguish the paternity claim.[296] Since the parents' marriage is not necessarily tied in with legitimation of the child – an express acknowledgment of paternity being required in many states – the child may again be the loser.[297] A recent case, however, held that an infant whose parents had married after his birth was entitled to a declaratory judgment establishing his legitimacy and changing his name to that of his parents.[298]

79. *France.* – Until a major revision in 1912, FRENCH law had flatly prohibited the judicial ascertainment of paternity,[299] with the strange exception of cases of abduction or rape – situations in which the establishment of paternity would seem especially unlikely to benefit the child. After 1912, FRENCH law still remained restrictive in defining the cases in which paternity could be ascertained judicially. Even the 1972 Law introduced only minor changes.[300] Most significantly, in contrast to earlier law which made severe distinctions between "natural simple", "adulterous" and "incestuous" illegitimates, the 1972 Law allows any illegitimate child to sue to have his paternity established. Nevertheless, if there is an incest prohibition on marriage between the child's parents, the child's parentage may be established only with respect to one parent (CC art. 334-10).

A paternity action may be brought under CC art. 340, as amended in 1972, only if at least one of the following special circumstances is present:

(1) The mother was *abducted or raped* by the alleged

285 Affiliation Proceedings Act, 1957, s. 5.

286 *Ibidem* s. 11.

287 *Griffith v. Evans* (1882), 46 L.T. 417 (Q.B.).

288 *Follit v. Koetzow* (1860), 2 E.&E. 730, [1843-60] All E.R. 761.

289 MINNESOTA Stat.Ann. § 257.28 (1965); VERMONT Stat.Ann. tit. 15 § 375 (1958).

290 In OREGON, the judge may make such compromise or arrangement with the putative father as the judge deems equitable and just, OREGON Rev.Stat. § 109.220 (1969). More common are provisions requiring judicial approval of settlements between the parties, *e.g.*, DISTRICT OF COLUMBIA Code Ann. § 16-2351 (1967); ILLINOIS Rev.Stat. ch. 106 3/4, § 59a (1969); Burns' INDIANA Ann.Stat. § 3-646 (1968); IOWA Code Ann. § 675.30 (1966); OHIO Rev.Code Ann. § 3111.07 (Page 1960); RHODE ISLANDS Gen.Laws Ann. § 15-8-7 (1970).

291 MARYLAND Ann. Code art. 16 § 66L (1966).

292 Not long ago, the illegitimate child in ILLINOIS lived with the minimum amount for a valid settlement set at $ 800. See *Haag v. Barnes*, 9 N.Y.2d 554, 216 N.Y.S. 2d 65, 175 N.E.2d 441 (1961).

293 See, *e.g.*, *In re Paternity*, 33 Ohio Op.2d 299, 211 N.E.2d 894 (Ct.Com.Pl. Hamilton Co. 1965), in which the illegitimate child unsuccessfully attempted to upset a compromise agreement between the putative father and its mother. But see *ABC v. XYZ*, 50 Misc.2d 792, 271 N.Y.S.2d 781 (Fam. Ct. 1966) in which an agreement between mother and putative father which specifically denies paternity but nevertheless allowed child support, was held not to bar child's later action to have paternity determined. The action was barred, however, by the statute of limitations.

294 *Clark* 173 n. 11.

295 MAINE Rev.Stat.Ann. tit. 19 § 258 (1965).

296 *Clark* 166. *Cf. Wadlington*, Shotgun Marriage by Operation of Law: 1 Ga.L.Rev. 183 (1967).

297 *Clark* 166 n. 40 and 177 n. 13. The OHIO statute would even disallow the paternity claim of the mother if, after the child's illegitimate birth, the mother marries another man. *Baston v. Sears*, 15 Ohio St.2d 166, 239 N.E.2d 62 (1968).

298 *Santana v. City of New York* (N.Y. S.Ct. Queens Co. 1969).

299 CC of 5 March 1803, art. 340: "*La recherche de la paternité est interdite*" (*supra* n. 30).

300 CC art. 340, as revised.

father during the probable period of conception. Physical violence has not been viewed as essential to a finding of "rape"; surprise, mental deficiency or any other circumstances showing the absence of the victim's consent may suffice.[301]

(2) The mother's *seduction* was accomplished by an abuse of authority, a promise of marriage or formal engagement, or other dishonest means. Under this provision the courts have allowed the judicial ascertainment of paternity when the promise of marriage (sincere or fraudulent) or the abuse of authority motivated the mother to permit sexual relations.[302]

(3) The alleged father has unequivocally *admitted* paternity in writing. No formal writing is necessary, a letter or any other writing of the alleged father may suffice.

(4) The alleged father and mother were living in *concubinage* during the period of conception. Under the pre-1972 provision which spoke solely in terms of a "notorious" concubinage, frequent and regular relations had sufficed,[303] and concubinage was held to be "notorious" if the relationship was known to several persons such as family, friends or neighbors.[304] The new provision confirms this trend expressly by providing that an action may be brought even if there is no common life, if only there is a continuous and steady relationship (CC art. 340 par. 1 no. 4).

(5) The alleged father has *contributed to the support* and education of the child. Under this provision the courts have searched for a tacit admission of paternity.[305] *Planiol* notes that "the law calls for both upkeep and education. Intermittent subsidies would not furnish sufficient proof... *A fortiori* mere promises to take charge of the child's upkeep would not suffice, if they did not constitute an avowal of paternity... But, the payment of a large sum upon the child's birth may be deemed to be participation in its upkeep..."[306] To exclude the benefactor who is motivated by affection for the mother, the subsidies must have been furnished by the alleged father himself, directly or indirectly, and he must have acted *en qualité de père*.[307]

As can be seen, FRENCH law limits the possibility to bring a paternity action by requiring that a *prima facie* case be built on predefined circumstances. In addition, it requires the paternity petition to be dismissed without review on the merits if the mother has been guilty of "notorious misbehavior" or has had intercourse with another individual during the legally defined period of conception. Under the 1972 law, this defense fails if, by blood test exclusions or other definite medical proof, it is established that the other man cannot be the father.[308] The judge may involve in the suit all men who might possibly be the child's father.[309] The court then makes its decision on the basis of relative probabilities of paternity.[310] This ends the reign of the defense of the *exceptio plurium concumbentium* which, according to *Planiol*, had simply required proof of "the fact of unfaithfulness, even an isolated act, committed during the legal period of conception, and intercourse with a given person."[311] The second ground on which the action must be dismissed is a showing that paternity is physically impossible.[312] This defense is defined narrowly and only includes failure to cohabit by reason of the absence of the alleged father or of physical impossibility (impotency by reason of accident or disease). Failure to cohabit by reason of natural impotency is not a defense. Moreover, the condition must have been present during the entire legal period of conception. Finally, the action is dismissed if non-paternity is established by blood tests or by other definite medical proof.[313] Blood tests may be ordered at the request of the mother or on the court's own motion. They must be ordered at the alleged father's request which may be made at any time, even on appeal.[314] Physical coercion is not applied if a party refuses to submit to a blood test but the court is free to draw its own conclusion.[315]

In FRANCE, the paternity action is solely the right of the child (CC art. 340-2). The right to bring the action is not transmitted to the child's heirs or successors. During the child's minority, the mother (even if she is a minor herself) may bring the action on behalf of the child, if she has acknowledged the child. If the mother is mentally incapacitated or deceased, the action is brought

301 Cass.civ. 6 Nov. 1961, D. 1961, 733.

302 Cass.civ. 23 Feb. 1960, D. 1960, 354.

303 *Planiol and Ripert* 843.

304 *Carbonnier* 531.

305 *Ibidem.*

306 *Planiol and Ripert* 843-844.

307 CC art. 340 par. 1 no. 5, as revised; *Carbonnier* 532.

308 CC art. 340-1 no. 1, as revised.

309 CC art. 311-11, as revised.

310 CC art. 311-12, as revised.

311 *Planiol and Ripert* 845.

312 CC art. 340-1 no. 2, as revised.

313 CC art. 340-1 no. 3, as revised.

314 Cass.civ. 13 Jan. 1959, D. 1959, 45.

315 See generally *Oppetit*, Les fins de non-recevoir à l'action en recherche de paternité naturelle: Rev.trim. dr.civ. 1967, 749 ss.

by the child's guardian if the family council gives authorization.[316] At majority, the child may bring his own action.

The mother must bring a paternity action within two years of the child's birth. However, if the alleged father and the mother have been living in concubinage or if the alleged father has contributed to the support and education of the child, the two year period begins to run only when the concubinage ends or when the alleged father stops rendering support. If no paternity action was brought during the child's minority, the child may bring the action during the first two years of his majority.[317] These periods of limitation are absolute and may not be extended or suspended for any reason.

If the plaintiff is shown to have brought the paternity action in bad faith, criminal penalties apply. These may include fines, imprisonment, or an order forbidding presence in a certain locality for a substantial period.[318] Civil damage remedies, roughly analogous to the COMMON LAW tort of malicious prosecution, are available. Paternity proceedings are not open to the public[319] and the record of a paternity trial is confidential.[320]

Such severe limitations undoubtedly account for the fact that, in 1962, when there were approximately 20000 children whose paternity was *not* recognized voluntarily, only 500 paternity actions were filed and of these, 316 succeeded and 184 failed.[321] The old prohibition on *la recherche de la paternité* thus remains quite alive, although it has lost some sting. First, the background threat of a possible paternity action may induce both voluntary acknowledgments and the voluntary rendition of support. Moreover, the restrictiveness of CC art. 340 has long been tempered by the courts in some cases. First, the courts sometimes have permitted the "seduced" mother to claim tort damages from the father and the measure of damages would include some of the cost of caring for the child.[322] The new law confirms this trend (CC art. 340-5).

More importantly, it had long been recognized that any parent owes his child a "natural" obligation of support even if parentage had not been or cannot be formally established.[323] Standing alone, this natural obligation was not legally enforceable. It might become enforceable, however, if put in the form of a reasonably explicit promise to render support. Although the Court of Cassation had refused to view a simple admission of paternity as a promise to render support, it did infer such a promise from a commitment "to take care of expenses of food, care and education".[324] The promise had to be evidenced by a writing.[325] Promises affirming this natural obligation were limited by their own terms, and the extent to which the support duty was enforced depended on the interpretation of the promise. The concept of a natural obligation subsists but has lost much of its importance as the 1972 Law allows the child whose paternal filiation has *not* been established to bring an action for support against any man who had intercourse with his mother during the legal period of conception (CC art. 342). Such an action may be brought even if, during the period of conception, the man or the child's mother could not marry because of some impediment.[326] The amount of the support varies in accordance with the needs of the child and the defendant's resources and family situation (CC art. 342-2). Several men may be joined in the action and also be held liable severally.[327] Blood test exclusions or other definite medical proof of nonpaternity or other proof of physical impossibility of paternity or proof that the mother lives in "debauchery" defeat the action (CC art. 342-4). The obligation of support arising from this action ceases when another man is established to be the father.[328] It may be expected that many mothers will continue to tap this source of support rather than risk their case by attempting to comply with the more stringent requirements of the paternity action, although the latter, among other things, would qualify the child under the inheritance laws.[329]

In the rare case in which maternity has not been established by acknowledgment, the court will declare maternal descent if the child proves a sufficient number of facts indicating the parent-child relationship and shows that he has the general and public reputation of being a natural simple child of the alleged mother. In the absence of *de*

[316] CC art. 340-2 par. 2-3.
[317] CC art. 340-4 par. 1.
[318] *Mazeaud*, Leçons no. 983.
[319] *Ibidem.*
[320] *Loi sur la liberté de la presse* art. 39 par. 1.
[321] *Carbonnier* 535; *cf. Savatier* 42.
[322] See *Mazeaud and Tunc* 371 no. 284 (1).
[323] *Mazeaud (-de Juglart)*, Leçons no. 1201 p. 550.
[324] Cass.civ. 14 Jan. 1952, D. 1952, 177.
[325] CC art. 1341, 1347, 1348.
[326] CC art. 342 par. 2, as revised. The child of a married woman may sue under CC art. 342 if his formal status as a legitimate child is not corroborated by actual status: CC art. 342-1, as revised.
[327] CC art. 311-11, 342-3.
[328] CC art. 342-8 par. 2.
[329] See *Mezger*, Der Siegeszug der Zahlvaterschaft in Frankreich: FamRZ 1970, 623.

facto status, maternity may be proved by means of the child's birth certificate (if it indicates the mother's name) or, failing that, by any relevant documentary or oral proof. Oral testimony tending to prove the child's identity must be corroborated by some documentary proof or by credible circumstantial evidence.[330]

80. *Norway, West Germany.* – Although the NORWEGIAN welfare authorities are primarily responsible for bringing the *mandatory*[331] paternity action against the putative father "without undue delay", the state is *not* a party. The action is brought in the names of the mother and the child.[332] The law requires the mother (as well as attending physicians and midwives) to furnish information to the welfare authorities relevant to the question of paternity in connection with each illegitimate birth.[333] This extends to information concerning the probable time of conception as well as the possible identity of the father.[334] However, no criminal sanctions are applied to compel disclosure. NORWEGIAN law does not recognize any settlements between the mother and the putative father relating to the child's rights. The mother has no authority to waive any of the child's rights to a paternity decision, inheritance or support.[335] A lump sum settlement may not take the place of the child's right to a monthly support payment.[336] The mother may waive the father's duty to pay through the "bailiff of alimony", and make private arrangements with him concerning the method of payment. Notwithstanding such arrangements, the mother or the child may request at any time that monthly payments again be made through the "bailiff of alimony".

An interesting special writ procedure is applied in many cases. It greatly reduces the formalities otherwise required for a determination of paternity. In essence, the writ served on the putative father states that he will be regarded as the father if he admits paternity or if he does not apply to the court for judicial determination of paternity within a period of four weeks.[337] The District Governor decides whether a paternity writ will be issued to the putative father.[338] For example, if there are several possible fathers, the District Governor may decide not to issue the writ. Another limitation is that the writ may be issued only if the putative father has been identified by the mother, but the mother's consent to the issuance of the writ is not required. If the father acknowledges paternity after having been served the writ, the case is closed.[339] However, if the putative father merely remains silent for a period of four weeks after having been served, the writ procedure will have the effect of a judgment in a paternity action. The writ procedure is an administrative process and does not involve the courts, unless the alleged father challenges the allegation in which case a court procedure follows.

Professor *Arnholm* has suggested that "the notion that one may become a father by inaction is rather strange" (p. 75). However, the putative father may have recourse to the courts even after the expiration of four weeks, if he can show that circumstances beyond his control or excusable error caused him to miss the four-week deadline or if he can show that he subsequently received information relevant to the question of paternity.[340]

If no man has acknowledged paternity and the writ procedure was not applied or has not produced a father for the child (as would be the case if the putative father challenges the allegation of paternity made in the writ), the courts will decide the question.[341]

The new WEST GERMAN law did not adopt the NORWEGIAN "writ procedure". The paternity action determines the paternity status of the child for all purposes.[342] The action is brought by the *child*, not his mother, which means that in the normal case a guardian will sue on behalf of the child. As in NORWAY, the paternity action in GERMANY is a civil action, although criminal sanc-

330 *Carbonnier* 526-528.

331 *Lov no. 10* § 10, 13, 17. The action is not brought "if it is impossible to establish the identity of the alleged father", or "if consideration for the mother or the child or public policy do not appear to render the issue of a writ necessary and provided that the Ministry agrees to the omission of the same" (§ 12 par. 1).

332 *Lov no. 10* § 17.

333 *Lov no. 10* § 8, 9, 35-37.

334 *Lov no. 10* § 8.

335 *Lov no. 10* § 28.

336 *Arnholm* 54.

337 *Lov no. 10* § 14.

338 *Lov no. 10* § 12.

339 *Lov no. 10* § 14.

340 *Lov no. 10* § 23.

341 *Lov no. 10* § 15.

342 CC § 1600 a, as revised; *Jansen and Knöpfel* 109; *Lüderitz*, Zur Reform des Verfahrensrechts in Kindschaftssachen: FamRZ 1966, 613, 617-619; *Göppinger*, Betrachtungen zum Referentenentwurf eines Unehelichengesetzes: FamRZ 1966, 418, 419-423; *Brüggemann*, Die verfahrensrechtliche Neuordnung des Unehelichenrechts: FamRZ 1969, 120. Conflicts aspects are thoroughly treated by *Siehr*, *passim*; *idem*, Die Vaterschaftsfeststellung im deutschen Internationalen Privatrecht: DAVorm. 1973, 126.

tions apply to non-compliance with a support decree (PC § 170 b).

In NORWAY, the trial judge takes a more active role in the paternity action than he takes in other types of cases. If information becomes available in the course of the proceeding which indicates that a person other than the defendant may be the father, he is brought into the case as a co-defendant.[343] All persons who may have information relevant to the case may be summoned as witnesses. The judge's duty to establish the child's paternity requires that he continue the action until all possible fathers have been tried.[344] Various special procedures expedite the paternity action. For example, a party failing to appear may be brought before the court by arrest, testimony given by a party or witness during the investigatory stages of the case may be read in court, and the mother and the putative father must testify in accordance with legislation relating to witnesses generally and are subject to the same sanctions.[345]

In WEST GERMANY, the paternity action relies on a presumption of paternity which is raised upon proof of cohabitation between mother and putative father at the critical time.[346] NORWEGIAN law proceeds similarly although there are no formal presumptions: Paternity is established by proof of a "positive" character – *e.g.*, proof that the putative father did have intercourse with the mother at the time of the child's probable conception, and "negative proof", meaning that no circumstances are established that make it seem "unlikely" that he is the father.[347] The legislative purpose is to ensure that paternity will not be declared unless a high degree of probability supports the determination.[348] During preparatory work on the paternity statute, it was emphasized that imposition of paternal obligations on the basis of weak evidence will cause unjust hardship to persons who are held liable and will not serve the interests of the child or those of society.[349]

A variety of circumstances may make it "unlikely" that the defendant is the father. His impotency or sterility are relevant, as are other circumstances that make it appear unlikely that intercourse between the mother and the alleged father led to conception of the child. The mother's personal conduct may raise doubts, especially if the period of gestation has been unusually short or long in relation to the act or acts of intercourse that have been proved. In contrast to WEST GERMAN law, however, NORWEGIAN law does not set specific limits for the period of gestation. Under GERMAN law one circumstance that may help rebut the presumption is a showing that the child's mother has had intercourse with other men at the critical time. The presumption is rebutted by a showing that paternity is impossible which may be made by blood tests or proof of the defendant's sterility or impotence. In turn, the child may use blood test exclusions to disprove a defense based on proof of the mother's intercourse with other men.[350] The court will consider any relevant evidence, including the mother's testimony, anthropological expert evidence which compares the alleged father and the child and blood test results, and medical testimony relating to the probable time of conception based on the child's condition at the time of birth.

Rather than resulting in an automatic dismissal of the action, the fact that the mother has cohabited with other men at the critical time is merely one circumstance tending to weaken the probability of the defendant's paternity.[351] Both WEST GERMAN and the NORWEGIAN courts employ improved blood testing methods and other scientific evidence which make it possible today to destroy a false defense based on the *exceptio plurium* in many cases where this would not have been possible even quite recently.[352] In general, parties must submit to the taking of blood and other relevant examinations to the extent reasonable and necessary for purposes of proof.[353]

If the *exceptio plurium* cannot be destroyed, the NORWEGIAN court may hold one of the men with whom the mother has had intercourse if it concludes that a substantial probability points to him

343 *Lov no. 10* § 17.

344 *Idsøe* 321, 325.

345 *Lov no. 10* § 19, 20. A refusal to testify or to give evidence under oath is punishable by fines and by the assessment of the additional trial costs thus caused. The giving of false, unsworn evidence is punishable by imprisonment of up to two years. Perjury results in imprisonment of up to six years.

346 Formerly CC § 1717; now CC § 1600 o. CC § 1600 o contains the same presumption as was contained in the old CC § 1717. However, according to CC § 1600 o par. 2 the presumption falls as soon as there "remain serious doubts concerning paternity".

347 *Lov no. 10* § 21.

348 *Arnholm* 80.

349 Innstilling til Odelstinget XXIII (Oslo 1956) 12.

350 See *Jansen and Knöpfel* 152–156.

351 CC § 1600 o, as revised, as compared with former CC § 1717 par. 1 sent. 1.

352 *Hummel*, Der Stand der medizinischen Wissenschaften in der Abstammungsbegutachtung und die Frage: Vaterschaftsfeststellung ohne Beweisregel?: FamRZ 1969, 19; *Lundevall* 123.

353 NORWAY: *Lov no. 8* § 1; WEST GERMANY: CC Proc. § 372 a.

as the probable father.[354] The purpose, however, is *not* to pick out from among the known competitors the man whose paternity is most probable (or least unlikely). NORWEGIAN law requires a substantial probability of the putative father's paternity. Thus, even if in a group of several possible fathers there is a relative preponderance of probability in favor of one man's paternity, that man will not be adjudged the father, if the court, on the basis of all the evidence, finds it "unlikely" that he is the father.[355] In WEST GERMANY, the *exceptio* has been eliminated in its traditional form, but the presumption of paternity normally arising from intercourse does not arise "if, considering all circumstances, there remain serious doubts concerning paternity."[356]

No statute of limitations applies in WEST GERMANY to the paternity proceeding.[357] As in the case of the legitimate child, however, past support may not be recovered,[358] unless demand has been made on the father or an action has been brought. Past support that has accrued prior to the formal ascertainment of paternity continues to be recoverable.[359]

Depending on the type of action that was brought, the WEST GERMAN paternity action previously involved the limited question of support *or* the determination of paternity for all purposes. Even in the latter "status" proceeding, the court could not declare the child legitimated or give the child a right of inheritance or the right to use the father's surname.[360] With the exception of the right of inheritance which now accrues by operation of law,[361] this remains true for the paternity action available under the reform statute.

NORWAY and WEST GERMANY require that the father make more far-reaching contributions to the mother of an illegitimate child than does the COMMON LAW. In NORWAY, the father must contribute to the mother's support for the last three months before the child's birth. He is liable for expenses incidental to the birth including the cost of medical care received by the mother during her confinement.[362] In exception to the general principle under which both parents are equally responsible for their child, these costs are chargeable only to the father.[363] In practice, however, because of the broad coverage of NORWAY's social security system, the mother's rights against the father are of minor importance. The social security insurance system provides mother's support and the general health insurance program typically covers all expenses incurred in connection with medical care related to the pregnancy.[364] In addition to full medical care, the mother of a child born out of wedlock automatically receives a cash allowance upon the birth of her child. She may be entitled to further support until she returns to work. Funds also may be available to improve her education and for other special purposes. The sole condition of eligibility is that the mother have been a resident of NORWAY for three years.[365] The mother is entitled to these benefits each time she has a child out of wedlock. There are no equivalent benefits in connection with the birth of legitimate children.

The WEST GERMAN statute of 1970 recognized, as did NORWEGIAN law, the growing importance of social security and private insurance arrangements, and the father's obligation to the unmarried mother is now limited to amounts actually expended by the mother. It no longer extends to the "usual" cost of childbirth and support for which he was liable under prior law.[366] The WEST GERMAN father must provide support to the mother for eight weeks after the child's birth. In exceptional cases, the father's support obligations may be extended to four months before and one year after the child's birth. For example, if the child cannot be cared for by the mother's relatives or in some other satisfactory manner, or if the mother is unable to pursue remunerative employment for reasons related to the child, the mother may be entitled to receive "extended" support from the father. However, unlike the absolute claim provided under prior law, the extended claim depends on the mother's need as well as the father's ability to pay (CC § 1615 l).

In contrast to NORWAY, where the mother's claim typically is joined with her child's claim,[368] WEST GERMAN law requires the mother to assert her

[354] *Lov no. 10* § 21; *Arnholm* 81, 82.

[355] *Lov no. 10* § 21; *cf. Arnholm* 80.

[356] As to what constitutes "serious doubts", see BGH 6 June 1973, BGHZ 61, 165, FamRZ 1973, 596. See also BGH 21 Sept. 1973, FamRZ 1973, 624; BGH 9 March 1973, 14 Nov. 1973, and 12 July 1974, FamRZ 1974, 85, 87, and 644, and *Büdenbender*, Die Rechtsprechung des Bundesgerichtshofes zur Vaterschaftsvermutung gemäss § 1600o Abs. II BGB: FamRZ 1974, 289.

[357] CC § 194 par. 2; *Jansen and Knöpfel* 148.

[358] CC § 1613; new CC § 1615a in connection with CC § 1613; see *Jansen and Knöpfel* 168-170.

[359] CC § 1615d, as revised; *Jansen and Knöpfel* 195.

[360] Generally, see *Dölle* II 495-515.

[361] CC § 1924-1929, 1934a, as revised.

[362] *Lov no. 10* § 27.

[363] *Arnholm* 54.

[364] *Lov no. 2* § 34, 52.

[365] *Lov no. 12* § 12.

[366] Formerly CC § 1715 par. 1; now CC § 1615k.

[367] Formerly CC § 1715 par. 1; now CC § 1615l par. 1.

[368] *Lov no. 10* § 29.

claim in an independent action.[369] Paternity is proved in the same manner as in the child's action for support. Even prior to the child's birth, the WEST GERMAN mother may obtain a provisional court order under which the putative father must deposit funds to cover the normal cost of childbirth and the mother's support for six weeks. These funds will be paid to her immediately after the child's birth. To obtain this order, the expectant mother must produce credible proof of the putative father's paternity, which will include her own sworn statement and proof to the effect that she cohabited with the putative father at a time at which the expected child probably was conceived.[370]

In WEST GERMANY, if a child is legitimated after the death of his father and thereby obtains the father's surname, the father's name must also be conferred upon the mother, upon her application, unless there are serious reasons to the contrary (CC § 1740 g). Furthermore, as under prior law, the mother may under certain other circumstances apply to have her name officially changed to that of the father.[371] Her child's name would be changed accordingly. In NORWAY, on the other hand, the out-of-wedlock mother may take the father's name only if she marries him. While it seems technically possible that, under the conditions applicable to name changes generally, the mother might apply for the father's name,[372] this does not appear to occur in practice.

81. In POLAND, CZECHOSLOVAKIA and EAST GERMANY, no limitations restrict the availability of the paternity action and there are no limitations on evidence. Paternity actions are civil and not criminal. In all three countries, the courts investigate the facts *ex officio* and paternity may be established by court action even after the death of the father.[373]

In EAST GERMANY, the action against the alleged father may be brought by the mother or the guardian of the minor child. If the child has reached majority, he may sue within one year after receiving knowledge of the facts which point to the defendant's paternity (FC § 56). In POLAND, the right of action vests in the child, the mother and the public prosecutor. The mother loses her right of action with the child's attainment of majority, but no time limitation applies to the child's suit. If the father is deceased, the action must be brought against a curator appointed for this purpose by the court of guardianship.[374] In CZECHOSLOVAKIA, mother or child may bring the paternity action independently of one another (FC § 54), and when either the mother or the child has commenced an action and dies during the pendency of the proceedings, the survivor of the two may continue the action (FC § 56). If the child's descendants can show an "interest" in establishing paternity, they may continue a suit commenced by the child within six months after the child's death (FC § 56). If the alleged father is deceased, a court appointed curator must be sued (FC § 56). EAST GERMANY expressly provides that a paternity action may not be commenced on behalf of a child whose paternity has been previously established by recognition or court action or whose paternity is presumed because he was born in wedlock as long as the ascertainment of paternity has not been annulled or the presumption rebutted by judicial decision.[375]

In each of the three EASTERN EUROPEAN systems under review, sexual intercourse of the defendant with the mother at the critical time raises a presumption of paternity. The defendant may defend himself by proving that it is impossible that he is the father.[376] If the "illegitimate" child was born during a valid marriage, the presumption that the mother's husband is the father must first be rebutted before a presumption of paternity arises from an adulterous relationship. None of the three codes recognizes the *exceptio plurium* in the sense that mere proof that the mother had sexual intercourse at the critical time with someone other than the defendant automatically ends the proceeding. Rather, the defendant is exonerated only if it is "more probable" or "obviously more probable" that the other man is the father.[377] CZECHOSLOVAKIA requires that the defendant's paternity be "excluded ... by important factors" (FC § 54),

369 The child's action for support may be (and usually is) combined with the mother's action. See CC Proc. § 147 and *Jansen and Knöpfel* 222-223.

370 Formerly CC § 1716 and now CC § 1615 o, in connection with CC Proc. § 936, 920 par. 2.

371 *Jansen and Knöpfel* 321-334.

372 *Lov no. 1* § 4, 5, 7, 9

373 CZECHOSLOVAKIA: FC § 54 par. 1, 55. EAST GERMANY: *Familienverfahrensordnung* § 28 par. 1, § 2 par. 2; FC § 56 par. 3; FC-Commentary § 54 no. 8, § 56 no. 3.1; *Krüger*, Das gerichtliche Verfahren in Familiensachen: NJ 1966, 132. POLAND: FC art. 84 par. 2; *Lasok* 162.

374 FC art. 84, 86.

375 FC § 58, 63 par. 3.

376 CZECHOSLOVAKIA: FC § 54; EAST GERMANY: FC § 54 par. 2; POLAND: FC art. 85.

377 EAST GERMANY: FC § 54 par. 2; *Halgasch* 79; *Schlicht* 169. POLAND: FC art. 85 par. 2.

whereas EAST GERMANY compares the "likelihood" of the defendant's and the other man's paternity.[378] If the paternity of a second man is *equally* likely, the defendant is declared to be the father.[379]

EAST GERMANY allows another man to be brought into the proceeding if there is sufficient indication that his paternity is more probable than the defendant's.[380] This permits the father to be found in a single proceeding. If any defendant's paternity can be excluded, the action against him is dismissed immediately.[381]

While it is recognized that the abolition of the *exceptio plurium* may lead to inaccurate and unjust results, the possibility of a limited number of unjust results is accepted in the interest of protecting the child.[382] Furthermore, only a small number of cases are resolved by the "probability" tests, since only some 10 per cent of all illegitimate births lead to court action and most disputed cases can be resolved by medical tests.[383]

The judgment declares the status of child and father and is valid against all. In POLAND, the court decides in the paternity action whether parental authority should be vested in the father,[384] and EAST GERMANY permits pecuniary claims to be enforced simultaneously with the paternity action.[385] In all three countries, of course, support rights may be enforced against the father by court action. In EAST GERMANY, only the public attorney may question a final paternity judgment and only if facts came to his knowledge indicating that the defendant is not the father.[386]

In POLAND, the father must contribute to the expenses arising from the mother's pregnancy and confinement and toward "losses" incurred in connection with the pregnancy, including the mother's maintenance for a total of three months before and after the child's birth. This is true even if the child was stillborn.[387] The mother must enforce these claims within three years of the child's birth. She may bring an action even before the birth if she can make out a *prima facie* case against the defendant.[388] CZECHOSLOVAKIAN law is similar, although the father may be held for a greater amount (FC § 95 par. 2).

In all three countries, paternity also may be established by voluntary acknowledgment, unless of course the law imposes a presumption of paternity to the contrary.[389] In CZECHOSLOVAKIA, there must be a joint declaration of both parents (FC § 52 par. 1, 2), unless the mother is mentally incompetent or her joinder in the acknowledgment cannot be procured without undue difficulty (FC § 52 par. 3). While in POLAND[390] and EAST GERMANY (FC § 55) only the father makes the declaration, the mother, rather than joining in it, must consent to the acknowledgment. In POLAND, the mother's consent may be dispensed with under certain circumstances (FC art. 77 par. 1, 3), but this may not be done in EAST GERMANY.[391] Specific formalities are prescribed in all three countries to make an acknowledgment effective.[392] In both CZECHOSLOVAKIA (FC § 53) and POLAND (FC art. 75) the child may also be acknowledged prior to birth.

82. *Soviet Union.* – In 1968, SOVIET law reintroduced the paternity action that had been abolished in 1944.[393] Its availability is limited:

> "In establishing paternity, the court takes into account cohabitation and the maintenance of a common household by the child's mother and the respondent before the child's birth or their joint rearing or support of the child, or evidence that reliably establishes the respondent's own acknowledgement of paternity."[394]

Apparently, the court may investigate paternity only if the listed conditions are present and the

[378] *Familienverfahrensordnung* § 28, 29.

[379] EAST GERMANY: *Familienverfahrensordnung* § 28 par. 1, 29 par. 2; *cf.* also FC-Commentary § 54 no. 4; *Schlicht* 229; *Bechthold* 8; *Halgasch* 79.

[380] *Familienverfahrensordnung* § 28 par. 2-4, 29; Directive no. 23 of the Supreme Court *sub* A II g; FC-Commentary § 54 no. 3.3; *Krüger* (*supra* n. 373) 134.

[381] See BezG Neubrandenburg of 10 Nov. 1969, NJ 1970, 375.

[382] *Plank* 41, 42; *Czachórski* 56; *Halgasch* 79.

[383] FC-Commentary § 54 no. 4; *cf. Schlicht* 169; *Bechthold* 8; *Halgasch* 79.

[384] FC art. 93 par. 2; *Lasok* 172.

[385] *Familienverfahrensordnung* § 27 par. 1. A preliminary order may be issued obliging the alleged father to make support payments before a final judgment establishes his paternity. See *Latka and Borkmann*, Einstweilige Anordnungen im Familienrechtsverfahren: NJ 1970, 205-206.

[386] FC § 60; FC-Commentary § 60 no. 1.

[387] FC art. 141; *Lasok* 165-166.

[388] FC art. 142; *Lasok* 161; *cf. Czachórski* 48-49.

[389] POLAND: FC art. 72; CZECHOSLOVAKIA: FC § 52 par. 1; EAST GERMANY: FC § 63 par. 3.

[390] FC art. 72, 77.

[391] FC-Commentary § 55 no. 3.1.

[392] POLAND: FC art. 78, 79; CZECHOSLOVAKIA: FC § 52 par. 2; EAST GERMANY: FC § 55 par. 3.

[393] Radical discrimination against illegitimate children was decreed by the Decree of the Presidium of the Supreme Soviet of the USSR of 8 July 1944, which continued in effect until 1 Oct. 1968. The 1944 decree abolished any kind of legal relationship between father and his illegitimate child, including the child's claim for support: *Bilinsky* 187.

[394] RSFSR FC art. 48 par. 2.

child of a casual union whose father does *not* recognize paternity or accept the child in some other way remains precluded from bringing a paternity action even if there is other, direct evidence of paternity.[395]

The Supreme Court of the USSR requires that the condition of living together and maintaining a common household prior to the child's birth be proved "by factors characteristic of normal family relations such as living in one apartment, having meals together, mutually caring for one another, acquisition of property for common use, and so forth." While this seems to limit the protection of the law to the children of *de facto* marriages, termination by the parties of their relationship prior to the child's birth is not of itself ground for rejection of a suit to have paternity established. Moreover, "joint upbringing" or "joint support" of the child need not necessarily involve a "normal family situation". For example, a father and a mother may live apart, but the father may fully accept his child and try his best to help raise and support his child.[396]

Paternity cases proceed on an adversary basis and the general rules of civil procedure apply.[397] After the alleged father's death, a special procedure may be employed.[398] Support may be awarded in a successful paternity action and would be granted as of the day the suit was filed.[399]

It is not clear what defenses may be available to the defendant in a paternity action. None of the four circumstances under which an action may be brought constitutes direct evidence of a blood-relationship between father and child. If a man cohabits with a woman or helps her to rear or support a child or even if he acknowledges himself to be the father, this need not mean that he is the father.[400] While proof of the circumstances under which the action may be brought is not tantamount to a finding of paternity, such proof weighs heavily.[401] By allowing an expert medical examination, the Supreme Court gives the putative father an opportunity to question his paternity.[402]

The putative father's acknowlegdment of paternity need not involve a formal or public recognition. Any private declaration, oral or written, suffices. The Supreme Court has taken the position that

> "As proof toward recognition of paternity by the respondent may be produced letters, forms, declarations by the respondent and other factual proof... which beyond all reasonable doubt point towards recognition of paternity of the respondent. Such recognition may be expressed either during the period of pregnancy of the mother or after the birth of the child."[403]

Since the Fundamentals do not specify whether anyone other than the mother may bring the paternity action,[404] this question is left to the Union Republics. The RSFSR allows the child, who has reached the age of majority, to bring the action (FC art. 48 par. 1). Since it is one of the aims of the new legislation to relieve pressure on public funds, it may be expected that public agencies will be authorized to initiate paternity actions.[405]

83. MEXICAN[406] and PHILIPPINE (CC art. 283) law show their FRENCH ancestry when they specify that a paternity action may be brought only (1) if the mother was kidnapped, seduced or raped by the alleged father and if the time of the crime coincided with the time of conception, (2) if the child is in possession of *de facto* status as a legitimate child of the alleged father, (3) if the child was conceived during a time when the mother lived with the alleged father as if married,[407] or (4) in MEXICO, if the child can show a beginning of written proof against the alleged father (CC art. 382). PHILIPPINE law may reflect AMERICAN influence in its liberalization of the last category. Unlike MEXICO, the corresponding provision of the PHILIPPINE Code speaks in terms of "any evidence or proof that the defendant is [the child's] father" (CC art. 283 par. 4). "Any evidence or proof" may include a school report card signed by the father,[408] a diary or love letters of the father recognizing the child,[409] as well as blood tests, the mother's testimony or the father's admission.[410]

395 Fundamentals of Family Law art. 16 par. 4.

396 Resolution no. 10 art. 3 par. 2-4.

397 Resolution no. 10 art. 5 par. 1; *Gorkin* 32.

398 Resolution no. 10 art. 5 par. 1. With regard to children born prior to 1 Oct. 1968, see art. 7.

399 Resolution no. 10 art. 6.

400 Public discussion in Izvestia, 7 May 1968 p. 5 (Current Digest of the Soviet Press 20 (1968) no. 19 p. 15); *Bilinsky* 198.

401 *Geilke* 150.

402 Resolution no. 10 art. 4.

403 Resolution no. 10 art. 3 par. 5.

404 Resolution no. 10 art. 5 par. 2 covers only the case where the father has died.

405 *Stone* 400.

406 CC art. 382, 384.

407 *Rojina Villegas* 477, 478.

408 *Joaquín v. Joaquín*, 60 Phil. 395 (1934).

409 *Varela v. Villanueva*, 95 Phil. 248 (1954); *Lagdameo v. Lagdameo*, (C.A.) G.R. No. 10166-R (19 Feb. 1954).

410 *Domingo v. Maliwat*, 3 Court of Appeals Reports 2d 913 (1963).

With these broad categories of permissible proof, PHILIPPINE law may be viewed as having all but overcome the FRENCH restrictions on the investigation of paternity. It appears to approximate the AMERICAN notion that paternity may be investigated freely and to the extent the Code still pays lip service to the FRENCH heritage, it obscures its liberal approach.

Of course, special concern for illegitimate children behooves a society whose law does not permit divorce. Mildly misreading the MEXICAN rules on this point, *Capistrano* says:

"In the old Code, investigation of paternity, except in the cases specified in its article 135, was not allowed by the *Ley de Bases* of said Code because generation is a mysterious act of nature and whatever is done to disclose it will lead to error, from which erroneous and deplorable consequences may follow, unlike pregnancy and delivery which are external acts susceptible of investigation and proof, as are all ordinary and visible facts of life.

The Code Commission, however, took note of the fact that investigation of paternity is generally allowed according to the modern tendency in legislation, of which the *Mexican Civil Code* is an example. Such investigation is also allowed in Anglo-American law. Even the *Law of Toro* allowed investigation of paternity. It now also appears untrue, at least debatable, that paternity is not capable of demonstration or proof especially with the aid of modern scientific tests and discoveries. It also appeared that while in monarchical Spain the nobles were interested in preventing investigation of paternity to protect themselves from the consequences of illicit relations with their maidservants and the daughters of their vassals, there are no nobles in the Philippines to protect. We have only high government officials and politicians, but in a democracy, their protection should consist of their own good moral character and honorable conduct, not of a law which will only cover up immorality and encourage the same to the detriment of the innocent offsprings. For these reasons, investigation of paternity is now allowed."[411]

Another significant aspect of the abandonment of the FRENCH heritage is that MEXICO does not distinguish between illegitimates by categories such as "natural" or "spurious". MEXICO permits the investigation of paternity in all cases which fall within the enumerated categories of proof. Even PHILIPPINE law, though still making the distinction, nevertheless allows parental recognition, voluntary or compulsory, of a spurious child just as fully as it allows the investigation of the paternity of a "natural" child. Note, however, that modern FRENCH law also has abandoned these classifications.

The investigation of maternity is permitted freely in both countries.[412] MEXICO excepts only the case of the married mother in which event the investigation of maternity is barred, unless maternity is indicated in a civil jugdment bastardizing the child as to the mother's husband or a criminal judgment such as the mother's conviction for adultery.[413] The PHILIPPINES, in such a case, would have her recognize the child as a spurious child.[414]

MEXICO provides that while rendering support alone does not prove or give rise to a presumption of paternity or maternity, it may serve as the basis for investigating paternity or maternity (CC art. 387). In both countries, paternity or maternity suits may be brought only during the life of the parent in question, unless the parent(s) have died during the child's minority. Then, the child may bring an action for declaration of his parentage within four years after reaching majority.[415] In view of generous presumptions of legitimacy established in MEXICAN law in the case of a deceased parent,[416] there will be only rare instances in which a child will need to bring a paternity (or maternity) action after the parent's death. The PHILIPPINES would also permit an action for recognition of parentage after the parent's death if, after the death, a document appears of which nothing had been heard before and in which the child is recognized (CC art. 285 par. 2).

Neither MEXICO nor the PHILIPPINES apply a period of limitation (other than the parent's lifetime, as discussed above) to the suit for ascertainment of the child's status.[417] In MEXICO, the heirs of the child may sue to have the child's status declared, if the child died prior to completing his 25th year of life, or lost his mental capacity prior to reaching that age and died in that condition (CC art. 348). In certain circumstances, the child's heirs may continue a suit brought by the child or continue to defend a suit that questions the child's legitimacy (CC art. 349). Similar rights are provided for creditors, legatees and donees if the child has not left enough property to satisfy their claims (CC art. 350). These rights must be exercised within four years of the child's death (CC art. 351).

In both countries, the legal effect of the paternity action equals that of voluntary recognition by the

[411] *Capistrano*, Civil Code of the Philippines I (Manila 1950) 266.

[412] MEXICO: CC art. 385; PHILIPPINES: CC art. 284.

[413] CC art. 385-386; *Rojina Villegas* 480.

[414] CC art. 289; *U.S. v. Yambao*, 4 Phil. 204 (1905).

[415] MEXICO: CC art. 388; PHILIPPINES: CC art. 285.

[416] CC art. 341-343.

[417] MEXICO: CC art. 347; PHILIPPINES: CC art. 285.

parent. In MEXICO, this means that – in the limited instances in which the paternity action may be brought – the result is essentially the equivalent of legitimate status. In the PHILIPPINES, on the other hand, while the investigation of paternity is permitted much more freely, the result of recognition differs from legitimate status and depends on whether the child is natural or spurious. The paternity suit is essentially an ordinary civil proceeding.[418] A complaint seeking "compulsory acknowledgment" may be combined with a request for support.[419]

The acknowledgment of an alleged natural child may be determined either in an ordinary civil action or in special proceedings for the settlement of the estate of the deceased parent.[420] All trials upon the merits are conducted in open court and, so far as convenient, in a regular court room. In its discretion, any court may exclude the public when the evidence to be adduced is of such a nature as to require confidentiality in the interest of morality or decency. The records of every court of justice are public and available for inspection by any interested person, unless the court has forbidden publicity in the interest of morality or decency.[421]

iii. *Comparative Summary*

84. *Paternity action.* – In addition to the voluntary establishment of the parent and child relationship by acknowledgment, as traditionally preferred by the FRENCH-based systems, most legal systems today also provide for the compulsory ascertainment of parentage. The rules under which the mother and child relationship is established – if there are specific provisions at all[422] – are largely the same everywhere. Usually, proof that the child was born to the mother harbors legally adequate proof of maternity.

Methods of establishing paternity by compulsory legal process show much more diversity. Two principles vie for dominance: One goal is to protect innocent men from harrassment or even the actual father's legitimate family. Accordingly, some strength remains in the time-honored phrase "*la recherche de la paternité est interdite*" with which *Napoléon* forbade paternity actions directly after the brief period of legal equality that had been legislated during the FRENCH revolution. Second, there is the opposite goal of seeking to find a father for each child born out of wedlock. This view of the matter has been especially influential in SCANDINAVIA. Nowhere is either of these basic positions realized to the fullest extent; everywhere both views influence applicable laws in varying degrees and detail.

85. *Conditions of ascertainment of paternity.* – By definition, the ascertainment of biological descent is the spoken or unspoken universal purpose of the paternity action. However, in many jurisdictions proof of biological descent is not enough. FRANCE and many FRENCH-based systems, such as those of MEXICO, but also BELGIUM, ITALY, SPAIN and others, require the presence of additional conditions, such as proof that the father committed a sexual delict against the mother (from rape to special cases of "seduction"), or concubinage or they require proof of certain facts tending to show acknowledgment of the child by the father before a "compulsory acknowledgment" (*reconnaissance forcée*) is decreed.[423] In addition, some of the FRENCH-based systems altogether exclude adulterous or incestuous bastards from acknowledgment and compulsory process to ascertain paternity, with some systems, however, allowing a claim for support to be made. In the latter case, paternity must be proved in the same manner as in the regular action.[424]

Recent reforms in the countries following the acknowledgment route generally show a tendency to reduce or eliminate these additional conditions.[425] The new, restrictive development in the SOVIET UNION – which holds since 1968 that paternity may be established only if there is a relationship resembling concubinage between the mother and the alleged father or if the alleged father has made moves toward acknowledging the child – must be understood in the context of the special history of the paternity action in the SOVIET UNION and definitely goes counter to the world-wide trend.

86. *Legal consequences of ascertainment of paternity.* – Many legal systems (most states in the UNITED STATES, ENGLAND) provide merely a support obligation, generally *in futuro*, in conse-

[418] PHILIPPINES: *Moran* I sec. 1 (rule 2).

[419] *Celis v. Crisostomo*, 46 O.G. 589; *Padilla* 409.

[420] CC art. 619; *Escoval v. Escoval*, 48 O.G. 616.

[421] *Moran* VI sec. 7 (rule 135), sec. 2 (rule 135).

[422] See FRANCE: CC art. 341; also, *e.g.*, ITALY: CC art. 272; SPAIN: CC art. 136 and art. 140 no. 3; PORTUGAL: CC art. 1857; ARGENTINA: CC art. 325, 326 (excludes action to establish maternity if the "putative" mother is married).

[423] BELGIUM: CC art. 340a; ITALY: CC art. 269; SPAIN: CC art. 135.

[424] BELGIUM: CC art. 340b; ITALY: CC art. 279; SPAIN: CC art. 140.

[425] For instance, ARGENTINA: Law no. 14367 of 30 Sept. 1954 art. 3 and CC art. 325. FRANCE: CC art. 342.

quence of a successful paternity action. A similar "minimum" solution is offered by SOVIET law, as well as by many FRENCH-based systems in cases where regular acknowledgment is forbidden.[426]

The modern trend is in the direction of having the ascertainment of paternity provide further rights to the child born out of wedlock. This trend was set early by the FRENCH-based systems that follow the acknowledgment route where the establishment of parentage provides regular status for the child, rather than just a bundle of specific rights. Today, an increasing number of systems permit the paternity action to establish full legal equality between children born out of wedlock and legitimate children. Other systems provide, in addition to support, inheritance rights or rights concerning the father's name and, conversely, may provide custodial or visitation rights to the father.[427]

87. *Procedure in paternity actions.* – Procedures for the ascertainment of paternity vary considerably. Generally, the paternity action is a regular civil proceeding, sometimes the judge is given special investigatory powers.[428] While the initiation of the action usually rests with the parties, the SCANDINAVIAN countries have pioneered automatic administrative processes which are set in motion upon the birth of each illegitimate child – sometimes earlier. A few systems (especially some states in the UNITED STATES, see s. 78 above) continue to relegate the paternity action to the criminal side of the courts (which provides broader protections for the accused, but imposes on the child a burden of proof that is not consistent with the establishment of a "civil" relationship) or they provide for a special, "quasi-criminal" level of proof in the civil action, such as "clear and convincing evidence".

88. *Potential plaintiffs.* – All three parties directly concerned – mother, father,[429] and child – as well as interested outsiders, such as welfare authorities or private persons or organizations who have furnished sustenance to the child, may be authorized to bring the paternity action. Some systems put their emphasis here, others there; few use one approach to the exclusion of other routes. For instance, the COMMON LAW typically has looked at the right to bring the action as belonging primarily to the mother (states in the UNITED STATES, ENGLAND, IRELAND)[430] and secondarily to the welfare authorities. Other systems (FRANCE, WEST GERMANY, EAST GERMANY, POLAND, CZECHOSLOVAKIA and many others, such as YUGOSLAVIA, AUSTRIA, BELGIUM)[431] have viewed the action as belonging primarily to the child. In practice, the distinction cuts less deeply than it would appear, because the child's action would still be brought by the child's representative who would usually be the mother. Where – as in the SCANDINAVIAN countries – the welfare authorities have an important role in the ascertainment of the paternity of children born out of wedlock, the interests of the child receive the broadest protection.[432]

89. *Statutes of limitation.* – Periods of limitation on paternity actions vary greatly. At one extreme, the action is never barred.[433] At the other extreme, the expiration of a few months after birth bars the action.[434] Between these extremes, many systems prefer periods of limitation ranging between one and five years.[435] The starting time of the period of limitation may vary with the person bringing the action. When the suit is brought by the mother, the starting point may be the child's birth, it may be the age of majority of the child, if the child is plaintiff, or it may begin with the first payment of welfare assistance, if the welfare authorities sue.

90. *Proof of paternity.* – One major trend relating to the proof of paternity is obvious: There is an increasing reliance on medical science, especially on blood typing, and the parties are increasingly asked to submit to appropriate tests. Beyond that, approaches vary substantially. Some systems continue to have binding rules of evidence to the effect, for instance, that proof of the mother's cohabitation at the probable time of conception with men other than the putative father forces dismissal of the action,[436] or that the action may

426 BELGIUM, ITALY, SPAIN (*supra* n. 424).

427 *Cf. infra* s. 102 ss.

428 *E.g.*, WEST GERMANY: CCProc. § 640 and 617, 622 par. 1.

429 WEST GERMANY: CC § 1600n par. 1. For the UNITED STATES, see also the Uniform Parentage Act.

430 IRELAND: Illegitimate Children (Affiliation Orders) Act, 1930, s. 2.

431 YUGOSLAVIA: Fundamental Law on the Relations Between Parents and Children art. 25; AUSTRIA: CC § 164c; BELGIUM: CC art. 341b par. 1.

432 NORWAY (*supra* s. 80); also DENMARK: *Lov no. 200* ch. 1 § 7 ss.; SWEDEN: *Föräldrabalk* ch. 3 § 4.

433 *E.g.*, WEST GERMANY: CC § 1600n; GUATEMALA: CC art. 220 par. 1.

434 IRELAND: Illegitimate Children (Affiliation Orders) Act, 1930, s. 2(2) (b) (six months).

435 One year: EAST GERMANY (FC § 56 par. 2) and SWITZERLAND (CC art. 308). Two years: ITALY (CC art. 271 par. 1). Three years: BULGARIA (FC art. 39). Five years: BELGIUM (CC art. 341b par. 2) and YUGOSLAVIA (Fundamental Law on the Relations between Parents and Children art. 25).

436 *E.g.*, BELGIUM: CC art. 340d.

be dismissed merely upon proof of the mother's general "immorality".[437] The current trend goes against binding rules of this sort (except, of course, for the increasing acceptance of the conclusiveness of blood typing results) and is moving in the direction of leaving the evaluation of all available proof to the court.[438]

91. *Conclusion.* – If anything is apparent, it is that the increasing sophistication and reliability of medical procedures have substantially changed the character of paternity proceedings. Science is helping both of the interests involved in the paternity action – that of the unjustly accused in being free of harrassment or being burdened with someone else's obligation, and that of the child in finding his father.

C. SCIENTIFIC EVIDENCE OF PATERNITY

92. We have just seen that most systems permit the investigation of paternity with more or less freedom. Even this limited resemblance is superficial, however. Variations are enormous in terms of the use of scientific evidence. An AMERICAN judge has observed that "without ... [blood grouping tests], the rules of evidence relating to proof of paternity have not changed much since our judicial ancestors threw witches into a New England pond and judged them according to whether they sank or swam."[439]

i. *Blood Tests*

93. *Introductory.* – It is clear that blood typing will establish non-paternity in all cases in which father, mother and child have a biologically impossible constellation of blood types.[440] Contrary to popular oversimplification, however, tests that do not result in exclusion of the alleged father show more than that any man with blood of the alleged father's type could be the father of the child in question. Whereas exclusions can be established with scientific, absolute certainty, inclusions can be established by degrees of probability. At the extreme end of the spectrum, paternity can be all but determined positively, because some genes are so rare that, if the same genes are found in the putative father and the child, in *Sussman*'s words, "the possibility of coincidence being responsible is so remote as to make the odds astronomical" (p. 83). In less extreme situations, the probability of paternity can be computed for any given case that did not produce an exclusion. Some systems have been more willing than others to trust the new techniques. Differences appear at two levels. In some countries, the scientific reliability of some of the newer findings remains in dispute. In other countries, though the courts may recognize the scientific value of blood typing tests, facilities are lacking to execute the tests reliably.

94. *United States.* – AMERICA is a suitable example of both categories. First, only a narrowly limited number of blood typing systems is now being accepted by most courts.[441] Second, reliable laboratory facilities for the execution of blood tests are a rarity. Dr. *Wiener* cautions that

> "there has been an unfortunate tendency to assume that these tests can be done by any blood bank or laboratory where clinical blood grouping tests are carried out ... This false belief has been fostered by the ready availability commercially of the antisera needed for conducting such examinations. This has led individuals with little or no experience in the field to accept the assignment from a court to conduct these examinations ..."[442]

This situation has led to conservative recommendations, made in 1957, by the Committee on Medico-Legal Problems of the American Medical Association that:

> "... routine medicolegal applications of blood grouping be restricted at present to tests for the four blood groups, O, A, B and AB of the A-B-O system; the three types M, N, and MN of the M-N-S system; and factors Rh, rh', and hr' of the Rh-Hr system. Tests for additional factors and systems are considered insufficiently established for routine use at present, although they may provide evidence in particular selected cases."[443]

437 *E.g.*, GREECE: CC art. 1543.

438 In addition to WEST and EAST GERMANY (both of which have repealed the *exceptio plurium*, old CC § 1717) NORWAY, and, among others, SWEDEN: *Föräldrabalk* ch. 3 § 3. Details are provided by *Malmström*, Die Rechtsstellung des unehelichen Kindes im schwedischen Recht: ZfRV 4 (1963) 142 ss.

439 *Judge Cook* in *Libertowski v. Hojara*, 228 N.E.2d 422, 425 (Ind.App. 1967).

440 For a brief review of the theory and practice of modern scientific techniques of ascertaining paternity, see *Krause* 123-136.

441 See AMERICAN sources in *idem* 129-132.

442 *Wiener*, Blood Grouping Tests in Disputed Parentage. Qualifications of Experts: 13 Acta Geneticae Medicae et Gemellologiae 340 (1964).

443 *Committee on Medicolegal Problems*, Medicolegal Applications of Blood Grouping Test: 164 J.A.M.A. 2036 (1957).

Many AMERICAN legislatures have been even more cautious and allow blood typing evidence only if a definite exclusion is established.[444] In the absence of statutes, many courts have taken the same view.[445] Moreover, even if an exclusion is established, only some AMERICAN statutes will accord it conclusive weight,[446] where others will regard it as just another item of evidence.[447] Whatever their weight, blood test results are admitted into evidence only when explained by expert testimony.[448] Only a few states allow the court to order that the parties submit to a blood test.[449] While such a requirement has been considered not to infringe constitutional guarantees relating to self-incrimination or unlawful search and seizure, many states remain half-hearted on this point.[450] The "Uniform Blood Test Act" has improved the law in the five states that have adopted it.[451]

This hardly admirable situation is expected to change drastically and soon. A joint committee of the American Medical Association and the American Bar Association has been charged with the evaluation of the theoretical and practical potential of the current state of the art and a detailed report is due in late 1975. This report will provide guidance to medical facilities, courts and lawyers in the medical use and judicial application of sophisticated modern techniques, it will set quality controls and generally tie in with the purposes of the Uniform Parentage Act as well as the 1975 federal legislation (P.L. 93-647) that is putting federal pressure behind the development and identification of adequate facilities to aid in the establishment of paternity.

95. ENGLAND's 1969 Family Law Reform Act provides for the utilization of blood tests in the ascertainment of paternity.[452] Any party to a civil proceeding, where paternity is to be determined, may request such tests. However, blood samples may not be taken from a person without his consent or that of his guardian. If a person fails to give his consent, or fails to take any other step necessary for compliance with the court's order, the court is permitted to "draw such inferences, if any, . . . as appear proper in the circumstances."[453] The expert who performs the tests is required to make a written report to the court.[454] The report should include the test results and state if an ex-

[444] CONNECTICUT Gen.Stat.Ann. § 52-184 (1968); MASSACHUSETTS Ann.Laws ch. 273 § 12A (1968); MICHIGAN Comp.Laws § 722.716 (1968); NEW JERSEY Rev.Stat. § 2A:83-2, -3 (1952); NEW YORK Fam.Ct.Act § 532 (McKinney 1963); WISCONSIN Stat.Ann. § 52.36 (Supp. 1969). Similar provisions are to be found in ALABAMA, ARKANSAS, INDIANA, MARYLAND, OKLAHOMA, RHODE ISLAND, TENNESSEE and WEST VIRGINA. – *Contra:* KENTUCKY authorizes a court, in its discretion, to admit tests that show a possibility of paternity: KENTUCKY Rev.Stat.Ann. § 406.11 (Supp. 1968). – In NEW HAMPSHIRE and COLORADO if the experts hold that the blood test shows a possibility of paternity, the court will rule as to admissibility on the basis of the frequency of the blood type involved: NEW HAMPSHIRE Rev. Stat.Ann. § 522:4 (1955); COLORADO Rev.Stat.Ann. § 52-1-27 (Supp. 1967). – In the DISTRICT OF COLUMBIA results are only admissible if not objected to: DISTRICT OF COLUMBIA Code Ann. § 16-2347 (1967). – OREGON and UTAH allow the court to exercise discretion where possibility of paternity is shown, depending upon the frequency of the blood type: OREGON Rev. Stat. § 109-258 (1967); UTAH Code Ann. § 78-45a-10 (Supp. 1969).

[445] See generally 10 Am.Jur.2d *s.v.* Bastards § 118-119 (1963). But *cf. Carpenter v. Goodall*, 224 N.E.2d 673 (Ind. 1969), which held, on appeal, that substantial evidence supported paternity and that it was not prejudicial (although not good practice) that the trial court had seen the blood test report which did not exclude defendant as a possible father.

[446] CALIFORNIA Evidence Code § 895 (West 1966); KENTUCKY Rev.Stat.Ann. § 406.111 (Supp. 1968); MISSISSIPPI Code Ann. § 383.11 (Supp. 1968); NEW HAMPSHIRE Rev.Stat.Ann. § 522:4 (1955) (if the experts agree); OREGON Rev.Stat. § 109.258 (1966); PENNSYLVANIA Stat. Ann. tit. 28 § 307.4 (Supp. 1970); WISCONSIN Stat.Ann. § 885.23 (1967).

[447] Judicial attitudes concerning the evidential value of blood typing tests are described by *Clark* 171; Note, Bastards – Evidentiary Weight of Blood Tests to Prove Non-Paternity: 98 U.Pa.L.Rev. 746 (1950); Note, A Trial of Bastardy is a Trial of the Blood: 34 Cornell L.Q. 72, 78-79 (1948); *Johnston*, Public Policy Considerations in Ruling on the Uniform Act on Blood Tests to Determine Paternity: 4 Wm. & Mary L.Rev. 149 (1963); Comment, The "Gap" Between the Law of Paternity and the Science of Serology. Blood Tests in Nonpaternity Proceedings: 16 Mercer L.Rev. 306 (1964). To be distinguished, of course, are cases which are given to the jury on the issue of whether the tests were expertly performed. *Cf.* Comment, Bastards – Accurate Blood Grouping Tests Which Negate Paternity Held Conclusive: 63 Harv.L. Rev. 1271 (1950).

[448] OHIO Rev. Code Ann. § 3111.16 (Page 1960).

[449] See, *e.g.*, ALABAMA Code tit. 27 § 12(5) (Supp. 1969).

[450] Note, Determination of Non-Paternity by Blood Tests: 23 Tul.L.Rev. 397, 398-399 (1949).

[451] See *Harris*, Some Observations on the Uniform Act on Blood Tests to Determine Paternity: 9 Vill.L.Rev. 59 (1963).

[452] Family Law Reform Act 1969, s. 20-25. Prior to the Act, a court had no power to order a blood test. *W. v. W.*, [1964] P. 67, [1963] 2 All E.R. 841. See, generally, *Lanham*, Reforms in Blood Test Law: 9 Medicine, Science and the Law 172-177 (1969).

[453] Family Law Reform Act 1969, s. 23.

[454] *Ibidem* s. 20(1), 21, 22(1) (i), 23.

clusion is shown. An exclusion now ends the case as a practical matter, although the statute does not so specify. The drafters seem to have thought that there might be rare cases in which an exclusion should be ignored.[455] If the man tested is not excluded, the report should state "the value, if any, of the results in determining whether that party is that person's father."[456] While the court may request an explanation or amplification of the report, it is not generally necessary that the doctor who conducted the test be called into court. A party to the proceeding may request it by serving an appropriate notice on all other parties within 14 days after he has received the report. In such instances, an opportunity for cross-examination will become available.[457] The Act also provides criminal penalties for impersonating another person, or substituting a child, for purposes of the blood tests.[458] Government authorities are authorized to make regulations concerning blood testing, for the specific purpose of assuring the reliability and uniformity of testing procedures.[459]

96. In SCANDINAVIA, the situation is drastically different.[460] Centralized blood typing facilities in Oslo, Copenhagen and Stockholm serve their whole countries and, over several decades, have developed great expertise. These laboratories are distinguished not only in terms of their use of complex and advanced blood typing systems, but also in terms of their highly developed safety procedures which assure accuracy of the results they report. This latter point may be the most crucial element of blood typing. We can agree quickly that it would be better not to admit blood tests into evidence at all than to admit unreliable evidence under the halo of scientific truth – as is done in many other places, including AMERICA where a re-check of even relatively simple tests revealed about one-third of them to have been in error![461] The safety procedures employed in SCANDINAVIA include specialization of and close supervision over highly skilled laboratory personnel, "blind" double testing of all samples with careful, independent rechecking by a third person of any discrepancies that are reported, careful maintenance and daily testing of testing agents, and tight control over the identification of samples and over other clerical aspects of the testing and reporting process.

The Scandinavian laboratories cooperate efficiently with the courts. Standardized routines govern the taking of blood samples, the transmission of samples to the laboratories and the reporting of findings to the courts. Most of this is accomplished by the use of well designed standard forms which keep the information compact and present it in a manner that is understandable to the court. The courts rely heavily on the medical evidence. The reputation for accuracy of the laboratories is such that the parties and their lawyers usually rest their case with the medical evidence.

SCANDINAVIA also leads the way in the variety of grouping systems used. Constant research seeks to develop new systems for practical use and years of testing precede the actual use of a new system. In contrast to the limited number of systems accepted for practical use in the American Medical Association's old (1957) guidelines, soon to be revised, the Copenhagen laboratory (and the practice in Stockholm and Oslo is similar) employs three sets of systems in "layers", by which an exclusion figure of approximately 90 per cent of non-fathers is reached.

97. *Computation of "probability" of paternity.* – That figure is indeed impressive. In addition, cases which do not produce an exclusion are pursued on the basis of a "blood group paternity index"

455 *Lanham* (*supra* n. 452) 172, 176.

456 Family Law Reform Act 1969, s. 20.

457 *Ibidem* s. 20(5).

458 *Ibidem* s. 24 (imprisonment not to exceed two years or a fine not in excess of £ 400, *i.e.* approx. $ 800).

459 *Ibidem* s. 22.

460 Information concerning SCANDINAVIAN practice was obtained through interviews with Professor *Lundevall* and Dr. *Lie* (University Institute of Forensic Medicine) and Judge *Aubert* (Paternity Court), Oslo; Drs. *Henningsen* and *Gürtler* (University Institute of Forensic Medicine), Judge *Mols* (Paternity Court), Mr. *Gronning-Nielsen* (Justice Ministry), and Mrs. *Thaulow* (Mother's Aid Center), Copenhagen; and Professor *Vamosi* (State Laboratory of Forensic Chemistry), Mr. *Lind* (Ministry of Justice), and Mrs. *Traung* (Social Welfare Department), Stockholm. Their most gracious and helpful cooperation is gratefully acknowledged! See generally also *Henningsen*, Some Aspects of Blood Grouping in Cases of Disputed Paternity in Denmark: 2 Methods of Forensic Science 209 (1963); *idem*, On the Application of Blood Tests to Legal Cases of Disputed Paternity: Revue de Transfusion 12 (1969) 137, 139; *Andresen*, Human Blood Groups Utilized in Disputed Paternity Cases and Criminal Proceedings (Springfield, Ill. 1952) 73; *Henningsen*, Die Bewertung blutgruppenserologischer Abstammungsgutachten vor Gericht in Dänemark, mit Erfahrungsbericht über die Abgabe positiver biostatistischer Indizien zur Vaterschaft (Paper delivered at meeting of Gesellschaft für Forensische Blutgruppenkunde, Travemünde 1969).

461 *Wiener*, Foreword in *Sussman*; see also *idem*, Problems and Pitfalls in Blood Grouping Tests for Non-Parentage: 15 Journal of Forensic Medicine 106, 126 (1968).

by means of which the "probability" of the named man's paternity can be estimated.[462] That index compares the frequency of a given father-mother-child blood constellation in a sample of actual fathers with the blood constellation in a sample of non-fathers and is related to the constellation obtained in the case in question. If the resemblance exceeds 95 per cent, the result is reported to the court. At the outer limits, *i.e.*, where the weight is very high, this approach produces *de facto* inclusions or exclusions. In less extreme cases, it produces interesting circumstantial evidence. It is of particular value when the relative likelihood of paternity of several possible fathers is being compared. Note that these methods all but obviate whatever need there once may have been for the *exceptio plurium*.

The use of statistical methods to estimate probabilities of paternity is not limited to SCANDINAVIA. For example, one WEST GERMAN case considered detailed blood tests to establish a 99.55 per cent probability of paternity[463] and, in a case reviewed in 1964, the WEST GERMAN Supreme Court decided that a blood test taken just nine years earlier that had failed to exclude defendant as a possible father was not conclusive in view of newly developed, more sophisticated methods of blood testing that now might result in excluding defendant as a possible father.[464]

In WEST GERMANY, the possibility of formulating a uniform method of using statistical computations in paternity cases has been under review by the Federal Ministry of Health. Official standards may eventually be formulated. While centralized laboratories following the SCANDINAVIAN model do not exist, a detailed set of regulations governs laboratory standards,[465] the identification of subjects, the taking and shipment of blood samples, the efficacy and maintenance of testing sera, other laboratory procedures, the typing systems that are deemed scientifically reliable, necessary qualifications of blood typing experts, and the proper evaluation of results.

The EAST GERMANS hold that if the level of probability of paternity or non-paternity reaches 99.8 per cent or 0.2 per cent, paternity is held to be "practically" established or excluded, respectively.[466] According to their calculations, this level of probability can now be reached in 90 per cent of all cases in which the defendant is *not* the child's father.[467] EAST GERMAN law allows a non-exclusion to speak as circumstantial evidence of paternity or non-paternity if the probability of paternity exceeds 90 per cent or is less than 10 per cent.[468] This is somewhat more daring than the 95 per cent or 5 per cent test of relevancy employed by the Scandinavian laboratories. Even in EAST GERMANY, however, lesser probabilities may not be used for any purpose, not even in a comcomparison of the relative probability of paternity of two possible fathers.

The statistical approach is not without pitfalls. First, Drs. *Henningsen* and *Gürtler* of the Copenhagen laboratory emphasize that knowledge of representative gene frequencies is a prerequisite of probability calculations. Moreover the population should be homogeneous. In SCANDINAVIA, of course, that condition is nearly fulfilled, although geographic variations are carefully taken into account. Second, there appears to be incomplete agreement on the formulae that should be used. The *Essen-Möller* formula is being used in SCANDINAVIA and WEST GERMANY,[469] but some experts dispute its value. Dr. *Alexander S. Wiener*, one of AMERICA's foremost blood typing experts (and co-discoverer of the Rh-Hr blood types) would calculate probabilities solely in terms of adding together the cumulative probability of arriving at an exclusion by means of the particular tests used. To illustrate, if the chance that none of the tests used would exclude the average innocent man is 15 per cent, then the probability that the non-excluded putative father actually is the father would be stated by him as 6 to 7 to 1.[470] In summary, it seems obvious that a careful, objective study of the whole subject of biostatistical evaluation of the "probability" of paternity is needed badly.[471]

[462] See, *Gürtler*, Principles of Blood Group Statistical Evaluation of Paternity Cases at the University Institute of Forensic Medicine, Copenhagen: 9 Acta Medicinae Legalis et Socialis 83 (1956).

[463] LG Köln 13 Oct. 1961, MDR 1962, 309.

[464] BGH 5 Feb. 1964, FamRZ 1964, 251.

[465] Richtlinien für Erstattung von Blutgruppengutachten: Bundesgesundheitsblatt 13 (1970) 149–153.

[466] Directive no. 23 *sub* A II 9.

[467] *Prokop*, Zur Berechnung der Wahrscheinlichkeit einer Vaterschaft: NJ 1967, 256.

[468] Directive no. 23 *sub* A II 9.

[469] *Essen-Möller*, Die Beweiskraft der Ähnlichkeit im Vaterschaftsnachweis (Vienna 1938); *Gürtler* (*supra* n. 462) 83–93. See, *e.g.*, *Hummel*, Biostatistical Opinion of Parentage (Stuttgart 1971).

[470] *Wiener*, Advances in Blood Grouping III (New York 1970) 616, 626.

[471] See *Glage*, Die Vaterschaftsfeststellung nach dem neuen Nichtehelichenrecht: NJW 1970, 1223, 1224 who distinguishes between several types of "probability" and considers "objective probability" to state what percentage of the male population could possibly be the father, given the mother-child blood constellation in the case. "Subjective probability" is defined as the relative probability of paternity of several possible

ii. *Other Methods*

98. *Anthropological investigation.* – Blood testing is not the only means of converting the ascertainment of paternity from a matter of opinion into a matter of fact. Other distinguishing and inheritable human characteristics are under investigation.[472] Very good prospects seem to lie in the development of knowledge in connection with transplant immunology.

In addition, recent anthropological research has resulted in a growing body of data concerning inheritable characteristics which may be of use in paternity proceedings.[473] Thus, *Keiter* has concluded that "the data at the disposal of the physical anthropologist contain sufficient information to determine in 19 out of 20 cases, at a level of three sigma significance (99.73 plus probability) whether a given individual is the parent of a child in question."[474] In essence, his approach compares a set of some 70 heritable traits, including blood group systems, dermatoglyphic traits, measurements and other factors. Many scientists consider the anthropological approach to be at a lesser level of scientific accuracy than has been achieved by blood grouping tests.[475] Others feel certain of its equal value.[476] Important experts discount its practical value altogether.[477] EAST GERMANY permits the use of anthropological evidence "as a last resort" and primarily in connection with the evaluation of the probability of paternity when there is more than one candidate. Still, in connection with other medical evidence, it may be accorded some weight in negating paternity.[478] Some use of anthropological techniques is made in POLAND.[479] Moreover, DANISH researchers employ anthropological traits as a supplement to inconclusive blood tests. The traits used include finger and palm prints, color and structure of the iris and a few physiognomic features. Correlation coefficients and other necessary data have been computed for all traits used, allowing an estimate of the value of a given comparison. The DANISH researchers caution that this type of investigation is not very valuable standing alone, but can be of great value in combination with blood test results. They estimate that an anthropological investigation raises the "probability" level of information to 95 per cent+ in about 80 per cent of the cases in which such an investigation is performed.[480]

In AMERICA, on the other hand, while the probative value of anthropological evidence remains in dispute, some courts still permit the simple "resemblance test" by which the jury is allowed to make a visual comparison between the baby and the man accused of being the father.[481]

99. *Duration of pregnancy.* – In addition to blood tests or anthropological evidence, the duration of a particular pregnancy (in relation to a proved act or acts of intercourse) may have probative value.[482] Most CIVIL LAW countries "solve" this question by specifying definite time limits. For example, EAST and WEST GERMANY consider that a pregnancy may last from 181 to 302 days, and FRANCE, POLAND, and CZECHOSLOVAKIA presume that the period of gestation lasts from 180 to 300 days.[483] Most AMERICAN states, on the other hand, have not imposed specific time limits, and the courts re-

fathers on the premise that actual father is among the men who are tested. A "mixed objective-subjective probability" is found in cases in which the relative probability of several possible fathers is computed in relation to the frequency of blood characteristics in the general population. See also *Hummel*, Nochmals – Vaterschaftsfeststellung nach dem neuen Nichtehelichenrecht: NJW 1971, 1072-1073, who suggests that a different formula be used for cases involving several possible fathers to take account of the likelihood (assumed to be 50 per cent) that the actual father is not among the men named as possible fathers.

472 Concerning "secretors" and "nonsecretors" see *Andresen* (supra n. 460); saliva and other secretions as indicators of blood types are discussed by *Sussman* 15, 16, 25-26, 29-31, 78, 107-108; *Nuzzo, Caviezel and de Carli*, Y Chromosome and Exclusion of Paternity: 1966-II Lancet 260.

473 See *Beitzke a.o.* 134-174; *Beky*, Rechtspolitische Probleme im Zusammenhang mit dem anthropologisch-erbbiologischen Gutachten (Bern and Frankfurt a.M. 1971) 43-46.

474 *Keiter*, Advances in Anthropological Paternity Testing: 21 Am.J.Phys.Anthropology 81 (1963).

475 See *Hummel*, Der positive Beweis der Abstammung in serologischen Gutachten; mögliche Auswirkung auf die forensische Praxis: Unehelichenrecht im Wandel (Schriften des Deutschen Instituts für Vormundschaftswesen no. 4) (Heidelberg 1967) 66.

476 See *Keiter*, Das Beweisgewicht des anthropologisch-erbbiologischen Gutachtens: NJW 1965, 1995, 1996.

477 *Wiener*, Book Review: 7 American Journal of Human Genetics 218-219 (1955).

478 Directive no. 23 *sub* A II 10, 11. BezG Neubrandenburg 10 Nov. 1969, NJ 1970, 375.

479 *Orczykowska-Swiątkowska and Wysłouchowa*, Badania antropologiczne w sądowym dochodzenia ojcostwa: PiP 1967 II 346 (Engl. summary no. 8/9, 7).

480 Memorandum prepared by Dr. *Hans Gürtler* (Copenhagen) for *Harry D. Krause*, 10 Jan. 1972.

481 See *Krause* 137-139.

482 Generally, see *Beitzke a.o.* (-*Hosemann*) 31.

483 EAST GERMANY: FC § 54 par. 3; WEST GERMANY: CC § 1592 par. 1; FRANCE: CC art. 311; POLAND: FC art. 85; CZECHOSLOVAKIA: FC § 54.

main free to evaluate all evidence that may be adduced.[484] Traditionally, COMMON LAW courts have operated within a very loose framework. Thus, "in the time of Edward II, the Countess of Gloucester bore a child one year and seven months after the death of the Duke, and it was pronounced legitimate. In the reign of Henry VI, Mr. Baron Rolfe expressed the opinion with apparent gravity, that a widow might give birth to a child seven years after her husband's death without injury to her reputation."[485] Modern AMERICAN courts are a little more conservative. In 1955, for example, the PENNSYLVANIA court upheld a paternity judgment on the basis of a 320 day pregnancy, agaiuts which some observers have put the scientific odds at millions to one.[486] There are but a few AMERICAN cases involving an unusually long or short pregnancy which have considered evidence of the child's weight and development in relation to a proved act or acts of intercourse. Typically, the courts have not concerned themselves with attempting to specify to the jury reduced probabilities of paternity at the outer limits of the scientifically possible but improbable duration of pregnancy.[487] While the SCANDINAVIANS do not do much with the length of pregnancy, probably because of their well developed blood testing techniques, in GERMANY tables on periods of gestation have been computed by statistical methods. In combination with information on the child's weight, length and other details showing whether the pregnancy was normal, short or long, these tables show the "probability" that a particular act of intercourse produced the child whose paternity is in question.[488]

100. *Lie detector tests.* – Although going slow on acceptance of blood typing evidence, some AMERICAN courts have pioneered in more exotic fare. For example, results of lie detector tests are usually admitted in evidence if the parties so stipulate and the use of such tests has led to startling conclusions concerning the veracity of typical parties and witnessess in paternity proceedings:

"... when the witnesses were given lie-detector tests, 57 per cent of them confessed to the lie-detector examiner that they had not had sexual intercourse with the mother during the conception period. In fact, many of them confessed that they never did have sexual intercourse with the mother.

Following their lie-detector tests, approximately 82 per cent of the paternity complainants, alleged fathers, and witnesses confessed to the lie-detector examiner that they committed perjury when testifying in court! The fact that over 40 per cent of the tested mothers confessed to having had sexual intercourse with others during the conception period is enough to warrant a more extensive use of the lie-detector in paternity proceedings."[489]

Concerning the accuracy of lie-detector test results, the authors of this study assert that

"... the latest estimation accords to the lie-detector technique, when properly used, an accuracy of 95% with a 4% margin of indefinite (inconclusive) determinations and a 1% margin of maximum possible error. In other words, in the examinations of 100 subjects the examiner can make a definite and accurate diagnosis as to the guilt or innocence of 95 of these subjects. The actual known error at the Reid laboratories for the past six years was less then .0007.

Far less accuracy will prevail, however, when the examiner is lacking in basic qualifications, adequate training, sufficient experience, general competence or complete honesty. The lie-detector is far from the automatic device some persons think it to be."[490]

Among other observers, however, it appears that the reliability of lie detector tests remains in dispute. The passage of time does not seem to have firmed techniques and settled doubts.[491] Many SCANDINAVIANS, for example, flatly disbelieve that these tests are useful and some express ethical concerns. It should be noted that the results of the study referred to above do not directly bring the accuracy of lie detector test results in issue. Rather, since the study reported confessions, the question is whether – and if so, how many – false admissions were stimulated by inaccurate lie

[484] But see WISCONSIN Stat. § 891.395 (1967), which presumes that the period of conception of a baby over 5½ pounds is 240 to 300 days before birth.

[485] *Dickinson's Appeal*, 42 Conn. 491, 501, 19 Am. Rep. 553, 555-556 (1875).

[486] *Commonwealth v. Watts*, 179 Pa.Super. 398, 116 A.2d 844 (1955).

[487] See *Krause* 139-142.

[488] WEST GERMANY: *Stegmann*, Feststellung der Vaterschaft. Tragzeitgutachten: *Ponsold* 509, 518-519; EAST GERMANY: Directive no. 23 *sub* A II 7; BezG Neubrandenburg 10 Nov. 1969, NJ 1970, 375; *Wagner*, Zum Tragzeitgutachten im Vaterschaftsfeststellungsverfahren: NJ 1969, 647.

[489] *Arthur and Reid*, Utilizing the Lie Detector to Determine the Truth in Disputed Paternity Cases: 45 J.Crim. Law, Criminol. & Police Sc. 213, 215 (1954).

[490] *Idem* 216 no. 5.

[491] See *Krause* 144-148.

detector test results. It seems reasonable to expect that number to have been low, certainly lower than the number of inaccurate tests. Of real interest in this connection, though still inconclusive, would be the incidence of continued denials in the face of polygraph results to the contrary. Unfortunately, that figure does not seem to be available.

iii. *Comparative Summary*

101. Medical procedures involving the ascertainment of paternity now are generally accepted in most systems. In terms of detail, however, the procedures used and the probative value of test results vary substantially.

Blood grouping tests are the most widely accepted method with which the paternity of an accused man may be disproved or, in some cases, proved. Some jurisdictions (such as states in the UNITED STATES) admit blood grouping tests into evidence only if the results *exclude* paternity; others (SCANDINAVIA, WEST and EAST GERMANY) allow blood grouping tests also for proof of paternity but only if the results show a high probability of paternity (usually to exceed 95 per cent) as computed by "biostatistical" formulae.

The reliability of the tests – essential of course to their value – is assured in the SCANDINAVIAN countries by reliance on central laboratories with highly qualified specialists, whereas WEST GERMANY and ENGLAND, among others, have set national standards for the execution of blood grouping tests and the qualification of individual experts. Where, as in the UNITED STATES and in most other systems, there is no official guidance concerning the execution of the tests and their use as evidence, abuses may easily result.

Some EUROPEAN countries employ further medical procedures, such as a genetic-anthropological examination, or they may compare the duration of pregnancy in the case at hand with "normal" periods of gestation as defined in medical tables. These procedures, however, are used only in supplementation of blood grouping tests and are considered valuable primarily in improving the probative impact of inconclusive blood tests.

Lie detector tests are used in a few jurisdictions in the UNITED STATES, but are elsewhere quite generally considered to be of doubtful value.

There can be no doubt that medical procedures are increasingly capable of making and are making a significant contribution in the ascertainment of paternity. This increased reliance on such procedures makes it all the more important that they be executed with the greatest possible care. While progress in the acceptability of medical evidence has been rather rapid, there has been significantly less progress in assuring that the reliability of that evidence measures up to the weight given to it.

IV. THE ILLEGITIMATE CHILD'S SUBSTANTIVE RIGHTS

102. The preceding sections have illustrated how the parent-child relationship is established. Now we shall be concerned with the substantive results that follow from the establishment of parentage under circumstances that fall short of legitimation. The principal incidents that are involved include rights to support and inheritance and questions relating to custody and to the child's name. These four categories will be discussed in detail – suffice it to mention that establishment of paternity also may affect the child's position under welfare laws or programs under which his father has earned eligibility, under the wrongful death acts of the COMMON LAW, under laws concerning citizenship and under certain tax laws.[492]

A. SUPPORT

i. *Principal Approaches*

103. The child's most elementary need is support. Reference to higher and lower animals, philosophers and cave men, the law of custom and that of civilized states, provides ample evidence that if there were just one "natural law", that law would require the parent to support his child.[493] Almost everywhere, modern man is held to this obligation. The married father is discussed in chapter 8 of this volume. The unmarried father may find himself in one of three situations. First, his illegitimate child may achieve legitimate status, by the father's own act or by means of a judgment or administrative act. Second, the law may impose a specific duty of support on the father of an illegitimate child, but paternity may not have been ascertained so that the obligation remains unenforceable. Third, the illegitimate father's duty may have been crystallized in a judgment or settlement. Regrettably, more often than not, laws are apt to pay lip service to the father's support obligation, but do little to enforce it. Here comparative *law* confuses the picture and comparative *practice* should be considered. Legal differences may loom as large as between TEXAS which, until 1973, flatly denied the illegitimate child any right of support and ILLINOIS which flatly gives him a right of support as if born in lawful wedlock. Practical differences, on the other hand, may be non-existent, or minor, if ILLINOIS fails to ensure enforcement of the support obligation – as is more or less the case. Whatever the legal duty of child support, experience shows that it becomes truly meaningful only when the state takes an active interest in enforcement – as is done in SCANDINAVIA and soon will be done in the UNITED STATES.

Variations among legal systems range from limitations on the duty of support in terms of time and amount, the permissibility of a lump sum settlement, the question whether the duty of support continues beyond the father's death, the question whether a support judgment establishes a father-child relationship for any purpose, and the extent to which paternal support is integrated into a system of social welfare.

Theoretically, the illegitimate *mother*'s legal duty of child support does not often vary from that imposed on the legitimate mother. It should be noted, however, that in many systems the married mother's support obligation will have been supplanted by her husband's primary duty. This means that, in fact, the illegitimate mother usually bears a greater *legal* burden – not to speak of the practicalities of the situation – with respect to her illegitimate child than her married counterpart bears with respect to a legitimate child.

ii. *Illustrations*

104. *England, United States.* – ENGLAND adopted her first support statute in 1576 and labeled it "An Act for Setting the Poor on Work."[494] Current ENGLISH law obligates the mother to support her illegitimate child until he attains the age of sixteen.[495] The father's obligation to maintain the

[492] *Krause* 36-42, 98-103.

[493] "A perfect obligation rests upon parents to maintain their children so long as they cannot take care of themselves, and ... this seems to be enjoined not merely by nature herself, but by the very act of the parents in begetting children and bringing them into the world ... Furthermore, maintenance is owed not merely to legitimate children but to natural children as well; nay, even to those born of incest. For why should a pitiable and innocent child perish of hunger for another's crime?" *Pufendorf*, De Jure Naturae et Gentium (1688) IV ch. XI at 428 (transl. by *Oldfather*: *J. Scott*, The Classics of International Law (Washington 1934) 627, 628). See also *Blackstone*, Commentaries on the Laws of England (London 1857) I 484.

[494] 18 Eliz. 1, c. 3, s. 2.

[495] National Assistance Act, 1948, s. 42, 64; Ministry of Social Security Act 1966, s. 22.

child commences with the entry of an affiliation order against him;[496] or when he has adopted his illegitimate child, either in fact,[497] or by an adoption order.[498] A maintenance order entered in connection with an affiliation proceeding operates until the child attains thirteen years of age unless the order specifically provides that the obligation shall continue until age sixteen.[499] Generally, the maintenance order is not affected by the marriage of the mother,[500] but it can be so limited.[501]

If the child is engaged in education or training beyond age sixteen, the father's support obligation may be extended, but not beyond age twenty one.[502] This provision places the illegitimate child on a parity with a legitimate child in respect to educational support.[503] Since the father's support obligation under a maintenance order is considered "personal", it is terminated by his death.[504]

In AMERICA the picture is varied.[505] Believing in the doctrine of *filius nullius*, TEXAS did not enact a paternity statute until 1975 and in MISSOURI the father's support obligation is expressed only in the criminal nonsupport statute.[506] The courts had long refused to derive a civil liability from that. Recently, however, MISSOURI changed her position dramatically in response to a UNITED STATES Supreme Court decision and today, still without a specific statute, imposes a support obligation in favor of the illegitimate child, equal to that owed a legitimate child.[507] TEXAS was forced to do the same.[508]

Most states impose a duty of support on the illegitimate father by means of their "bastardy act" or "paternity statute." Many or most of these statutes, however, do not run in favor of the child but speak in terms of the mother's right to child support.[509] This is also true in ENGLAND.[510]

Under the AMERICAN statutes, the level of support at which the father must maintain his illegitimate child is quite generally left to the court's discretion, rarely the jury's.[511] Sometimes it is expressly fixed by the statute. A number of statutes have gone some distance toward the ideal arrangement for the illegitimate by providing that a judgment in a paternity action establishes equality in support matters with legitimate offspring of the father.[512] Many statutes expressly provide that the mother must assist in providing support.[513] The length of time during which support must continue ranges from ages twenty-one,[514] twenty,[515] eighteen,[516], sixteen,[517] and fourteen,[518] or to such period of time as the child is likely to be unable to support itself,[519] or to a period not exceeding six years.[520] The amount of time *prior* to judgment for which support and similar payments may be awarded ranges from four years[521] to such proportion of expenses already incurred as the court deems just.[522] There also are provisions that award the cost of support from the time of birth,[523] and others that limit it to one year next preceding the action.[524] In INDIANA, the support obligation extends beyond the father's death, with the proviso that the child cannot take more than if he had been an heir.[525] Whether the support obligation owed the illegitimate child extends to higher education is in doubt. Some states impose a legal duty to support a destitute parent on the illegitimate child.[526]

The support obligation is enforced through the contempt power of the court or through criminal provisions which make it a misdemeanor to

[496] Affiliation Proceedings Act, 1957, s. 4 (3); Legitimacy Act, 1959, s. 3(2).

[497] *Hesketh v. Gowing* (1804), 5 Esp. 131, 170 E.R. 762.

[498] Adoption Act, 1958, s. 13.

[499] Affiliation Proceedings Act, 1957, s. 6.

[500] *Sotheron v. Scott* (1881), 6 Q.B.D. 518.

[501] *Pearson v. Heys* (1881), 7 Q.B.D. 260, [1881-85] All E.R. 554.

[502] Affiliation Proceedings Act, 1957, s. 7.

[503] Matrimonial Proceedings Act, 1960, s. 2.

[504] *In re Harrington*, [1908] 2 Ch. 687, [1908-10] All E.R. 235.

[505] See AMERICAN sources in *Krause* 22-25.

[506] *Helmbrock v. Stevenson*, 387 S.W.2d 263 (Mo. 1965); *James, etc. v. Hutton*, 373 S.W.2d 167 (Mo. 1963).

[507] *R. v. R.*, 431 S.W.2d 152 (Mo. 1968).

[508] *Gomez v. Perez*, 409 U.S. 535 (1973).

[509] See, *e.g.*, INDIANA Ann.Stat. § 3-625 (1968).

[510] Affiliation Proceedings Act, 1957, s. 5(1), 5(4).

[511] See *e.g.* NEW YORK Family Court Act § 513 (McKinney 1963).

[512] MINNESOTA Stat.Ann. § 257.23 (1959). Accord, ARIZONA Rev.Stat.Ann. § 14-206 (1956).

[513] MAINE Rev.Stat.Ann. ch. 166 § 29 (1954); MARYLAND Ann. Code art. 16 § 66 H (1966).

[514] NEW YORK Family Court Act § 545 (McKinney 1963).

[515] HAWAII Rev. Laws § 332-4 (1955).

[516] CONNECTICUT Gen.Stat.Ann. § 52-442 (1960).

[517] ARKANSAS Stat.Ann. § 34-706 (1962).

[518] GEORGIA Code Ann. § 74-303 (1964).

[519] COLORADO Rev.Stat.Ann. § 22-6-5 (Supp. 1967).

[520] MASSACHUSETTS Ann. Laws ch. 273 § 5 (1955).

[521] KENTUCKY Rev.Stat.Ann. § 406.031 (Supp. 1968).

[522] MICHIGAN Comp. Laws § 722.717 (1968).

[523] NORTH DAKOTA Cent. Code § 32-36-21 (1960).

[524] MISSISSIPPI Code Ann. § 383-03 (Supp. 1967).

[525] INDIANA Ann.Stat. § 3-629 (1968).

[526] ALASKA Stat. § 25.20.030 (1962).

default on support payments.[527] The penalty may be a fine or imprisonment or both.[528] While imprisonment for debt is constitutionally prohibited, courts have not viewed imprisonment resulting from failure to comply with a judicially imposed support obligation as imprisonment for debt.[529] Many statutes require the father to give bond, or permit the court to require bond or security or to attach his wages.[530] The support obligation also may be enforceable by a lien against the father's property.[531] A few states have interpreted their statutes which make non-support a criminal offense to apply to legitimate children only.[532] In the UNITED STATES, the recent heavy involvement of the Federal Supreme Court with the law of illegitimacy has established a rapid movement toward full legal equality between legitimate and illegitimate children and may be expected to speed the achievement of national uniformity as envisioned by the Uniform Parentage Act.

ENGLAND provides that where payments under a maintenance order are in arrears for at least four weeks or two payments which are due on a basis other than weekly, the person entitled to such payments may obtain an attachment of earning order. However, such an order will issue only if the arrearage is due to "willful refusal" or "culpable neglect."[533]

Throughout the systems here reviewed the losing party in a paternity action usually is permitted to take an appeal, if appropriate grounds exist. It should be noted, however, that in those AMERICAN states in which the paternity proceeding remains a criminal action, the prohibition of double jeopardy may prevent an appeal to be taken from a verdict of "not guilty".

105. In FRANCE, the support obligation that parents owe their legitimate children is a consequence of marriage (CC art. 203). Nevertheless, the courts had long enforced a mutual support obligation between parents and their natural simple children in amounts variable in accordance with the needs of the child and the parent's resources.[534] This obligation rested on the ancient maxim of pre-Code FRENCH law, never abandoned, to the effect that "*qui fait l'enfant doit le nourrir*".[535] In 1955, legislation expressly granted support rights to adulterous and incestuous children, and this persuasive analogy had been carried over to the case of the natural simple child.[536] The 1972 Law has confirmed and surpassed this evolution. All illegitimate children whose paternity has been established now have the same right of support as legitimate children.[537]

106. *Norway, West Germany.* – The central feature of the new GERMAN law is to make the child's claim for support against his father depend on ascertainment of paternity. If the father does not acknowledge the child, his paternity must now first be judicially ascertained.[538] Also in contrast to earlier GERMAN law under which the father owed support to his illegitimate child regardless of his ability to pay or the child's need, the new WEST GERMAN statute conditions the illegitimate child's claim for support on the father's ability to pay as well as on the child's need.[539] The new WEST GERMAN rule mirrors NORWEGIAN law.[540] The WEST GERMAN father's liability (which was primary) has become equal in rank with that of the mother,[541] as it is in NORWAY.[542] This approximates the legal position of the legitimate child in matters of support.[543] Nevertheless, in WEST GERMANY and NORWAY, the mother normally will fulfill her obligation by providing personal care for the child rather than by providing money (CC § 1606 par. 3). As did earlier law, the new WEST GERMAN statute burdens the father with the full range of the child's needs, including food, shelter and education.[544]

527 NORTH CAROLINA Gen.Stat. § 49-2 (Supp. 1966).

528 DELAWARE Code Ann. tit. 13 § 502 (1953).

529 See, *e.g.*, *Bradley v. Superior Court*, 48 Cal.2d 509, 310 P.2d 634 (1957).

530 CONNECTICUT Gen.Stat.Ann. § 52-445 (1960) (wages); GEORGIA Code Ann. § 74-303 (1964).

531 *E.g.*, FLORIDA Stat.Ann. § 742.08 (1964).

532 *Linda R. S. v. Richard D.*, 410 U.S. 614 (1973) (TEXAS).

533 Maintenance Orders Act, 1958, s. 6.

534 *Marty and Raynaud* 495-500.

535 He who makes the child, must feed it.

536 *Carbonnier* 543; *Mezger* (*supra* n. 329).

537 CC art. 334. Concerning the special right of support of children who are not acknowledged, see CC art. 342 through 342-8.

538 CC § 1600a sent. 2; BGH 25 May 1973, NJW 1973, 1336, 1337.

539 CC § 1615a, 1615c in connection with CC § 1602, 1603; see *Knöpfel*, Der Regierungsentwurf zum Unehelichenrecht: FamRZ 1967, 581, 585; *Lange*, Ein Reformvorschlag zum Unehelichenrecht: JZ 1966, 727, 730; *von Hülsen*, Das materielle Unterhaltsrecht des unehelichen Kindes im Reformentwurf: FamRZ 1966, 431, 436.

540 *Lov no. 10* § 2.

541 CC § 1615a, 1606 par. 3.

542 *Lov no. 10* § 25.

543 WEST GERMANY: *Jansen and Knöpfel* 186-189; *von Hülsen* (*supra* n. 539) 431-433. NORWAY: *Lov no. 10* § 5.

544 Formerly CC § 1708, now CC § 1615a in connection with CC § 1610 par. 2. NORWAY: *Lov no. 10* § 5.

Since the new WEST GERMAN statute strives for equality for legitimate and illegitimate children, the father's duty to support his illegitimate child is not limited in point of time. The primary consequence of the elimination of earlier law (CC § 1708) is that the father now must subsidize the child's post-high school education if the child merits higher education.[545]

The NORWEGIAN father's duty to support his child is similarly governed by the rules that apply to children born in wedlock. The support burden is shared by both parents in proportion to their financial resources and, insofar as possible, the child is brought up and educated according to the circumstances of the parent in the better financial position. If one parent is unable to contribute, the whole obligation falls upon the other.[546] The father normally must provide support until the child reaches the age of eighteen, although the District Governor may make an exception. If circumstances warrant, support payments may be reduced or discontinued when the child attains the age of fifteen. On the other hand, the support obligation may be extended beyond age eighteen, if this seems reasonable in view of the financial resources of the parents, the interests and abilities of the child and other relevant circumstances which may include a physical or mental disability which prevents the child from providing for himself.[547]

An interesting innovation brought by the new WEST GERMAN statute is the concept of "minimum support". The law specifically prescribes that a minimum amount of support must be paid until the child's eighteenth birthday,[548] unless unusual hardship results for the father or unless the child has other income, in which case the minimum support required of the father is adjusted downward (CC § 1615 h). The minimum rate is set periodically by the federal government and may vary with the child's age and local differences in the cost of living (CC § 1615 f par. 2). This concept resembles the NORWEGIAN arrangement by which the Department of Social Welfare stipulates minimum monthly rates that are chargeable upon illegitimate fathers. The applicable statute provides expressly that contributions are to be increased above the minimum rate, if and to the extent the father's financial resources permit.[549] Other than through the illegitimate child's right of inheritance and the child's possible eligibility under pension plans or social security arrangements, the father's support obligation does not survive his death.[550]

107. *Czechoslovakia, East Germany, Poland.* – In POLAND and CZECHOSLOVAKIA, the father's obligation to support his child is the same whether or not he is married to the child's mother.[551] Similarly, the EAST GERMAN father's support obligation follows the rules dealing with maintenance of the child of separated married parents (FC § 46). Specifically, this means that the child must be in need of support, the father's obligation is limited by his capacity to pay, the support must be paid monthly in advance, and the child may not renounce prospective support rights.[552] The natural child is favored by the statute of limitation in that support arrearages are barred after four years whereas a one year period applies to the legitimate child.[553] The father's death ends the support obligation, but, as discussed below, the child inherits from his father.

108. Under SOVIET and MEXICAN law the child who has not been acknowledged by his father has no right of paternal support. The right of the acknowledged child, on the other hand, is equal to that of the child born in wedlock.[554]

109. In the PHILIPPINES, a recognized natural or spurious child has the same legal right to receive support from the parent recognizing him as has a fully legitimate child (CC art. 282 no. 2). The Code defines support as including everything that is "indispensable for sustenance, dwelling, clothing and medical attendance, according to the social position of the family" (CC art. 290 par. 1). It includes the education of the person entitled to be supported until he completes his education or training for some profession, trade or vocation,

545 *Jansen and Knöpfel* 185-186.

546 *Lov no. 10* § 25.

547 *Lov no. 10* § 26.

548 CC § 1615f; *Brühl*, Das allgemeine Verwandten-Unterhaltsrecht und der Unterhaltsanspruch des unehelichen Kindes gegen den Vater: FamRZ 1966, 541, 542; *von Hülsen* (supra n. 539) 431, 434-435.

549 *Lov no. 10* § 25.

550 NORWAY: *Arnholm* 43; WEST GERMANY: CC § 1615a, 1615.

551 CZECHOSLOVAKIA: While the Family Law of 1949 specifically declared in its preamble that it was ntended to grant all children rights regardless of their descent, the current (1963) Code contains no special provisions on illegitimacy. The normal rules governing child support apply: FC § 85 par. 1. POLAND: *Lasok* 140, 162, 165. Normal rules governing child support apply: FC art. 128 ss.

552 FC § 46 par. 1, 19, 20-22.

553 FC § 108, 20 par. 2; for details see *Janke*, Zur Verjährung des Anspruchs eines ausserhalb der Ehe geborenen Kindes auf Erhöhung des Unterhalts für die Vergangenheit: NJ 1970, 585.

554 SOVIET UNION: *Bergmann and Ferid*, *s.v.* UdSSR 33; MEXICO: *Bergmann and Ferid*, *s.v.* Mexiko 34 n. 2.

even beyond the age of majority (CC art. 290 par. 2). Except for the reference to "social positions" in fixing the level of support, no attempt at discriminating between categories of illegitimates is apparent. The support obligation is reciprocal (CC art. 291).

iii. *Comparative Summary*

110. *Generally.* – In the first instance, the comparative study of child support shows that some legal systems do discriminate between legitimate and illegitimate children in support matters and others do not. In countries which do not discriminate, all children either are treated equally with regard to support (CZECHOSLOVAKIA, POLAND, SOVIET UNION) or special rules apply to children of parents living apart (EAST GERMANY). In countries which do discriminate between the two classes of children, the illegitimate child almost universally is worse off than the legitimate child and more or less detailed provisions define the support owed illegitimates. In some states of the UNITED STATES, the child's right to support may be enforceable only indirectly, by criminal prosecution of the father who fails to render support. In addition to these basic differences, substantial variations exist concerning the conditions, duration and extent of the support obligation.

111. *The mother's support obligation.* – Universally, the mother is obliged to support her child. Normally, the illegitimate's right to support from the mother is the same as that of the legitimate child. The right, however, may terminate when the child attains a certain age. Some countries provide expressly that the mother's support obligation is fulfilled by providing personal care and education for her child (NORWAY, WEST GERMANY). In many systems, the parents' support obligations are equal (NORWAY, WEST GERMANY, and, further, ITALY[555]), whereas elsewhere the mother's liability is secondary to that of the father (states in the UNITED STATES, also AUSTRIA[556]).

112. *The father's support obligation.* – Generally, the right to receive support from the father comes into existence or, at least, becomes enforceable only when paternity has been established either by acknowledgment or judgment. In most legal systems examined here, there is no right to support until paternity has been determined (MEXICO, SOVIET UNION, WEST GERMANY). Under FRENCH law, however, the child may claim support from any man, even though paternity has not been legally established, with whom the mother had sexual intercourse at the probable time of conception as defined by law.[557] Some countries which normally require the ascertainment of paternity as a condition to imposing a support obligation provide that three months' support may be claimed for the child even before birth, simply upon showing a *prima facie* case of paternity (*e.g.*, AUSTRIA, POLAND, SWITZERLAND, WEST GERMANY).[558]

113. *Extent of the support obligation.* – Most laws describe the factors which determine the amount of the support obligation in very general terms. Hence, the courts or public authorities are left to exercise broad discretion in individual cases. Typically, the economic situation of each parent and, if appropriate, of the child is taken into consideration (FRANCE, NORWAY, WEST GERMANY and, among others, AUSTRIA[559]). Statutes may provide specifically or courts may hold that the illegitimate is entitled to the same level of support as the legitimate child (some states of the UNITED STATES, probable national trend under UNITED STATES Supreme Court decisions.) A few countries provide obligatory minimum support levels (NORWAY, WEST GERMANY). In many countries, the public authorities or courts strive to develop guidelines for the calculation of support awards which are more or less binding.[560]

114. *Duration.* – In some countries, the father's support obligation does not end when the child reaches a specific age, but continues for so long as the child is needy or until the child is able to support himself (WEST GERMANY, FRANCE, AUSTRIA).[561] Other countries have specific age limitations, such as an absolute maximum of 18 years (SWITZERLAND),[562] or a general limit of 18 years which may be exceeded in exceptional cases (NORWAY), or a maximum of 21 years (ENGLAND). In many countries, the age limitations range from 14 to 21 years. In legal systems in which the

555 ITALY: CC art. 261, 441 par. 1.

556 AUSTRIA: CC § 166a par. 2.

557 FRENCH CC art. 342, as revised 1972. – Under certain conditions, for instance if there is a clear written declaration of paternity or maternity, ITALIAN law recognizes a right to support even though parentage may not be established: CC art. 279.

558 AUSTRIA: CC § 168; POLAND: FC art. 142; SWITZERLAND: CC art. 321; WEST GERMANY: CC § 1615 o par. 1.

559 AUSTRIA: CC § 166a par. 1.

560 A particularly high degree of precision combined with restriction of discretion is reached by Guideline no. 18 of the Supreme Court of East Germany of 14 April 1965 (GBl. II 331).

561 FRANCE: CC art. 342-2 par. 2; AUSTRIA: CC § 166a par. 1.

562 CC art. 319 par. 2.

illegitimate may himself become an heir of the father, the support obligation terminates and is not assumed by the father's heirs (*infra* s. 115 ss.), but where the illegitimate child does not inherit from the father or has only a very limited inheritance claim, the father's support obligation may pass to his heirs (AUSTRIA and SWITZERLAND,[563] but not in the UNITED STATES).

B. INHERITANCE

i. *Principal Approaches*

115. Contrasted with support rights, inheritance rights are somewhat of a luxury. By the time parental inheritance becomes due, the typical child can take care of himself. Moreover, inheritance rights traditionally have been viewed as a family affair and may have taken on a social meaning transcending blood lines. Even jurisdictions that have equalized the legal status of the legitimate and illegitimate child have sometimes hesitated to take the final step and have failed to assimilate the illegitimate child into the family as an heir.[564] An equal inheritance may be provided, but "family status" remains denied.

When comparing the inheritance treatment of the illegitimate and that of the legitimate child in different legal systems, it is a point of crucial importance whether the law permits the parent to disinherit his child. Typically, CIVIL LAW countries do not. In contrast, even today, a parent may disinherit his minor, supportless child in most COMMON LAW jurisdictions. For current purposes, it is essential to keep in mind this difference. A right of intestate succession is one thing when it is defeasible by a simple will, and quite another when a will is ineffective to destroy an inheritance relationship created by law.

In the interpretation of wills, trusts, and similar instruments, the question may arise, whether the words "child", "issue" or their equivalents include an illegitimate child. Inheritance rules also may be important in determining a child's rights under social welfare programs or private pension plans.

A worrisome aspect of inheritance rights is related to the practice of ascertaining paternity. Unless efforts are made early to ascertain an illegitimate child's paternal descent, the administration of estates will be burdened unduly with the task of sorting out dubious claims of persons claiming illegitimate relationships. Many fair claims will forfeit for lack of proof. The efforts of the SCANDINAVIAN countries to ascertain each illegitimate child's paternity shortly after birth go a long way to eliminate this problem.

ii. *Illustrations*

116. At COMMON LAW, *Blackstone* said, "the incapacity of a bastard consists principally in this, that he cannot be heir to any one, neither can he have heirs, but of his own body; for, being *nullius filius*, he is therefore of kin to nobody, and has no ancestor from whom any inheritable blood can be derived."[565] In older days, this disability was the most serious consequence of illegitimate status and was seen as a necessary by-product of the uncertainty of illegitimate paternity. Since the child's relationship to his mother normally is beyond doubt,[566] statutes have long provided in nearly all AMERICAN states that, in matters of inheritance, the illegitimate occupies the same position with respect to his mother as a legitimate child.[567] Discrimination between legitimate and illegitimate offspring with respect to inheritance from the mother has become very uncommon.

117. UNITED STATES. – In most states, however, the illegitimate child still cannot inherit from his father other than by will.[568] Few states have enacted statutes permitting the illegitimate child to inherit from his father as if the child were legitimate.[569] Some ground has been occupied between these extreme positions. Thus, the inheritance laws of a substantial number of states specifically provide that the child may inherit if the father subsequently marries the mother and acknowledges the child.[570] (Of course, even in states that do not expressly provide this in their inheritance statutes, such a child would have been legitimated by his parents' marriage and normally would be entitled to inherit for that reason). A few states would give the child his inheritance on the basis of a judgment in a paternity suit.[571] Mere acknowledgment or recognition of the child on the part of the father, by some laws required to

563 AUSTRIA: CC § 169; SWITZERLAND: CC art. 322.

564 See *Aksoy* II 660 ss.

565 *Blackstone* (*supra* n. 493) 485.

566 Except in LOUISIANA. See Comment, 6 La.L.Rev. 268 (1945). But see, *Levy v. Louisiana*, 391 U.S. 68 (1968); *Glona v. American Guarantee & Liability Ins. Co.*, 391 U.S. 73 (1968).

567 Generally see *Krause* 25-28.

568 See, *e.g.*, HAWAII Rev. Laws § 330-12 (1955).

569 ARIZONA Rev.Stat.Ann. § 14-206 B (1956).

570 See, *e.g.*, MISSISSIPPI Code Ann. § 474 (1957).

571 INDIANA Ann.Stat. § 6-207(b) (1953).

be in writing and before a competent witness, may[572] or may not[573] suffice; sometimes it is effective only if the father actually had the intent to give the child the capacity to inherit.[574] The father's admission of paternity in open court may have the same effect.[575]

In 1971, the UNITED STATES Supreme Court turned back an attempt to use the federal constitution to provide equality for legitimate and illegitimate children in matters of inheritance.[576] Recently, the ruling was severely limited,[577] but it may be expected to stand for some time, thus leaving the issue to state law. The Uniform Probate Code, approved in 1969, and the Uniform Parentage Act, approved in 1973, of the National Conference of Commissioners on Uniform State Laws both insist on full equality in matters of inheritance.[578]

Statutes permitting inheritance from the mother's family are more frequent than those permitting inheritance from the father's side.[580] As to inheritance from the illegitimate himself, there is no question about his own issue. If he has no issue, the mother and her line usually will take,[581] and there may be a specific prohibition against the father and his line.[582] Provisions permitting the father to inherit,[583] and statutes passing property from the illegitimate to the father's family are uncommon.[584]

Another vehicle of discrimination is the definition of "heir", "descendant," "child," "issue," and similar terms under statutes as well as under private instruments such as wills and trusts. Usually, these terms have been construed by courts to refer to legitimate children only.[585]

Moreover, especially in interpreting wills and trusts, the courts do not always concern themselves with the testator's or settlor's actual intent but often apply a flat exclusion that may defeat the giver's clearly obvious desires.[586]

118. ENGLAND effected a substantial change in the illegitimate child's rights *vis-à-vis* his intestate father in 1969 and now provides full equality. In addition, when an illegitimate person dies intestate, each surviving parent takes whatever interest he would have taken had the child been legitimate.[587] Formerly, only the mother could inherit from her intestate illegitimate child.[588]

ENGLISH law now also specifically prescribes rules of construction for the use of terms such as "children", "related persons", "issue" and, with the exception of the words "heir" or "heirs" used in the creation of an entailed interest, presumes that such references include illegitimate children and persons related through illegitimate children, unless a contrary intention is expressed. The anti-lapse provision of the Wills Act of 1837 was amended to protect issue of illegitimate and legitimated children of the testator. Illegitimate children are now counted as dependents under the Inheritance (Family Provision) Act of 1938.[589]

119. Under pre-1972 FRENCH law, the inheritance rights of acknowledged natural simple children were somewhat inferior to those of legitimate children. Incestuous and adulterous illegitimates had no intestate succession rights at all. The 1972 Law has brought a drastic change. The illegitimate child now has nearly the same inheritance rights as a legitimate child, including the right to an indefeasible *légitime* (CC art. 913). The rights are reciprocal and extend to the parents' relatives.[590] Of course, formal establishment of parentage remains a prerequisite under the intestacy laws (as for all other purposes) (CC art. 756).

Although the 1972 Law provides full equality for all classes of illegitimate children in most particulars, it does not fully do so in the inheritance field. Special rules govern inheritance by illegitimate children conceived while their father or mother were married to a third person.[591] In short, the inheritance law retains the notion of "adulterous child", although the new discrimination is not absolute. The special provisions apply to limit the adulterous child's rights only if, at the time of the inheritance, the illegitimate child competes with a surviving spouse or legitimate children. Some limitations concern the amount

572 CALIFORNIA Probate Code § 255 (West Supp. 1968).

573 DELAWARE Code Ann. tit. 13 § 1304 (Supp. 1967).

574 NEW MEXICO Stat.Ann. § 29-1-18 (1954).

575 WISCONSIN Stat.Ann. § 237.06 (Supp. 1969).

576 *Labine v. Vincent*, 401 U.S. 532 (1971).

577 *Weber v. Aetna Cas. & Surety Co.*, 406 U.S. 164 (1972).

578 Uniform Probate Code § 2-109; Uniform Parentage Act § 1, 2.

579 IDAHO Code Ann. § 14-104 (1948); ILLINOIS Rev. Stat. ch. 3 § 12 (1967).

580 ARIZONA Rev.Stat. § 14-206 (1956).

581 ALABAMA Code tit. 16 § 8 (1959).

582 KENTUCKY Rev.Stat.Ann. § 391.090 (1963).

583 INDIANA Ann.Stat. § 6-207 (1953); NORTH DAKOTA Cent. Code 56-01-05 (1969).

584 INDIANA Ann.Stat. § 6-207 (1953).

585 *Clark* 179.

586 *E.g.*, *Wilson v. Ingram*, 207 Ga. 271, 61 S.E.2d 126 (1950).

587 Family Law Reform Act 1969, s. 14(1)(2).

588 Legitimacy Act, 1926, s. 9.

589 Family Law Reform Act 1969, s. 15, 16, 18.

590 CC art. 757, 758.

591 CC art. 759–764, 908, 908-1, 915, 915-2.

the adulterous child may take[592] and others concern the right of the surviving spouse or the legitimate child to take specific property from the estate (CC art. 761). If there is no surviving spouse or legitimate child, or if they renounce their right to inheritance, the adulterous child is restored to a fully equal position.

The new law provides that the adulterous child may be given an advance in an amount up to the intestate share so as to make it unnecessary to involve him in the estate proceedings.[593] However, the advance must be sufficient and its sufficiency reviewed when the estate is divided.[594]

The "adulterous" child's indefeasible share amounts to one-half of what he would have been entitled to if all children, including himself, had been legitimate (CC art. 915). A child whose inheritance is thus limited, may renounce his inheritance rights and claim support from the estate. To do that, he must show need. The heirs may deny the claim for support and may opt to give him the share he would have received if the estate were shared normally (CC art. 915-2). In order to avoid a possible preferential treatment of the illegitimate child to the disadvantage of the widow and legitimate children of the deceased father, illegitimate children may not receive more by way of gift or bequest than provided by law.[595] On the other hand, CC art. 908-2 makes it clear that terms such as "children and grandchildren" include illegitimate children and grandchildren.

120. Under the NORWEGIAN scheme of equality, the illegitimate child has fully the same inheritance relationships with his mother and his (ascertained) father as a legitimate child.[596] This equality extends to their respective families. Inheritance flows in both directions, without regard to illegitimacy, and equal treatment extends to the obligatory statutory share in a parent's estate that NORWEGIAN law provides to a child. An exceptional provision denies the father a right of inheritance from a child conceived as a result of rape.[597] Another relatively minor exception relates to the inheritance of certain rural property (*odel*).[598] If the father actually wants his illegitimate child to have such property, he must take the affirmative step of acknowledging the child in a formal public declaration.[599] If the father wishes to make certain that his illegitimate child will take over his farm or other kind of rural property (giving the right to *aasete*),[600] he must declare in writing that the child is to be his heir.[601]

121. WEST GERMAN law provides the equivalent of equality in a more complicated manner. A full right of inheritance is given to the illegitimate child only if the father does not leave legitimate children or a wife.[602] If the father leaves a wife or legitimate children, the illegitimate child does not become an heir in the technical sense but obtains a mere money claim against the estate in lieu of the normal statutory share of inheritance.[603] The net effect of this distinction is that the illegitimate child cannot participate in (or interfere with) the administration and distribution of the father's estate as an heir. Reciprocally, GERMAN law gives the father a right of inheritance from his illegitimate child, but limits it in most cases (if the child leaves a wife, mother or descendants of his mother) to a money claim against the illegitimate's estate.[604] Even prior to his father's death, the illegitimate child who has reached the 21st but has not completed his 27th year of age may request an "early inheritance settlement" (CC § 1934 d par. 1). The amount of the settlement is determined without reference to the inheritance that might actually have come to the child and is equal to three times the average annual amount of support paid by the father to the child during the preceding five years (CC § 1934 d par. 2). If the child takes advantage of this settlement procedure, he retains no claim to inheritance at the time of the father's death (CC § 1934 e).

122. *Czechoslovakia, East Germany, Poland.* – In POLAND and CZECHOSLOVAKIA, the illegitimate child's right to inherit from his father or his father's relatives differs in no way from that of the legitimate child.[605] Mild differences continue in EAST GERMANY, where the illegitimate child's right to inherit from his father and his father's parents was first introduced in 1965.[606] The le-

[592] CC art. 759, as revised, combined with art. 765, 766; CC art. 760.

[593] CC art. 762, 763, 908.

[594] CC art. 762, 763-1.

[595] CC art. 908 par. 1, 759, 760.

[596] *Lov om arv* § 4 par. 1.

[597] *Ibidem* § 4 par. 2.

[598] *Lov angaaende odels- og aasetesretten*; NORWEGIAN Const. art. 107.

[599] *Lov angaaende odels- og aasetesretten* § 2.

[600] "*Aasete*" is the eldest son's right to take over the possession of the whole farm by buying out the other heirs at a reasonable price and on reasonable terms.

[601] *Lov angaaende odels- og aasetesretten* § 10a.

[602] CC § 1934a par. 1, as inserted by the Law of 19 Aug. 1969 (BGBl. I 1243); see *Lutter* 23 ss.

[603] CC § 1934a par. 1; see *Lutter* 28 ss.

[604] CC § 1934a par. 2, 3.

[605] CZECHOSLOVAKIA: CC § 526; POLAND: *Lasok* 165.

[606] *Einführungsgesetz* § 9; CC § 1924. The mother's right to inherit from her child follows from CC § 1925.

gislator apparently considered that the illegitimate child typically grows up in the mother's home and thus lacks the close relationship with his father that the legitimate child enjoys.[607] Compromising with the interests of the father's legitimate family, EAST GERMANY restricts the illegitimate child's[608] intestate succession after his father and the father's parents. Succession is limited to cases in which the child is a minor or in need of support after majority or, during minority, the child had lived primarily in the father's household or did so upon the death of the father or the father's parents, or his father's wife, parents, and legitimate children and their descendants do not survive or have lost their right to succeed.[609] These provisions do *not* restrict the father's or his parents' rights to provide for the child by will.[610] The regulation was intended to be temporary and it has been speculated that the inheritance rights of the illegitimate child will be broadened,[611] when a new civil code for EAST GERMANY is promulgated.

123. *Soviet Union, Mexico, Philippines.* – The SOVIET and MEXICAN position is simple – if parentage has been established, the child inherits as if legitimate. If not, no right of inheritance exists.[612]

In accordance with the CIVIL LAW tradition, both MEXICO (CC art. 1599 ss.) and the PHILIPPINES (CC art. 886 ss.) recognize the *légitime*, that part of the testator's property of which he may not dispose because the law has reserved it for certain heirs who are, therefore, called compulsory heirs. In contrast to MEXICO, however, where any acknowledged child inherits as a legitimate child, PHILIPPINE law provides only a limited inheritance for acknowledged natural and spurious children.[613] The PHILIPPINE Code deems the child of an attempted bigamous or incestuous marriage to be a "natural child by legal fiction" (CC art. 89). The *légitime* of each acknowledged natural child or natural child by legal fiction is one-half of that of each legitimate child or descendant. The *légitime* of a recognized spurious child is equal to four-fifths of the *légitime* of an acknowledged natural child (CC art. 895).

iii. *Comparative Summary*

124. *Issues.* – The basic situations that need be considered are intestate and testate succession, and in the latter more particularly the institution of the *légitime* or indefeasible share of inheritance and the testator's right to disinherit his or her children.

125. *Intestate succession.* – In one group of systems, the illegitimate inherits from his intestate parent on the same basis as does the legitimate child (CZECHOSLOVAKIA, MEXICO, NORWAY, POLAND, SOVIET UNION, FRANCE with some restriction). Other countries grant a limited right of intestate succession to the illegitimate child whose affiliation has been acknowledged or determined by a court (ITALY).[614] Many countries distinguish between inheriting from the mother and the father and usually give the illegitimate child the same right of inheritance from the mother as has a legitimate child (UNITED STATES, WEST GERMANY and, further, AUSTRIA and SWITZERLAND).[615] In addition, the illegitimate child frequently is entitled to inherit from maternal relatives on the same basis as a legitimate child (most of the UNITED STATES and, among others, SWITZERLAND, and to a degree AUSTRIA).[616]

In legal systems which discriminate between legitimates and illegitimates, the illegitimate's right to inherit from his intestate father varies greatly. Some systems deny the illegitimate child any right of intestate succession (many of the UNITED STATES) and others acknowledge a full or limited right of intestate succession, often predicated upon paternity having been ascertained during the father's lifetime (states in the UNITED STATES). Satisfaction of specific formal requirements regarding acknowledgment or ascertainment of paternity occasionally is required (some of the UNITED STATES). EAST GERMANY grants illegitimates intestate succession rights as a matter of course only during minority and requires satisfaction of special criteria after the child has reached majority.

The illegitimate child's right to inherit from his father often depends upon the presence or ab-

[607] FC-Commentary § 46 no. 1; *Halgasch* 81; *cf.* also *Bechthold* 7.

[608] As to what constitutes a "child born out of wedlock" within the meaning of the *Einführungsgesetz*, see FC-Commentary, note on *Einführungsgesetz* § 9, and *Schrodt* 299, 300.

[609] *Einführungsgesetz* § 9; FC-Commentary, note on *Einführungsgesetz* § 9; *Schrodt* 301-302; *Ansorg*, Weitere Probleme der Rechtsbeziehungen zwischen Eltern und Kindern: NJ 1965, 248; *Hauschild and Schmidt*, Die Bedeutung des Einführungsgesetzes zum Familiengesetzbuch: NJ 1966, 13.

[610] *Einführungsgesetz* § 9 par. 5.

[611] *Benjamin* 7; *Schrodt* 299; *cf. Halgasch* 81.

[612] See *supra* n. 554.

[613] CC art. 887, 888, 895.

[614] CC art. 573 ss. Same, with respect to acknowledged children, SPAIN: CC art. 931 ss.

[615] AUSTRIA: CC § 754 par. 1; SWITZERLAND: CC art. 461.

[616] SWITZERLAND: CC art. 461 par. 1; AUSTRIA: CC § 754 par. 1.

sence of legitimate children or a surviving spouse. The presence of legitimate children may preclude any right to inherit on the part of the illegitimate (AUSTRIA).[617] Elsewhere, the illegitimate may be entitled to inherit only half as much as a legitimate child (*e.g.* ITALY, SPAIN, SWITZERLAND)[618]. Occasionally, the law discriminates especially harshly against certain classes of illegitimates. For example, in FRANCE the illegitimate's intestate share is reduced by half if the child was adulterous and the parent also had legitimate children (CC art. 760 par. 1). In WEST GERMANY, on the other hand, the illegitimate's share is not reduced even in the presence of legitimate siblings or a surviving spouse, but the illegitimate is not technically an heir, but receives instead a pecuniary claim against the heirs amounting to the value of the normal statutory share of inheritance.

The parents' right to inherit from the illegitimate child normally mirrors the child's right to inherit from them. Under many systems, the parents inherit from the illegitimate as if he were legitimate (ENGLAND, NORWAY, FRANCE). Other countries give the parents inheritance rights only if they have acknowledged the child (ITALY, SPAIN).[619] In those systems in which the illegitimate may inherit only from his mother, typically only she may inherit from the illegitimate. Few systems provide the father a right to inherit from the illegitimate (a few of the UNITED STATES). Where the illegitimate has merely a pecuniary claim against the heirs, the father is similarly limited to a claim against the illegitimate's heirs (WEST GERMANY).

126. *Testamentary succession.* – Some systems presume that a testator's reference in his will to "children" includes illegitimates (ENGLAND, FRANCE), but others do not (*e.g.* some states of the UNITED STATES). A specific bequest to an illegitimate typically is honored, unless it violates another heir's rights. If, however, the father fails to provide in his will for his illegitimate child, the law must face the question whether the child should be protected. In CIVIL LAW countries which have eliminated discrimination between legitimates and illegitimates, the answer generally is positive, although questions of proof of paternity remain to cause problems and provide diversity.

A basic distinction between CIVIL LAW and COMMON LAW countries cannot be overemphasized: CIVIL LAW countries typically provide children with a *légitime* (an indefeasible share of inheritance), whereas COMMON LAW countries traditionally do not. In the latter, the parent remains free to disinherit his child at will, even his minor child. This distinction, of course, carries over into the right of succession of the illegitimate child. What this means is that even if a COMMON LAW country recognizes the illegitimate child's right to inherit, the parent may easily defeat it simply by providing otherwise by will. If, on the other hand, a CIVIL LAW country recognizes the illegitimate child's claim to inheritance, that claim typically would not be defeasible by the parent, although some countries provide different statutory shares for legitimate and illegitimate children, to the disadvantage of the illegitimate child (*e.g.*, PHILIPPINES and, further, ITALY[620]) or burden the right of succession with special conditions, as summarized in preceding sections.

It is thus quite a different thing to speak of the illegitimate's right to succession in CIVIL and COMMON LAW countries. It should be noted finally that in FRANCE the illegitimate child may demand support payments from the estate, instead of claiming an inheritance, and in ENGLAND, the Inheritance (Family Provisions) Act of 1938 gives the minor child at least a support claim against the estate. In the UNITED STATES, only very few states recognize a similar claim.

127. *Conclusion.* – The illegitimate's right to inherit from his mother generally is recognized. Occasional restrictions burden the right to inherit from maternal relatives. The modern trend is to recognize the child's right to inherit from an intestate father. Often, however, the illegitimate remains subject to discrimination if a wife or legitimate children survive. Similar trends may be observed with respect to the illegitimate's right to an indefeasible share in or right of support from the father's estate.

C. CUSTODY, VISITATION

i. *Principal Approaches*

128. Custody has been the stopping point of the illegitimate child's march toward a broader legal relationship with his father. Everywhere, the illegitimate child remains primarily in his mother's custody. While most systems now provide the child paternal support and some provide paternal inheritance, very few allow the illegitimate father any parental rights or custody. In the typical fact situation confronting the illegitimate

[617] CC § 754 par. 2.

[618] ITALY: CC art. 574 par. 1; SPAIN: CC art. 840 par. 1, 942; SWITZERLAND: CC art. 461 par. 3. *Cf.* GREECE: CC art. 1539.

[619] ITALY: CC art. 578 par. 1; SPAIN: CC art. 944.

[620] *Cf.* CC art. 539, 537.

mother and her child, this makes sense. Many jurisdictions, however, have made inroads on the exclusiveness of the mother's role by providing the father rights of visitation. Some fathers may be allowed to adopt their illegitimate children, some will be given custody if fit as a parent, especially if the mother is deceased. Closely related to the issue of parental authority is the question whether the father's consent to the adoption of his illegitimate child by a third party is needed. This point will be dealt with in the later sections on the law of adoption (s.170 ss.).

In the area of custody, the factual circumstances of the illegitimate child differ most directly from those of the legitimate child. While the law can order equality between legitimate and illegitimate children in terms of support or inheritance, its hands are tied in matters of custody. Family life cannot be legislated. On the other hand, the child of divorced parents is a legitimate model of increasing incidence. Some systems now seek to approximate the situation of the illegitimate child to that of the child of divorce.

Loss of parental authority involves the same criteria in the context of illegitimacy as are involved if a legitimate child is concerned. Since statutes dealing with the loss of parental authority typically refer to fitness of a person to fulfill a parental role, illegitimacy enters through the backdoor – as a matter of fact, many illegitimate mothers are not well equipped to rear their illegitimate children. Furthermore, to the extent some of these statutes deal in terms of conventional morality, illegitimacy as such may help "prove" parental unfitness.[621]

ii. *Illustrations*

129. *England, United States.* – The ENGLISH court may make orders for the custody, guardianship, and visitation rights in respect to an illegitimate child as may be made for the legitimate child.[622] This liberal rule is not yet consistently followed in AMERICA. Typically, if she is a suitable person, the mother of the illegitimate child is considered entitled to his custody and guardianship.[623] She is considered to be the child's "natural guardian".

Liberal trends giving consideration to the illegitimate child's father culminated in a 1972 decision of the UNITED STATES Supreme Court which, as a matter of constitutional law, held that the father of illegitimate children cannot flatly be presumed to be unfit to have custody of his children, but must be granted a hearing on the issue of his fitness.[624] For the future, this case sets the boundaries for permissible state laws, ruling out any laws that wholly exclude the illegitimate father from custodial rights. It may also be expected that this case will play a role in extending the illegitimate father's right of visitation.[625]

130. FRENCH law distinguishes between parental authority and the administration of the minor's property,[626] although the same person will generally have both.[627] Parental authority is defined as power over the child's person and is roughly comparable to the COMMON LAW concept of custody.

The parent who acknowledges the illegitimate child exercises parental authority (CC art. 374 par. 1). This usually brings the mother into the picture early. If both mother and father have acknowledged the illegitimate child, parental authority is exercised by the mother alone (CC art. 374 par. 2). If one of the parents or the state's attorney requests, the court may decide that parental authority is to be exercised either by the father alone or by both parents. If both parents have joint authority, the provisions concerning legitimate children apply (CC art. 374 par. 2).

Parental authority over an out-of-wedlock child is subject to the same judicial control that applies in the case of legitimate children.[628] Parental authority extends from the right to custody to the obligation to educate the child. The custodial parent must allow visitation if the other parent's parentage has been ascertained formally.[629] Confirming a long line of cases, the 1970 Law gave grandparents a right of visitation which the parents may oppose only for "serious" reasons. The 1970 Law gives the court power to allow

[621] See *Krause* 284-295, 339-342.

[622] Legitimacy Act, 1959, s. 3; see, generally, *infra* this volume ch. 7.

[623] Generally see *Krause* 28-30; 95-97.

[624] *Stanley v. Illinois*, 405 U.S. 645 (1972).

[625] *Vanderlaan v. Vanderlaan*, 405 U.S. 1051 (1972).

[626] Parental authority is regulated in CC art. 371 to 381 as modified by Law no. 70-459 of 4 June 1970 (JO 5 June p.5227). The administration of the minor's property is governed by CC art. 382 to 475 as modified by the same Law and by Law no. 64-1230 of 14 Dec. 1964 (JO 15 Dec. p. 11140); see *Madlener* 133 ss.

[627] CC art. 382, 389, 390.

[628] Parental rights may be fully or partially terminated under CC art. 378-381 (*supra* n. 626). In addition, the *juge des enfants* may take measures of *assistance éducative* when needed to safeguard the well-being of the child: CC art. 375 to 375-8, as revised (*supra* n. 626).

[629] *Madlener*, Das französische Familienrecht nach dem Gesetz v. 3.1.1972: FamRZ 1972, 336, 340.

visitation and mail privileges to any person, whether a parent or not, in exceptional situations (CC art. 371-4).

The Court of Cassation had long refused to allow the adulterous or incestuous parent a right to visit the child he supports,[630] but finally came to recognize such a right, if there is no conflict with the child's best interests and no interference with the exercise of parental authority.[631] It may be assumed that the 1972 Law brought no change in this. As a practical matter, the courts grant visitation on one or two days a month and may allow a longer visit during school vacations. Rather than calling it "right of visitation" (*droit de visitation*) the courts tend now to speak of permission to visit (*permission de visitation*) or a right of contact (*droit de contact*).[632]

If a minor illegitimate child's parentage has not been ascertained on either side, a *tutelle* is created (CC art. 390 par. 2). The law provides that a "guardian takes care of the minor's person and represents him in all legal acts, except when law or custom authorize minors to act for themselves" (CC art. 450). It should be noted that this guardianship does not differ from that arranged for legitimate children who are orphaned on both sides.

131. *Norway, West Germany.* – The NORWEGIAN father may obtain custody of his illegitimate child, if the mother agrees, is unable or unfit to have custody or dies, and if the child welfare committee[633] does not consider this inadvisable. In WEST GERMANY, the illegitimate father may achieve a right of custody only through a declaration of legitimacy or adoption,[634] but he may have visitation with his child if the child's mother or guardian consents or if the best interests of the child require visitation.[635] Since the person having custody would normally be the mother and since earlier law did not *forbid* the father to see his child, the statute does not seem to change the earlier situation materially; the primary channel between the father and the child continues to be a voluntary agreement between the mother and the father. To facilitate agreement between the father and the mother, the mediation of youth welfare authorities may be invoked (CC § 1711 par. 2).

NORWEGIAN law, on the other hand, has moved substantially further toward equality in this respect. Each parent specifically is provided a right to visitation that substantially resembles the visitation right given divorced spouses. If the non-custodial parent demands to see his child, the child welfare committee decides whether visitation should be allowed and defines the extent of the right of visitation. Visitation is granted only if, in the opinion of the committee, it will not have an unfavorable effect on the child. If the custodial parent refuses to allow visitation ordered by the committee, the other parent's right may be enforced by invoking the aid of the courts which may levy a fine.[636] Decisions rendered by the child welfare committee concerning the custody of the child and rights to visitation may be appealed to the District Governor[637] and the latter's decision may be appealed to the Department of Social Welfare.[638] When circumstances change, the committee may modify or reverse its earlier decisions according to the best interests of the child.[639]

132. *Czechoslovakia, East Germany, Poland.* – In EAST GERMANY, the mother retains full parental authority even if paternity has been established; however, the father may obtain parental authority if the mother is deceased or if she has been divested of her parental rights (FC § 46 par. 2). In POLAND and CZECHOSLOVAKIA, the mother alone exercises full parental authority unless the paternity of the alleged father has been established.[640] In POLAND, if the father recognizes his child, he exercises full parental authority together with the mother (FC art. 93). Most far-reaching is CZECHOSLOVAKIAN law which does not distinguish between married and unmarried parents in the exercise of parental authority.[641]

---

[630] Cass.civ. 3 Jan. 1964, J.C.P.1964.II.13521.

[631] Cass.civ. 4 June 1966, D.S. 1967, 65 (visitation granted the father of a child adulterous on both sides) and Cass.civ. 29 March 1966, D.S. 1966, 369 (visitation granted the father of a child adulterous as to him only).

[632] *Cf.* Cour Paris 9 Jan. 1969, D.S. 1969, 144 (child adulterous on both sides).

[633] *Lov no. 10* § 3; *cf. Lov no. 3* § 3.

[634] Formerly CC § 1707, 1708, 1736, 1738; now CC § 1705, 1736, 1738 par. 1, 1742a; *Jansen and Knöpfel* 289-291, 299, 338.

[635] New CC § 1711, as revised; *Jansen and Knöpfel* 281-287; *cf. Grasnick*, Der Verkehr des Vaters mit seinem unehelichen Kinde: NJW 1966, 1298; *Reuther*, Verkehrsrecht für den unehelichen Vater?: FamRZ 1967, 258.

[636] *Lov no. 10* § 4.

[637] *Lov no. 10* § 3, 4.

[638] In accordance with the procedures prescribed in *Lov no. 10* § 39.

[639] *Lov no. 10* § 3, 4.

[640] CZECHOSLOVAKIA: FC § 34 par. 1, 36, 37; *Radvanova*, The Czechoslovak Family Code: Rev.Contemp.L. 12 (1965) no. 2, 62. POLAND: *Lasok* 171-172.

[641] FC § 34 par. 1; *cf.* limitations applicable both to married and unmarried parents in case of misuse of parental rights or if the parents do not live together: FC § 44-50.

133. Under SOVIET law, if parentage is established, no special regulation applies and the child has the same legal status with regard to both mother and father as a legitimate child.[642] If the illegitimate child's descent from his father has not been established, the mother alone exercises full parental authority.[643] Normally, a public guardian or caretaker is not appointed.

134. MEXICAN law provides that if the parents jointly recognize their out-of-wedlock child and are living together, they will share parental authority (CC art. 415). If they are not living together, they must decide among themselves who is to have parental authority. If they fail to agree, the local judge will determine this question in the best interests of the child after hearing the parents and the state's attorney (CC art. 380). If recognition by the parents occurs separately, the parent who first recognizes the child obtains parental authority, unless the parents have agreed otherwise. In the latter case, the local judge may modify or change their agreement to conform to the child's best interests (but only for important reasons) after hearing all interested persons and the state's attorney (CC art. 381). It should be emphasized, however, that the recognized out-of-wedlock child of a married man may enter his household only if his wife consents (CC art. 373).

135. In the PHILIPPINES, a minor, recognized, natural child, as well as a natural child by legal fiction,[644] is under the authority of the parent who has recognized him. While parents exercise their authority jointly, the father's decision prevails in case of disagreement (CC art. 311). Spurious illegitimates, on the other hand, come under the sole authority of the mother (CC art. 228). In all questions on the care, custody, education and property of children, the latter's welfare is considered paramount and the Code provides expressly that no mother shall be separated from her child under seven years of age, unless the court finds compelling reasons for such action (CC art. 363).

iii. *Comparative Summary*

136. *Generally.* – To be distinguished are the case in which only one parent is ascertained from the case in which both are ascertained. In countries such as FRANCE where maternity must be acknowledged or ascertained it may be possible that neither parent is known in which case the child will be put under guardianship.

137. *One parent ascertained.* – In a country relying on acknowledgment, if only one parent is ascertained that parent takes custody (FRANCE and, further, ITALY and SPAIN).[645] In countries which do not require formal ascertainment of maternity, the mother has custody as of birth (CZECHOSLOVAKIA, POLAND, SOVIET UNION, COMMON LAW countries, WEST GERMANY). However, statutes often restrict the mother's custodial rights by requiring the participation of a guardian or advisor in decisions of legal significance (*e.g.*, WEST GERMANY). In some countries, a guardian is formally appointed in all cases, but the mother usually serves as guardian, and only if she fails, the father (AUSTRIA).[646] In still other countries, the mother becomes the guardian as a matter of law (*e.g.*, NETHERLANDS).[647]

138. *Both parents ascertained.* – If both parents are ascertained, custody is granted either jointly to both or exclusively to one parent. The first parent to acknowledge the child usually gets custody but that rule may be overturned by court decision or agreement between the parents (MEXICO). Parents have joint and equal custodial rights in several SOCIALIST countries (CZECHOSLOVAKIA, POLAND and, among others, HUNGARY and RSFSR).[648] Other countries provide for joint custody only if the parents cohabit (MEXICO). Some systems qualify the spouses' "equality" in joint custody by providing that, in the event of disagreement, the father's decision prevails (PHILIPPINES). Although occasionally the letter of the law vests sole custody in the father (ITALY),[649] it is more often granted to the mother (COMMON LAW countries, FRANCE, EAST and WEST GERMANY and, further, AUSTRIA[650]). In some countries, the father may gain custody if the mother consents, if she is proved unfit or dies (*e.g.*, NORWAY and, further, SWEDEN[651]), or if her parental rights are terminated (*e.g.*, EAST GERMANY). In other countries, the court may confer joint custody upon the father's request (FRANCE). Still other jurisdictions preclude the father of the illegitimate child from custody (states in the UNITED STATES, although of doubtful constitutionality under recent Supreme

[642] *Cf.* Fundamentals of Family Law art. 18 par. 1; RSFSR FC art. 50; see *Korkisch* 21 ss.

[643] *Cf.* Fundamentals of Family Law art. 16 par. 1; RSFSR FC art. 47 par. 1, 52 ss.

[644] CC art. 89; *supra* s. 123.

[645] ITALY: CC art. 260 par. 1; SPAIN: CC art. 154 par. 2.

[646] CC § 198 par. 2.

[647] New CC art. 287 par. 1.

[648] RSFSR FC art. 54-56; HUNGARY: FC § 72.

[649] CC art. 260 par. 2. Court may override, par. 3.

[650] AUSTRIA: CC § 170 par. 1 (with restrictions).

[651] *Föräldrabalk* ch. 12 § 2.

Court decisions), and in some he may obtain custody only by adopting or legitimating the child (WEST GERMANY).

139. *Visitation rights.* – If the father does not have custody, he may have other rights. Unless deemed against the best interests of the child, many countries give the non-custodial parent visitation rights in appropriate circumstances (ENGLAND, FRANCE, NORWAY, WEST GERMANY). Occasionally, the father may have the right to be heard before important decisions are made on the child's behalf (AUSTRIA).[652] Some countries extend visitation rights to the grandparents (FRANCE and, further, AUSTRIA[653]).

D. THE SURNAME OF THE ILLEGITIMATE CHILD

i. *Principal Approaches*

140. The name question allows one of four answers: The child may bear the mother's or the father's surname or a combination of both or a name may be provided by a public agency, in the case of a foundling, for instance. Since the illegitimate child's relationship is normally established first with the mother, he usually takes the mother's name at birth. Upon legitimation by the father, the child's name usually changes to that of the father. If an unlegitimated child continues to live with his mother, most systems have thought it sensible to continue the child's identification with his mother through her name. With the advent of "equality", however, some jurisdictions have allowed the illegitimate child to take his father's name when paternity is established, automatically or through a special judicial procedure.

In considering the name question, it should be kept in mind that legal attitudes on names vary greatly.[654] For instance, the AMERICAN[655] Common Law is all but unconcerned with names, and allows anyone to use any name for any reason he may please, short of a fraudulent purpose. In many other countries, on the other hand, the surname is a highly personal and carefully regulated right.

ii. *Illustrations*

141. *England, United States.* – Long ago in ENGLAND, a Norman father who wished to recognize his bastard son would give the child his name preceded by the prefix "Fitz". Today few COMMON LAW jurisdictions make specific provision permitting the illegitimate child to bear his father's name,[656] absent a subsequent marriage between his parents. Nevertheless, courts have allowed the illegitimate child to change his name. To illustrate, a recent NEW JERSEY case gave a minor, out-of-wedlock child the name of his married father, despite objections from the father's wife, since there was no "unworthy motive, the possibility of fraud on the public, or the choice of a name that is bizarre, unduly lengthy, ridiculous or offensive to common decency and good taste."[657]

Where paternity is clear, the original birth record may show the father's name even though paternity has not been formally established.[658] Upon legitimation, whether through the marriage of his parents or otherwise, many AMERICAN states allow the child to have his birth records changed so as to delete any open reference to his former illegitimate status.[659] In a number of states, the original birth certificate may be amended or a new certificate is issued when paternity is established.[660] A state may provide that a new, revised certificate may not be identified as amended.[661] To prevent the information that a child was born out of wedlock from becoming generally available, many statutes specifically provide that all official proceedings relating to the child's status must remain confidential.[662]

The ENGLISH Family Law Reform Act of 1969 provides that the father's name may not be entered on the child's birth registration, either at birth or subsequently, unless there is a joint request by the mother and the person acknowledging himself to be the father or the mother requests the entry and produces a declaration of paternity from the father.[663]

142. In FRANCE, the illegitimate child receives the surname of the parent with whom his relationship is established first. While this typically

652 CC § 170 par. 2.

653 CC § 170a par. 2.

654 See *supra* this volume ch. 2 subch. II.

655 Generally, see *Krause* 32.

656 GEORGIA Code Ann. § 74-103, 88-1111 (1964); ALABAMA Code tit. 27 § 12 (1958).

657 *In re M.*, 91 N.J.Super. 296, 298, 219 A.2d 906, 907 (Mercer Co. Ct. 1966).

658 IOWA Code Ann. § 675.36 (1950). But see CONNECTICUT Gen.Stat.Ann. § 7-50 (1960).

659 *E.g.*, ALASKA Stat. § 25.050 (1962).

660 ARKANSAS Stat.Ann. § 82-519 (Supp. 1967).

661 VIRGINIA Code Ann. § 32-353.24 (1964).

662 IOWA Code Ann. § 675.35 (1950); MISSOURI Rev. Stat. § 193.240 (1959).

663 Family Law Reform Act 1969, s. 27.

means that the child receives the mother's name, the child receives the name of his father if both parents acknowledge their parentage simultaneously (CC art. 334-1). If the paternal link was established later than the maternal relationship, the child may nevertheless take the father's name, if both parents file an appropriate petition. The child's consent is required if he is older than fifteen (CC art. 334-2). In all other cases, the court must authorize a change of name. The action may be taken during the child's minority or within two years after reaching majority (CC art. 334-3). If paternity has not been established, the mother's husband may transfer his name to the child, if the mother consents (CC art. 334-5 par. 1).

143. In NORWAY and WEST GERMANY, a child born out of wedlock automatically takes the mother's surname at birth.[664] It is worth adding that, in WEST GERMANY, the father or the mother's husband may confer his surname on the child if mother and child consent (CC § 1618) and that, in NORWAY, the child may petition the Ministry of Justice for the right to use his father's surname if he is known.[665]

144. An interesting feature of POLISH, CZECHOSLOVAKIAN and EAST GERMAN law is that the married woman, as a point of equality, does not necessarily adopt her husband's name. Thus, while EAST GERMAN spouses are required to have a common name, they may choose either the wife's or the husband's name (FC § 7). In consequence, even legitimate children may bear their mother's surname. In POLAND, the wife has the option to keep her own name, adopt her husband's name or add the husband's name to her own (FC art. 25). Legitimate children bear their father's name, unless the mother has kept her own name or has added her husband's name to hers and the spouses declared at the time they married that their children would take the name of the wife (FC art. 88 par. 1). In CZECHOSLOVAKIA, spouses may adopt either the wife's or the husband's name as their common name or they may keep their separate names. In the latter case, they must declare which of their names their children will take (FC § 8).

If the parents are not married and do not marry after the child's birth, there are different solutions in POLAND, CZECHOSLOVAKIA and EAST GERMANY to the name problem. In EAST GERMANY, the child normally obtains his mother's name.[666] In CZECHOSLOVAKIA, unmarried parents must agree which of their names the child will take and, if they fail to agree, the child's name will be determined by court order.[667] In POLAND, the law distinguishes between recognition and establishment of paternity through court action. Upon recognition, the child takes his father's name, unless the father declares that the child shall keep his original (*i.e.*, normally the mother's) name. If paternity is established by court action, the court may confer the father's name upon the child if his legal representative (normally the mother) so requests. The child's own consent is required if he is over thirteen years of age (FC art. 89).

145. In SOVIET RUSSIA, the child's birth certificate and the information it gives concerning the father are of great importance. Before 1 October 1968, the child's illegitimacy was held out publicly by a blank space in the birth certificate where the patronymic would normally be entered.[668] While the reform legislation did not accept a proposal to register the father's name in the child's birth certificate according to the mother's instructions,[669] the discriminatory blank space was eliminated. If the illegitimate child's paternity is established, the father's true name is recorded in the child's birth certificate.[670] If the child's parentage is not established, a fictitious male form

[664] NORWAY: *Lov no. 1* § 2; WEST GERMANY: CC § 1617, as revised.

[665] *Lov no. 1* § 9.

[666] FC § 64 par. 2; but see the exception under FC § 65.

[667] FC § 38 par. 2, 3.

[668] This "blank space" was under heavy attack before 1968. *Cf.* letters to the editor: Literaturnaya Gazeta no. 16, 17 April 1968, p. 12 (Current Digest of the Soviet Press vol. XX no. 16, 8, 9). See also discussion of the draft Fundamentals at the USSR Academy of Sciences' Institute of State and Law: Literaturnaya Gazeta no. 17, 24 April 1968, p. 11 (Current Digest of the Soviet Press vol. XX no. 17, 4, 5); discussion of the draft Fundamentals: Izvestia 7 May 1968, p. 5 (Current Digest of the Soviet Press vol. XX no. 19, 17); Izvestia 18 May 1968, p. 5 (Current Digest of the Soviet Press vol. XX no. 21, 15); Izvestia 23 May 1968, p. 5 (Current Digest of the Soviet Press vol. XX no. 21, 16, 17); *Waehler* 562.

[669] See discussion at the USSR Academy of Sciences' Institute of State and Law (*supra* n. 668); discussion of the draft Fundamentals: Izvestia 18 May 1968, p. 5 (Current Digest of the Soviet Press vol. XX no. 21, 16, 17); Report of the Council of the Union's Legislative Proposals Committee: Izvestia 27 June 1968, p. 2, 3 (Current Digest of the Soviet Press vol. XX no. 27, 17).

[670] As the child of a marriage, the illegitimate child may bear the name of the father or the mother or a combined name as the parents may agree, RSFSR FC art. 51.

of the mother's name is registered as the father's name.[671]

146. *Mexico, Philippines.* – Under MEXICAN law, the child obtains the name of the parent who has recognized him, *i.e.*, if paternity is established, the child will bear the father's name, if not, the mother's (CC art. 389). In the PHILIPPINES, a recognized natural child has the right to bear the surname of the parent recognizing him.[672] In case of joint recognition of a natural child or in the case of a child who is natural by legal fiction (CC art. 89), the child "shall principally use" the surname of the father.[673] The illegitimate spurious child, on the other hand, bears the surname of the mother (CC art. 368). Since the rights of an illegitimate are solely derived from voluntary or compulsory recognition by the parent(s), a child's petition for change of surname from that of his mother to that of his father will be denied in the absence of evidence that the child was duly recognized by the alleged father.[674] Even if the father is willing to allow the child to use his name, the appropriate procedure is not a petition for change of name, but an action for recognition.[675]

iii. *Comparative Summary*

147. In the countries requiring acknowledgment of parentage, the child usually takes the name of the parent first ascertained, typically of course the mother (FRANCE, MEXICO and, among others, ITALY, SPAIN).[676] If paternity is ascertained subsequently, the child may continue to use his mother's name (FRANCE) or adopt his father's (ARGENTINA, ITALY).[677] If both parents acknowledge the child simultaneously, the child usually receives the father's name (FRANCE and, further, ARGENTINA, ITALY).[678] In some countries, the child bears the mother's name by law, but may use the father's name upon acknowledgment (GREECE, NETHERLANDS, SWITZERLAND).[679]

In the other major group of countries, the child receives the mother's name at birth and retains it regardless of subsequent ascertainment of paternity (EAST and WEST GERMANY, NORWAY and, among others, AUSTRIA, SWEDEN).[680] In a few countries, the parents are expected to agree which name the child will take, and in case of disagreement, the child's name is determined by the court (CZECHOSLOVAKIA).

Many countries facilitate a change of name for illegitimate children. Where the child begins life with the mother's name, there often is a possibility that it may adopt the father's name later.[681] Typically, such a change requires a petition by the father and the consent of the mother (FRANCE), that of the child (NORWAY), or that of both (WEST GERMANY and, further, AUSTRIA[682]). Another possibility is that the mother's husband who is not the child's father may give his name to the child (FRANCE, WEST GERMANY and, among others, AUSTRIA, SWEDEN).[683] These options supplement regulations that otherwise might be too rigid and, in effect, often allow the child a choice between the surnames of his parents.

671 *Waehler* 562.

672 CC art. 282 par. 1, 366.

673 CC art. 366, 367.

674 *Manuel v. Republic*, L-15811, 27 March 1961.

675 *Lerma García v. Republic*, L-16058, 29 Nov. 1961.

676 ITALY: CC art. 262; SPAIN: CC art. 134 no. 1.

677 ARGENTINA: *Ley del nombre* art. 5 par. 2; the previous name may be retained by permission of the court. ITALY: CC art. 262.

678 ARGENTINA: *Ley del nombre* art. 5 par. 2; ITALY: CC art. 262.

679 GREECE: CC art. 1531, 1537; NETHERLANDS: New CC art. 5 par. 2; SWITZERLAND: CC art. 324 par. 1, 325 par. 1.

680 AUSTRIA: CC § 165; SWEDEN: *Namnlag* § 2 par. 1.

681 SWEDEN: *Namnlag* § 2 par. 2.

682 CC § 165a.

683 AUSTRIA: CC § 165a; SWEDEN: *Namnlag* § 4 par. 1.

V. ADOPTION

148. A few comments concerning adoption have already been made in the Introduction (s. 20, 21). The discussion that follows will deal first with the legal nature of adoption, then concern itself with the persons who may adopt and who may be adopted and identify those who must consent to an adoption. The varying legal effect of adoption in various systems will be dealt with in detail. The discussion closes with an investigation of whether, when and how an adoption may be revoked.

A. THE NATURE OF ADOPTION

i. *Principal Approaches*

149. Some systems view adoption as a contract between the parties. Others view adoption as a governmental (administrative or judicial) act. Actually, the difference is less than meets the eye. Systems that treat adoption as a contract usually involve the court in a supervisory capacity. Systems that view adoption as a governmental act cannot get away from the fact that no adoption can take place until an intending adopter, a person to be adopted, and persons whose consent is needed, agree that there is to be an adoption. In other words, the practical difference is one of emphasis, and the apparent worldwide trend is away from the contract approach. But if court involvement is generally required, its purpose is not uniform. Originally, court involvement probably had much to do with assuring that the legal prerequisites of adoption were observed and was geared to protect the adopter's collaterals and possible future heirs. Today, court supervision emphasizes the best interests of the child and seeks to assure that these are served by the adoption. While adoption thus has changed from a device primarily intended to perpetuate a family to one which has child welfare as its principal purpose, some statutory reminiscences of the past linger on.

ii. *Illustrations*

150. *England, United States.* – The COMMON LAW treats adoption as a judicial process. The court order confers the new status and terminates the old blood ties. The court, at least in theory, is heavily involved in a supervisory capacity. Thus, in ENGLAND, it is a condition precedent to the entry of an adoption order, that the intending adopter have filed a written notice with the local authority,[684] unless he is a parent of the child or the child is above the age limit for compulsory school attendance.[685] This notice allows the local authority to conduct an investigation of the proposed adoption and also constitutes the child a "protected child".[686] Similar provision for agency notice is made in all states of the UNITED STATES.[687] In most of the states such notice and investigation is mandatory,[688] unless the petitioner is the spouse of the natural parent or another relative of the child.[689] In other states, investigation is left to the discretion of the court in any case.[690] Most statutes specify who shall make the investigation,[691] but some statutes simply empower the court to appoint someone competent.[692]

Following the required notification and investigation, the court proceeds with the hearing. Some states handle adoption as a two-stage proceeding involving the initial hearing and an interlocutory decree; a waiting period under supervision and a final hearing with the entry of a final decree.[693] In a few states an adoption may not be finalized unless and until the child has resided with

684 Adoption Act, 1958, s. 3, 12, 28.

685 The age limit is 15 unless extended to 16, Education Act, 1944, s. 35.

686 Adoption Act, 1958, s. 37.

687 See *Leavy* 50–56.

688 *E.g.*, ARIZONA Rev.Stat.Ann. § 8-111 (1973); CALIFORNIA CC § 226 (1957); CONNECTICUT Gen.Stat. Ann. § 45-63 (1958); DELAWARE Code Ann. tit. 12 § 912 (1953); GEORGIA Code Ann. § 74-410 (1973); MISSOURI Ann.Stat. § 453.070 (1949).

689 *E.g.*, DISTRICT OF COLUMBIA Code Ann. § 16-307 (1966); ILLINOIS Rev.Stat. (1974) ch. 4 § 9.1-6.

690 ARKANSAS Stat.Ann. § 56-105 (1971); HAWAII Rev. Laws § 578-8 (1968); MAINE Rev.Stat.Ann. tit. 9 § 533 (1964); MISSISSIPPI Code Ann. § 93-17-11 (1972).

691 *E.g.*, FLORIDA Stat.Ann. § 63.091 (1969) (state welfare board or agency having custody of the child).

692 *E.g.*, ILLINOIS Rev.Stat. ch. 4 § 9.1-6 (1974).

693 *E.g.*, ALABAMA Code tit. 27 § 4 (1958); ARKANSAS Stat.Ann. § 56-108 (1971) (six months from interlocutory to final decree); CONNECTICUT Gen.Stat.Ann. § 45-63 (1958); DISTRICT OF COLUMBIA Code Ann. § 16-309 (1966) (interlocutory becomes final not more than one year nor less than six months from entry thereof); ILLINOIS Rev.Stat. ch. 4 § 9.1-14 (1974) (final decree may be obtained only after six months have elapsed since entry of interim order); MISSISSIPPI Code

the petitioner for a prescribed period.[694] In a few states the court is empowered to appoint, on the filing of a petition, a guardian *ad litem* to protect the child's interests throughout the proceedings.[695]

At the hearing, the court will consider all available information regarding the adoption in order to determine what is in the best interests of the child.[696] Since the aim of agency investigation and supervision is to provide the court with as much information as is possible, agency reports generally are required by statute to include information about the child, the adopting parents and the natural parents.[697] In order to ensure that the agency report has a factual basis, it frequently is specified that an agency representative must have visited the home several times during the period of supervision.[698] The final report generally is advisory only, with the agency recommending for or against entry of a final decree.[699] However, in at least one state, the agency may effectively block an adoption because the agency's consent is required to effect the adoption.[700]

The ENGLISH Adoption Act requires the appointment of a guardian *ad litem* with extensive duties not only to the child but also to the court. The guardian is required to gather relevant information about the applicants and the child and submit a confidential report. The Act also requires that the infant have resided continuously with the applicants for at least three consecutive months before an adoption order may be entered and provides that the appropriate local authority shall visit the child during the period of supervision and shall give advice concerning his care and maintenance. In addition, the local authority is empowered to prevent a person from receiving a child if such placement would be detrimental to the child and the placement took place outside of a registered agency or local authority.[701]

151. FRANCE broke with the CIVIL LAW tradition which sees adoption as a contract in 1958, and now bases adoption directly on a court order.[702] Previously adoption had rested on a judicially approved adoption contract. The Civil Code of 1804 had made adoption difficult and had limited its effects. This continued until 1923 when a new statute, intended to deal with the legacy of orphans left by World War I, simplified adoption greatly. Even then adoption was given only limited effect. In 1939, a new form of adoption was created under the name "adoptive legitimation" and this procedure made the adopted child into the near equivalent of a legitimate child.[703] Current FRENCH law dates from 1966 and modifies all provisions of the Civil Code concerning adoption under the heading "adoptive filiation".[704] To be distinguished now are full adoption (*adoption plénière*) and limited adoption (*adoption simple*). Adoption procedure is not complex. The intending adopter goes before the court and the court orders whatever investigation it thinks necessary,[705] primarily concerning the adopter's social background and medical facts. A national public child welfare agency is usually involved.

152. *East and West Germany.* – GERMAN adoption law historically derives from ROMAN concepts of adoption.[706] Adoption had been known to GERMAN law prior to the Civil Code of 1900 and was covered in PRUSSIA's *Allgemeines Landrecht* of 1794,[707] in BAVARIA's *Landrecht* of 1756,[708] in SAXONY's Civil Code of 1865 (§ 1784 ss.) and in the BADISCHE *Landrecht* of 1809[709] which differed only insignificantly from FRANCE's *Code civil.*

In WEST GERMANY, today, adoption remains a contract, although court approval is required (CC § 1741). EAST GERMANY, on the other hand, has

Ann. § 93-17-15 (1972) (final decree may not be entered less than six months after entry of interlocutory order, unless the period of supervision is waived by the court *or* the child has already resided in the home of the adopter).

694 *E.g.*, KENTUCKY Rev. Stat.Ann. § 199.470 (1971); NEVADA Rev.Stat. § 127.110 (1967); MASSACHUSETTS Gen. Laws Ann. ch. 210 § 5A (Supp. 1972); MISSISSIPPI Code Ann. § 93-17-156 (1972); NEW YORK Domestic Relations Law § 116 (1964).

695 *E.g.*, MISSOURI Ann.Stat. § 453.020 (1949).

696 *E.g.*, ARIZONA Rev.Stat.Ann. § 8-116 (1973); COLORADO Rev.Stat.Ann. § 4-1-9 (1963). See also *Leavy* 51. ENGLISH law directs that an order will be entered only when the welfare of the infant is served, Adoption Act, 1958, s. 7 (1), (2).

697 *Leavy* 49; *Clark* 616.

698 *E.g.*, ALABAMA Code tit. 27 § 4 (1958); LOUISIANA Rev.Stat.Ann. § 9.430 (1964).

699 *Clark* 616 ss.

700 CALIFORNIA CC § 226 (1957).

701 Adoption Act, 1958, s. 3, 9, 38, 41; *Bromley* 255.

702 CC art. 353, 361.

703 CC art. 368-370.

704 Law no. 66-500 of 11 July 1966 (JO 12 July p. 5956), modifying CC art. 343 to 370-2.

705 CC art. 353 par. 1, 361.

706 *Cf. Dölle* II 563 ss.; *Staudinger (-Engler)* no. 6 before § 1741.

707 II, 2 § 666-716. The earlier *Sachsenspiegel* did not mention adoption, *cf. Staudinger (-Engler)* no. 15 before § 1741.

708 *Cf. Staudinger (-Engler)* no. 10-12 before § 1741.

709 *Landrecht* rules 343 ss. as cited by *Staudinger (-Engler)* no. 14 before § 1741.

wholly broken with the contract view[710] and sees adoption as an administrative decision.[711] Specifically, in EAST GERMANY, the intending adopter applies to the youth welfare authorities who must satisfy themselves that the adopter is fully able to act as a parent and that the adoption is in the interest of the child (FC § 68 par. 2).

In WEST GERMANY, the adoption contract must be unconditional, without time limit (CC § 1742) and authenticated by a notary public (CC § 1750). The court may deny its approval only if a statutory condition has not been fulfilled or if there is considerable doubt whether the adoption will lead to a true parent-child relationship (CC § 1754 par. 2). The contractual approach to adoption raises the question of capacity. A child who is wholly without legal capacity or who is less than 15 years of age, may enter into an adoption contract only through his legal representative (CC § 1751 par. 1). A child who has completed his fourteenth year of age and does not lack legal capacity for a reason other than age, must himself enter into the adoption contract, although the approval of his legal representative as well as the consent of the court of guardianship continue to be required (CC § 1751 par. 2).

In EAST GERMANY, where the contract view is rejected, the same is accomplished by requiring the consent to his own adoption of a child older than 14 years of age, in addition to the consent of his parents (FC § 69 par. 1). Both GERMANIES conceive the principal purpose of adoption to be the welfare of the child,[712] although only EAST GERMAN law states this as a condition of adoption (FC § 68 par. 2). In pursuance of this goal, adoption seeks to provide normal conditions for the development of the adopted child by giving him substantially all the rights of a legitimate child *vis-à-vis* the adopter.[713]

153. *Soviet Union.* – Adoption has experienced contrasting treatment under SOVIET rule. In the early years after the October Revolution, the RSFSR Family Code of 1918 prohibited adoption outright. It was provided expressly that any purported adoption would not produce any rights or duties on the part of either the adopter or the adopted person (art. 183). The alleged reason behind this rigorous rule was that, at that time, no effective state supervision over adoption was available. The legislature seemed to believe that only outright prohibition of adoption would protect children from exploitation by adoptive parents.[714] This proved to be a temporary solution. The RSFSR Family Code of 1926 favored adoption as a means of providing homes for the orphans of war and the revolution who had become a threat to public order.[715] Today, the principal questions concerning adoption are regulated in the SOVIET UNION Fundamentals on Family Law of 1968[716] which may be implemented, but not contradicted, by the law of the individual republics of the SOVIET UNION. Procedurally, adoption is an administrative act and is accomplished by decision of the executive committee of the district or city Soviet at the request of the adopter.[717]

154. The history of MEXICAN and PHILIPPINE laws on adoption traces back to SPAIN and FRANCE. While the origin of adoption lies in the contract approach in both systems, court approval of an adoption has long been required in all cases.[718] In both countries, the purpose of adoption is perceived to be the welfare of the child,[719] and "solace to those who have no children or to those who have lost them, so that the void which exists in a childless home may be filled."[720]

iii. *Comparative Summary*

155. Two typical approaches govern the nature of adoption: The contract of the parties may be deemed to be of primary significance (although the contract remains subject to judicial scrutiny, *e.g.*, WEST GERMANY, MEXICO, PHILIPPINES), or it may be the act of the state through an appropriate court (as for instance in ENGLAND, FRANCE, the UNITED STATES and, among others, ARGENTINA, the NETHERLANDS, SWEDEN)[721] or through an

[710] See generally FC § 66-78, which is largely based on the decree concerning adoption of 1956.

[711] FC § 68 par. 1; *cf. Benjamin* 6; *Schlicht* 178. The adopter is given a certificate of adoption, *cf.* FC § 68 par. 1.

[712] WEST GERMANY: *Staudinger (-Engler)* § 1751 no. 24; EAST GERMANY: FC-Commentary § 66 no. 1.

[713] WEST GERMANY: CC § 1757; *cf. Staudinger (-Engler)* no. 22 before § 1741. EAST GERMANY: FC § 66, 72 par. 1; FC-Commentary § 66 no. 2.

[714] *Kourilsky* 267 with further references. Despite the prohibition, *de facto* adoptions were not uncommon, *cf. idem* 267.

[715] *Geiger* 72 ss.; *Kourilsky* 267.

[716] Fundamentals on Family Law art. 24-25; for earlier law see *Stone* 404.

[717] Fundamentals on Family Law art. 24 par. 2.

[718] See *de Pina* 368-370; *Paras* 680-681.

[719] *De Pina* 366; *Paras* 680.

[720] *Paras* 680.

[721] ARGENTINA: *Ley de adopción* art. 1 par. 1; NETHERLANDS: New CC art. 227 par. 1; SWEDEN: *Föräldrabalk* ch. 4 § 1.

administrative agency (as in the SOVIET UNION, EAST GERMANY and, further, DENMARK and NORWAY)[722] that is considered to effect the adoption.

Quite generally, an investigation is made to assure that the proposed adoption will serve the best interests of the child (for instance, ENGLAND, UNITED STATES, FRANCE, WEST GERMANY and, further, SWEDEN, DENMARK).[723] Relevant are the suitability of the intending adopter(s) including the material circumstances that will be offered to the child. This investigation may be made entirely by an official agency (as in many states in the UNITED STATES) or by a guardian *ad litem* (or children's officer or probation officer) appointed by the court (as in ENGLAND).

In order to safeguard the child's best interest some provisions require that the intending adopters must first have cared for the child for a specified period of time to prove their suitability (as in several states in the UNITED STATES and, among others, the NETHERLANDS and SWITZERLAND).[724] The probationary period may be three months (ENGLAND), may run to a year (ARGENTINA[725]), or be two years (the NETHERLANDS, SWITZERLAND). FRANCE has developed a special procedure governing foster care with the ultimate purpose of adoption.

The modern trend is in the direction of having adoption provide a full reciprocal parent and child relationship.[726] This is especially important to children who have no functioning natural family, such as orphans or neglected children.

B. WHO MAY ADOPT WHOM?

i. *Principal Approaches*

156. Variance in the purpose of adoption dictates variety in restrictions on who may adopt whom. These restrictions take many forms. Common are age requirements. These range from insistence that the child to be adopted be a minor to provisions requiring the adopter to be older than the person to be adopted. Some laws state that a specific age differential must exist between adopter and adopted person, others prescribe a minimum or maximum age for the adopter and the child. Worth mentioning are GREEK and PERUVIAN age prescriptions which set a minimum age for the adopter of 50[727] and CHILE which sets a minimum of 40 and a maximum age of 70.[728] HOLLAND requires the age difference between the adopter and adopted person to be at least 18 and no more than 50 years,[729] whereas BOLIVIA asks that the child to be adopted be at least 14 years old (CC art. 183). In IRELAND the child must be at least 6 months but not more than 7 years old.[730] An unborn child may be adopted in ETHIOPIA although the mother is given an opportunity to cancel the arrangement within three months of the child's birth (CC art. 799).

Adult adoption is possible in many countries and categorically prohibited in others. Many systems prohibit adoption if the intending adopter has children of his own. GREECE allows no further adoptions during the lifetime of the first adopted child, but would allow several children to be adopted at once (CC art. 1570). COLOMBIA does not permit the adoption of the adopter's own acknowledged natural child (CC art. 272), and GREECE and VENEZUELA extend that prohibition to any illegitimate child of the adopter.[731]

While practice in many countries disfavors adoption by a single person, it is usually allowed, but often limited to persons of the same sex (*e.g.*, COLOMBIA CC art. 273). Adoption by married persons, in any event, is more common and regulations range from the requirement that a married adopter's spouse must consent, to a requirement that the spouse join in the adoption, to a requirement that spouses who seek to adopt jointly have been married for a given period of time, often set at five years,[732] but extending to 18 years in SOUTH VIETNAM (CC art. 136 par. 2). HOLLAND, however, forbids one spouse to adopt the other's child or grandchild.[733]

Aside from age requirements, IRELAND allows only illegitimates or orphans to be adopted,[734] whereas SPAIN, until 1970, allowed the full

722 DENMARK: *Adoptionslov* § 1; NORWAY: *Lov om adoption* § 1 par. 1.

723 DENMARK: *Adoptionslov* § 2; SWEDEN: *Föräldrabalk* ch. 4 § 6.

724 NETHERLANDS: New CC art. 228 *lit.* f; SWITZERLAND: CC art. 264.

725 *Ley de adopción* art. 6.

726 ARGENTINA: *Ley de adopción* art. 14 ss. (*adopción plena*); BOLIVIA: FC art. 233 ss. (*arrogación*); ITALY: CC art. 314-2 ss. (*adozione speciale*); FRANCE: CC art. 343 ss. (*adoption plénière*).

727 GREECE: CC art. 1568; PERU: CC art. 326 par. 1.

728 Adoption Act art. 2.

729 New CC art. 228 *lit.* c.

730 Adoption Act, 1952, s. 10 (b).

731 GREECE: CC art. 1569; VENEZUELA: CC art. 249.

732 FRANCE: CC art. 343; HOLLAND: New CC art. 228 *lit.* g.

733 New CC art. 228 *lit.* b.

734 Adoption Act, 1952, s. 10 (c).

adoption only of children under 14 years of age who had been abandoned for at least three years.[735] Concern with religion varies from ILLINOIS' admonition that the court "shall, whenever possible, give custody through adoption to a petitioner . . . of the same religious belief as that of the child"[736] to ISRAEL's categorical proscription of all adoptions among persons of varying religions.[737] In AUSTRIA, persons who have taken a holy vow of celibacy may not adopt at all (CC § 179 par. 1).

ii. *Illustrations*

157. AMERICAN statutes typically provide that any person[738] or any proper person[739] or any adult person[740] may petition for adoption. NEW JERSEY requires the petitioner to be a citizen of the UNITED STATES or to have declared his intention to become one.[741] Some states simply require the petitioner to be a resident of the state[742] and even where the statute does not define eligible petitioners in terms of residency, there may be a residency requirement.[743] In addition, adoption may be dependent upon residence of the child with the petitioner for a specified period. Some states require the adopter to be older than the person to be adopted.[744] Adoption by a single person is generally permitted, but most, if not all, of the states require the petition to be joint if the petitioner is married.[745]

All AMERICAN states allow the adoption of minors or children.[746] A substantial number of states also allow the adoption of adults.[747] In some of the latter, adult adoption is viewed as a separate category,[748] and additional requirements may be imposed, such as a prohibition on adopting a spouse.[749] In some states, the adoption of an adult is allowed only if adoption failed to occur during minority because of inadvertence, mistake, or neglect and the petitioner has maintained the position of parent for more than 15 years,[750] or if the adult to be adopted has resided with the adopter for two years prior to the filing of the petition,[751] or if the person to be adopted is ten, twenty years or at least a day younger than the petitioner,[752] or if the person to be adopted is unmarried and childless.[753] A requirement that the adopter and the person to be adopted be of the same race is unconstitutional.[754] Several states require that the child be placed with a petitioner of the same religion when that is practicable.[755] If the necessary consent (of the mother) can be obtained, there usually is no obstacle to the adoption of an illegitimate child by his father.[756]

158. Under the ENGLISH Adoption Act, unrelated adopters must be at least 25 years old (s. 2 (1)(c)). No age requirement applies to a parent seeking to adopt his own child (s. 2 (1)(a)), and a relative of the child is eligible to adopt when he is at least 21 years old (s. 2 (1)(b)). Two persons may jointly adopt a child if they are married (s. 1 (2)), and a married adopter may adopt only with the consent of his spouse (s. 4 (1)(6)), unless the spouses are living apart and are likely to remain apart (s. 5 (4)). A female may be adopted by a single man only under exceptional circumstances, by permission of the court.[757] The Adoption Act allows solely for the adoption of persons under age 18 who have never been married and who are residents of ENGLAND or SCOTLAND at the time of the application.[758]

159. In FRANCE, if the adopting person is a bachelor, he must be older than 35 years of age (CC art. 343-1) and at least 15 years older than the person to be adopted.[759] Exceptions to this rule may be granted by the President of the Republic in appropriate cases. If a married person wishes to adopt singly, he must be older than 35 years of

[735] CC art. 178 par. 2, as revised by Law of 24 April 1958, but now superseded by the new revision effected by Law of 4 July 1970.

[736] ILLINOIS Rev.Stat. ch. 4 § 9.1-15 (1971).

[737] Adoption Act s. 5.

[738] DISTRICT OF COLUMBIA Code Ann. § 16-302 (1966).

[739] ILLINOIS Rev.Stat. ch. 4 § 9.1-2 (1974).

[740] ALABAMA Code tit. 27 § 1 (1962).

[741] NEW JERSEY Rev.Stat. § 9:3-22 (1937).

[742] DELAWARE Code Ann. tit. 13 § 903 (1970).

[743] See, *e.g.*, ARIZONA Rev.Stat.Ann. § 8-103 (1971).

[744] See, *e.g.*, CALIFORNIA CC § 221 (1957).

[745] See, *e.g.*, COLORADO Rev.Stat.Ann. § 4-1-3 (1963).

[746] See *Leavy* 20-24.

[747] See, *e.g.*, ARKANSAS Stat.Ann. § 56-101 (1971).

[748] See, *e.g.*, FLORIDA Stat.Ann. § 63.061 (1969) (minors), § 63.241 (1969) (adults).

[749] CALIFORNIA CC § 221 (1957).

[750] IDAHO Code Ann. § 16-1501 (1947).

[751] ILLINOIS Rev.Stat. ch. 4 § 9.1-3 (1974).

[752] CALIFORNIA CC § 227p (1957).

[753] CALIFORNIA CC § 221 (1957).

[754] *Loving v. Virginia*, 388 U.S. 1 (1967); *Compos v. McKeithen*, 341 F.Supp. 264 (E.D.La. 1972).

[755] ILLINOIS Rev.Stat. ch. 4 § 9.1-15 (1973).

[756] For AMERICAN sources, see, generally, *Clark* 602-671; *Leavy*.

[757] *Bromley* 249.

[758] Adoption Act, 1958, s. 1 (1), 57 (1).

[759] CC art. 344. The age differential may be reduced to ten years if a spouse seeks to adopt the child of his spouse.

age[760] and needs the consent of his spouse.[761] If a married couple wishes to adopt jointly, at least one of the spouses must be older than 30 and they must have been married to each other for at least five years (CC art. 343). Morever, a married couple may not adopt if they have a legitimate child (CC art. 345-1). While this limitation has been under attack, it was reiterated in the latest statute. However, exceptions may be granted by the President of the Republic (CC art. 345-1). The presence of previously adopted children, on the other hand, is no obstacle to a new adoption. Moreover, an adoption is not affected if the adoptive parents have a legitimate child after the adoption.[762]

Adoption is permitted between blood relatives as well as between persons related by marriage with the exception of spouses. For example, adoption is possible between uncle and nephew, and special rules govern the adoption of the child of an adopter's spouse (CC art. 344). While limited adoption does not involve an age limitation (CC art. 360 par. 1), a child who is to be adopted by full adoption generally must be under 15 years of age.[763] Under special circumstances, full adoption may be awarded until the child is twenty-one.[764]

FRENCH law does not impose specific conditions concerning the sex, religion or nationality of adopting or adopted persons. The principal issue for consideration by the court is the moral and social condition of the adopter's home and the focus is on the interest of the child (CC art. 353). This represents a change from the Napoleonic concept of adoption which, true to the ROMAN model, saw adoption primarily as a means to continue the family name and tradition.

FRENCH law permits the adoption of an illegitimate child by a parent thereby affording the parent an unembarrassing method of conferring legitimacy on his offspring.[765] Until the change in the illegitimacy law in 1972, adoption provided the only method by which a parent could confer legitimacy on his adulterous or incestuous child, and thus escape the restrictive rules which barred the acknowledgment of such children.[766]

160. EAST (FC § 67 par. 1) and WEST GERMANY (CC § 1744) specify that an adopter must have full legal capacity. In contrast to EAST GERMANY, where the adopter need merely have attained majority and that means he must be 18 years of age,[767] WEST GERMANY requires the adopter to be at least 25 years old, but this requirement may be waived.[768] As a safeguard, EAST GERMAN law provides that an "appropriate" age differential should exist between the adopter and the person to be adopted.[769]

While EAST GERMAN law is silent on this point, WEST GERMAN law still maintains that a person who has a legitimate or illegitimate child of his own may not adopt another child.[770] A person's own illegitimate child, however, may be adopted even if there are other children (CC § 1742a). In

760 CC art. 343-1; *cf. Mazeaud (-de Juglart)*, Leçons 404-405; *Marty and Raynaud* 519.

761 CC art. 343-1 par. 2.

762 CC art. 345-1 par. 2.

763 CC art. 345 par. 1. The statute of 1939 required the child to be under five, the statute of 1958, under seven. Full adoption requires further (art. 345 par. 2) that the child to be adopted have lived in the household of the adopter for at least six months, *cf. Ferid* 1349. This residence requirement should be distinguished from temporary placement for future adoption which may be ordered under CC art. 351 ss. The latter is intended to protect intending adopters against arbitrary conduct (especially demands for the child's return) on the part of the natural parent(s) before the adoption is completed. Before the temporary order is granted, all conditions for adoption, with the exception, of course, of the six months' residence period, must be fulfilled and all necessary consents must be in hand. *Cf. Ferid* 1350-1351.

764 CC art. 345 par. 2. If the child is older than 15 years of age, but younger than 21, full adoption may be ordered only if the person to be adopted was living with a person not qualified to adopt him before he reached 15 years of age. This might be the case if the child reached 15 years before the intending adopter reached 35 years of age, or where the child had been previously adopted by limited adoption either by the person who now intends or by someone else, now deceased. *Mazeaud (-de Juglart)*, Leçons 422; see also *Ferid* 1349.

765 *Carbonnier* 586 records that in 1961 there were 163 adoptions of natural simple children who had, and 178 adoptions of children who did not have, status as to the adopting parent.

766 See *Carbonnier* 573. The first decision allowing a father to adopt his acknowledged natural simple child was rendered in 1846, Cass.civ. 1 April 1846, D.P. 1846.1.81.

767 FC § 67 par. 1; *cf. Schlicht* 178.

768 CC § 1744, 1745b, as amended by Law of 14 Aug. 1973 (BGBl. I 1013).

769 FC § 67 par. 1. The standard is whether the person to be adopted could be the adopter's natural child: FC-Commentary § 67 no. 1.

770 CC § 1741, *cf. Staudinger (-Engler)* § 1741 no. 27ss. This principle seems rooted in the ancient GREEK concept of adoption which had the sole purpose of maintaining a family which had no natural offspring. *Meinecke*, Gesetzesinterpretation und Gesetzesanwendung im attischen Zivilprozess: Rev.int.dr. antiquité (third series) XVIII (1971) 296 ss.

addition, the court may dispense with this requirement under certain other conditions.[771] The birth of a child after the adoption contract is executed or the presence of a child adopted earlier does not prevent an adoption.[772] Whereas WEST GERMANY allows a married person to adopt a child singly but requires the consent of his spouse (CC § 1746), EAST GERMANY expresses a preference for spouses to adopt jointly.[773] A spouse may adopt the child of his spouse,[774] and a father may adopt his illegitimate child.[775] If the adopter seeks to adopt his illegitimate child or the child of his spouse, WEST GERMAN law all but requires the court to grant exception from the requirement that an adopter be 25 years of age (CC § 1745 b).

The guardian of a minor's person or of the estate may not adopt the minor in his care so long as he continues as guardian or his guardianship accounts remain open (CC § 1752).

Both GERMANIES freely allow the adoption of minor children but frown on the adoption of an adult, who is defined in both countries as a person over 18 years of age.[776] EAST GERMANY's prohibition is categorical,[777] whereas WEST GERMANY allows the adoption of an adult in exceptional circumstances, if his adoption is "morally justified". This must be accomplished by special court order.[778]

161. In the SOVIET UNION the Fundamentals on Family Law of 1968 are silent on who may adopt. In the RSFSR, any person may adopt who has reached the age of majority and has not been deprived of parental rights or been found to be wholly or partially incompetent in accordance with applicable legal procedures (FC art. 99). Only minors may be adopted and the law expressly requires that adoption be in the child's best interest (FC art. 98).

162. MEXICAN law was amended in 1970 to provide that a person 25 years of age, unmarried and in full exercise of his civil rights, may adopt one or more minors or a person without legal capacity, if he is at least 17 years older than the person to be adopted and has adequate means to provide for the support and education of the minor, or the care of the incompetent, as if he were his own child according to his (financial) circumstances.[779] Other conditions are that adoption must be beneficial for the person to be adopted and that the adopter must be a person of good habits (CC art. 390). In special cases, the judge may allow the adoption of two or more incompetents or of minors and incompetents simultaneously (CC art. 390). A husband and wife may adopt jointly when both wish to consider the child to be adopted as their own. In such a case, only one of the spouses need fulfill the requirement that there be a 17 year age difference between adopter and adopted (CC art. 391). The case of adoption by a married couple is the only situation in which more than one person is allowed to adopt another (CC art. 392). A specific prohibition expressed by the MEXICAN Civil Code bars the guardian from adopting his ward until after the guardianship accounts have been finally approved (CC art. 393).

163. In the PHILIPPINES, every person of age, married or unmarried, who is in full possession of his civil rights, may adopt (CC art. 334), if he is at least 16 years older than the person to be adopted (CC art. 337). An important exception bars persons who have legitimate, legitimated, acknowl-

[771] CC § 1745, 1745a. The possibility of a dispensation was added through the Law of 8 Aug. 1950. The standard for granting a dispensation is whether the interests of a child of the intending adopter would suffer or whether the interests of the adopted child would suffer by reason of the existence of legitimate children (CC § 1745a).

[772] *Staudinger (-Engler)* § 1741 no. 33; CC § 1743.

[773] EAST GERMANY: FC § 67 par. 1. WEST GERMAN law does not specify a preference for spouses to adopt jointly, but implies it in CC § 1745a par. 2 which allows the requirement that the adopter have no child to be waived only in the case of a joint adoption by spouses who have children and are living together.

[774] EAST GERMANY: FC § 73 par. 2; FC-Commentary § 73 no. 2. WEST GERMANY: *cf.* CC § 1745b.

[775] EAST GERMANY: FC-Commentary § 67 no. 2. Under certain conditions parental authority may be conferred upon the father other than through adoption: FC § 46 par. 2. In contrast to adoption the conferral of parental authority on the father under these provisions does not destroy the legal relationship between the child and the mother and her relatives: FC-Commentary § 67 no. 2. WEST GERMANY: CC § 1742a, 1745b.

[776] EAST GERMANY: FC § 67 par. 1; *cf. Schlicht* 178. WEST GERMANY: CC § 1744 in connection with CC § 2, as revised by Law of 31 July 1974 (BGBl. I 1713).

[777] The character of a socialist society is thought to rule out the possibility of adult adoption, FC-Commentary § 67 no. 1.

[778] CC § 1745c. The court will usually grant a dispensation if the adopter intends to adopt a younger relative or a foster child living in his house, in order to take a deceased child's place or because he does not have a natural child; *cf. Staudinger (-Engler)* § 1745c no. 3, 5.

[779] CC art. 390, as revised by *Decreto* of 23 Dec. 1969 (DO 17 Jan. 1970, 2).

edged natural children, or natural children by legal fiction,[780] and nonresident aliens or resident aliens from countries with which the PHILIPPINES have broken diplomatic relations.[781] On the other hand, a natural child, a step-child and even a spurious illegitimate child may be adopted by his father or mother (CC art. 338). An *acknowledged* natural child may also be adopted and such an adoption is not barred by the requirement that an adopter have no children of his own (CC art. 335).

The case of the married couple is covered by two provisions. First, as in MEXICO, husband and wife may adopt jointly (CC art. 336), and this is the only case in which more than one person may adopt jointly (CC art. 339 par. 3). In contrast to MEXICO, however, even one spouse may adopt singly, if his spouse consents (CC art. 335 par. 3). The MEXICAN prohibition on the guardian's adoption of his ward before the accounts are approved is taken over intact, and the MEXICAN requirement that the adopter have good habits is expressed more precisely in the PHILIPPINE provision making a person ineligible to adopt if he has been convicted of a crime involving moral turpitude, when the penalty imposed was six months' imprisonment or more (CC art. 335).

iii. *Comparative Summary*

164. *Introductory.* – The question of "who may adopt whom" generally is answered in accordance with the legislators' view as to the purpose of adoption.

165. *Limitations concerning the person to be adopted.* – Most limitations dealing with the person to be adopted concern age. Some systems impose rather strict limitations on the child's age, such as the maximum age of seven years in IRELAND, but most systems are more generous. Other countries prohibit the adoption of adults (several states of the UNITED STATES, EAST GERMANY, RSFSR). Elsewhere, the adoption of adults may be possible only if special requirements are met, such as proof of a specially close relationship between the intending adopter and the person to be adopted, with the exclusion, typically, of relationships resembling marriage (*e.g.*, WEST GERMANY and, further, SWITZERLAND[782]). Systems which recognize several different forms of adoption typically permit the form of adoption that is intended primarily for the benefit of children only up to a certain age (FRANCE and, among others, ITALY, BOLIVIA).[783]

While many systems permit the adoption of the adopter's own illegitimate child (*e.g.*, PHILIPPINES, ENGLAND, WEST GERMANY, states of the UNITED STATES, also SWEDEN[784]), others prohibit such adoptions or permit adoption only of children who have not been acknowledged previously (COLOMBIA CC art. 272).

The adoption of children of a spouse often is facilitated, sometimes prohibited (*infra* s. 167). Other restrictions may consist of requirements that the intending adopter and the child must be of the same religion (ISRAEL; many states of the UNITED STATES, "where practicable") or that only illegitimate children and orphans may be adopted (IRELAND) or may prohibit the adoption by a person of one sex of a child of the other sex (*e.g.*, COLOMBIA).

166. *Restrictions on intending adopters.* – Again, restrictions applicable to persons intending to adopt – other than their general suitability as adoptive parents – generally relate to their age, their own this time, and many other factors, ranging from religion (see *supra* s. 165) to requirements that adopters be married or have been married for a specific period of time (FRANCE: 5 years and one partner over 30 years of age), or that they have been married for a specific period if a child of the other spouse is to be adopted (SWITZERLAND: 2 years[785]). Some systems provide a specific minimum age for adopters, such as 25 years (ENGLAND, WEST GERMANY, MEXICO and, further, DENMARK, SWEDEN)[786] with appropriate exceptions, for instance, applying to the case where a natural child of the adopter is to be adopted (ENGLAND) or to the case where the adopter's natural child or the child of his or her spouse is to be adopted (SWEDEN: 18 years of age[787]).

In some jurisdictions, a single person who wishes to adopt must be more than 35 years old (FRANCE and, further, SWITZERLAND[788]), and other jurisdictions still require rather high minimum ages for

[780] CC art. 89, *supra* s. 123; a corresponding limitation relating to "descendants" was repealed in MEXICO in 1970.

[781] CC art. 335, 339 par. 2.

[782] CC (as revised by Law of 30 June 1972, AS 1972, 2819) art. 266 par. 1.

[783] BOLIVIA: maximum of 6 years for the *arrogación* (FC art. 233), of 18 years for the *adopción* (FC art. 217 no. 2). FRANCE: maximum of 15 years for the *adoption plénière* (CC art. 345); ITALY: maximum of 8 years for the *adozione speciale* (CC art. 314-4 par. 1).

[784] *Föräldrabalk* ch. 4 § 1.

[785] CC (see *supra* n. 782) art. 264a par. 2 and 3.

[786] DENMARK: *Adoptionslov* § 4; SWEDEN: *Föräldrabalk* ch. 4 § 1 sent. 1.

[787] *Föräldrabalk* ch. 4 § 1 sent 2.

[788] CC (see *supra* n. 782) art. 264b par. 1.

all adopters, such as 40 years (CHILE) or 50 years (GREECE, PERU). Another quite common requirement relates to a minimum age differential between adopter and adoptee. This may range from the legislative caveat that the difference be "appropriate" (EAST GERMANY) to specific spans, such as 15 years (FRANCE), 16 years (PHILIPPINES and, further, SWITZERLAND),[789] 17 years (MEXICO) or 18 years (NETHERLANDS). If children of the adopter's spouse are concerned, the required differential is sometimes reduced (FRANCE: from 15 to 10 years). A maximum age differential is prescribed only rarely (NETHERLANDS: 50 years).

Some jurisdictions insist that adopters may not have children (*e.g.*, WEST GERMANY). Others merely require that there be no legitimate descendants (FRANCE), or they are concerned with the existence of natural children only where the adoption of an adult is proposed (SWITZERLAND[790]).

167. *Adoptions by married couples.* – Most of the systems here reviewed provide somewhat specialized rules for adoption by couples. It often is a basic proposition that a married person may adopt only if the spouse joins in the adoption (general rule in the UNITED STATES, EAST GERMANY, MEXICO and among others, DENMARK, SWEDEN, SWITZERLAND).[791] Exceptions are made if a spouse is absent or lacks mental capacity, as well as for the adoption of the adopter's natural child or the child of the spouse for which, of course, the latter's consent is required.[792] Many systems do not require that the spouse actually join an adoption by a married person, but do require the spouse's consent (ENGLAND, FRANCE, PHILIPPINES, WEST GERMANY). Here again exceptions are admitted, for instance when the spouse is incapacitated.

168. *Trends.* – It appears that the more a legal system comes to view adoption from the perspective of the child, the more traditional limitations on adoption disappear, such as the requirement that the adopter have no natural children or be of what now seems to be an unreasonably high minimum age (the high age presumably having been set originally to give the adopter a chance to have his or her own children). Modern adoption laws and practice seem to be guided by the notion that the adoptive child will find optimal conditions where the natural family situation is simulated most closely. This, of course, would favor relatively young parents. At the same time, the emphasis on adoption as a child welfare device seems to increase legislative interest in setting a maximum age for adoption and to permit adoption of adults only in exceptional cases.

C. WHO MUST CONSENT?

i. *Principal Approaches*

169. In most of its variations, adoption involves taking a person out of his own family and placing him into the adopter's family. Therefore it comes as no surprise that all systems require the consent of a minor child's parents and many ask for the consent of the child himself, after he has reached a certain age. In systems which view adoption as a judicial or administrative act, consent is given by the natural parents directly, usually in writing and sometimes in blank. In systems which take the contract view, the consent of the natural parents is obtained indirectly, by having the parent represent his minor child in the adoption contract. Parental consent usually is unnecessary when the parent has formally lost parental authority, or when circumstances show his unsuitability as a parent or when he has abandoned the child. Sometimes the illegitimate father is involved in the adoption process by giving him a hearing, but his consent is rarely required.

Other variations on this theme go to the question of *when* an effective consent may be given. For example, some systems prohibit a mother from issuing a valid consent prior to the birth of her child or within periods ranging from days to months after the birth. The idea is that the mother cannot fully appreciate what she is doing until the child has arrived and she has recovered from the immediate trauma of birth. The countervailing argument is that a required delay in the surrender of the child will aggravate the psychological difficulty experienced by the mother and thus prevent or impede an adoption which may be in the child's best interests. Similar arguments have been mustered in connection with the question of revocation of consent. At the extremes are jurisdictions disallowing revocation altogether and those that allow revocation freely and without grounds until the adoption becomes final.

789 CC (see *supra* n. 782) art. 265 par. 1.

790 CC (see *supra* n. 782) art. 264, 266 par. 1; similarly ARGENTINA: *Ley de adopción* art. 4.

791 DENMARK: *Adoptionslov* § 5 par. 1; SWEDEN: *Föräldrabalk* ch. 4 § 3; SWITZERLAND: CC (see *supra* n. 782) art. 264a par. 1.

792 DENMARK: *Adoptionslov* § 5 par. 1; SWEDEN: *Föräldrabalk* ch. 4 § 3; SWITZERLAND: CC (see *supra* n. 782) art. 264b par. 2.

ii. *Illustrations*

170. *England, United States.* – All but three of the AMERICAN states require the consent of the person to be adopted if he is over 10 to 14 years old.[793] In a few of the states where such consent is required it may be waived by the court. The consent of the infant is not required under the ENGLISH Adoption Act, except in SCOTLAND.[794]

Generally, the AMERICAN states require the consent of the parents if the child is legitimate.[795] The same is true under the ENGLISH Adoption Act.[796] The required consents may be waived upon certain grounds. The most common grounds include abandonment or neglect of the child, incapacity of the parent, a parental failure to support the child, or the court's inability to locate the parent.[797] Less common statutory grounds for waiving the consent requirement include the fact that the parent is imprisoned at the time of the petition and has been imprisoned for three years or more,[798] that the parent has failed to maintain a reasonable degree of interest in the child or that he has engaged in open and notorious adultery or fornication,[799] that the parent is a habitual drunkard,[800] that the parent has failed for at least one year to communicate with his child (where the child is in the custody of another person),[801] that the parent is an inmate or a keeper of a house of ill fame,[802] or that the parent "has been convicted of being a common night walker or a lewd, wanton and lascivious person, and neglects to provide proper care and maintenance for the child."[803] These illustrations show a good deal of variance. In addition, parental consent generally is not necessary if parental rights have been judicially terminated or if the parents have placed the child with an agency for adoption.[804] Finally, many state statutes do not require the consent of a parent who has been deprived of custody through divorce proceedings.[805] This last rule is especially significant in view of the high rate of divorce and helps to facilitate the adoption by a new spouse of the child of his spouse's former marriage. If the child is placed through an agency, the consent of the agency is generally required.[806] If the child is in the custody of a guardian, his consent is necessary.[807]

Most AMERICAN statutes do not require the consent of the father of an illegitimate child, but a few require his consent if paternity has been established, if he has care of the child or if the child has been legitimated. For example, INDIANA provides that the father's consent is required if his paternity has been established by a court proceeding, he has contributed to the care and support of the child and his address is known or can be found without an expenditure exceeding five dollars.[808] A substantial increase in the unwed father's rights to control the adoption of his illegitimate child will result from a recent decision of the UNITED STATES Supreme Court which declared the father to hold constitutional rights to the custody of his child.[809] The ENGLISH Adoption Act has been interpreted to require the consent of the father of an illegitimate child only if an affiliation order has been entered or maintenance decreed.[810]

At least one AMERICAN state requires the consent of the parents of the mother of an illegitimate child if she is under eighteen[811] and another state makes such consent discretionary.[812] In addition to the many specific provisions concerning consent, AMERICAN courts may be empowered to dispense with required consents when to do so would be in the best interests of the child.[813] The ENGLISH Act specifically provides that any required consent may be dispensed with if it is withheld unreasonably.[814] In ENGLAND, the consent must be attested on the date of execution before a proper officer.[815] In AMERICA, consents are usually required to be in writing[816] and may be required to be acknowl-

793 For AMERICAN sources, see *Clark* 620–29; *Leavy* 45; ILLINOIS Rev. Stat. ch. 4 § 9.1-2 (1971).

794 See Adoption Act, 1958, s. 4.

795 See, *e.g.*, ALABAMA Code tit. 27 § 3 (1958); ILLINOIS Rev.Stat. ch. 4 § 9.1-8 (1973).

796 Adoption Act, 1958, s. 4; *Bromley* 249.

797 See *Clark* 620; *Bromley* 251.

798 ALASKA Stat. § 20.10.40 (1962).

799 ILLINOIS Rev.Stat. ch. 4 § 9.1-8 (1974).

800 MONTANA Rev.Codes Ann. § 61-205 (1947).

801 INDIANA Ann.Stat. § 3-120 (1968).

802 IOWA Code Ann. § 600.3 (1949).

803 MASSACHUSETTS Gen. Laws Ann. ch. 210 § 2 (Supp. 1972).

804 See, *e.g.*, CALIFORNIA CC § 224 (1957).

805 See, *e.g.*, ALABAMA Code tit. 27 § 3 (1959).

806 See, *e.g.*, COLORADO Rev.Stat.Ann. § 4-1-6 (1963).

807 See, *e.g.*, ARIZONA Rev.Stat.Ann. § 8-106 (1956).

808 INDIANA Ann.Stat.§ 3-120 (1956).

809 *Stanley v. Illinois*, 405 U.S. 645 (1972).

810 *In re M.*, [1952] 2 Q.B. 479.

811 MINNESOTA Stat.Ann. § 259.24 (1971).

812 NEW HAMPSHIRE Rev.Stat.Ann. § 461.3 (1968).

813 See, *e.g.*, ARIZONA Rev.Stat.Ann. § 8-106 (1956).

814 Adoption Act, 1958, s. 5.

815 Adoption Act, 1958, s. 6.

816 See, *e.g.*, ARIZONA Rev.Stat.Ann. § 8-107 (1956).

edged or notarized.[817] Often, the required consents must accompany the adoption petition.[818] In ILLINOIS, a valid consent may not be given until after 72 hours from the birth[819] and in NEVADA a consent executed prior to the birth is void.[820] The ENGLISH Adoption Act emphasizes the time factor even more and disregards the consent of a mother if the consent was given when the child was less than six weeks old.[821] In many AMERICAN states, a consent to adoption may not be executed in blank and must identify the intending adopter, unless the consent is given to an authorized adoption agency.[822]

Some AMERICAN statutes specify when and how a consent may be revoked. In a few states, a consent to adoption, once given, may be revoked only upon court approval.[823] In many others, consent to adoption is irrevocable, unless it was obtained by fraud or under duress.[824] In some states the consent becomes final after the entry of an interlocutory adoption decree.[825] Still others may use a combination of these approaches.[826] ENGLISH and NEW YORK law hold that the consent may be revoked at any time prior to the adoption order.[827]

171. In FRANCE, if a child's parentage has been established on both sides, both parents must consent to the adoption, unless deceased or otherwise unable to consent.[828] In the case of an illegitimate child, only the parent whose parentage has been established need give his consent (CC art. 348-1). If parentage has not been established, the family council may authorize adoption (CC art. 348-2). The court may allow adoption without the consent of parents or family council if there is evidence of a lack of interest in the child that jeopardizes the child's health or morality (CC art. 348-6). Parental (or family council) consent to the adoption by a non-relative of a child less than two years old is valid only if the adoption is handled by the child welfare authorities or by a recognized adoption agency.[829] In that case, consent to adoption may be given in blank, so that the agency may choose adoptive parents (CC art. 348-4). If the person to be adopted is 15 years of age or older, he must himself consent to his adoption (CC art. 360).

Consent to adoption must be in the form of an official writing[830] and need not necessarily reveal the identity of the adopter. A consent to an adoption may be revoked within three months of the date of the document by means of a registered letter to that effect directed to the person to whom the consent was given.[831]

172. Both GERMANIES require that both parents consent to the adoption of their minor legitimate child by a third party.[832] EAST GERMANY (FC § 69 par. 1) also asks the consent of the child if he is more than 14 years of age, whereas WEST GERMANY accomplishes the same result by requiring a child who is more than 14 years old to agree expressly to the adoption (CC § 1751 par. 2). In EAST GERMANY, if a child has a legal representative other than his parents, he must consent also, whereas in WEST GERMANY, the child's guardian represents the child in the adoption contract, if the child is under 14 years of age, and the guardian needs to consent to the adoption, if the child is more than 14 years old.[833]

If the child is illegitimate, only the mother need consent to his adoption. EAST GERMANY requires the natural father's consent only if he has been given parental authority (FC § 69 par. 1) which, however, is possible only after the mother has lost her parental authority or if she is deceased (FC § 46 par. 2). In WEST GERMANY, the court will hear the natural father before approving an adoption, but typically without disclosing to the father

[817] See, *e.g.*, ARKANSAS Stat.Ann. § 56-106 (1971).

[818] See, *e.g.*, DELAWARE Code Ann. tit. 13 § 906 (a) (1970).

[819] ILLINOIS Rev.Stat. ch. § 9.1-9 (1974).

[820] NEVADA Rev.Stat. § 127.070 (1967).

[821] Adoption Act, 1958, s. 6.

[822] See, *e.g.*, ILLINOIS Rev.Stat. ch. 4 § 9.1-10.

[823] See, *e.g.*, DELAWARE Code Ann. tit. 13 § 909 (1974).

[824] See, *e.g.*, GEORGIA Code Ann. § 74-403 (1964); see ILLINOIS Rev.Stat. ch. 4 § 9.1-11 (1974).

[825] See, *e.g.*, MARYLAND Ann. Code art. 16 § 74 (1966).

[826] MONTANA Rev. Codes Ann. § 61-206 (1962).

[827] ENGLAND: "Order" does not include an interim order, Adoption Act, 1958, s. 8. The consent may not be withdrawn as of right on the ground that the identity of the applicant was not known. If that is the ground the court may dispense with the consent as it is deemed unreasonably withheld. Adoption Act, 1958, s. 5(3). NEW YORK: *Scarpetta v. Spence-Chapin Adoption Serv.*, 28 N.Y.2d 185, 269 N.E.2d 787 (1971).

[828] CC art. 348 par. 1, 2.

[829] CC art. 348-5. This formality has been criticized (especially when applied to the case of a child already living in the household of the intending adopter) but is considered necessary to protect the interests of the child. *Raynaud*, La réforme de l'adoption: D.S. 1967, Chr. 77 ss.; see also *Ferid* 1343.

[830] *Acte authentique*, CC art. 348-3.

[831] CC art. 348-3 par. 2, 3.

[832] WEST GERMANY: CC § 1747; EAST GERMANY: FC § 69 par. 1.

[833] EAST GERMANY: FC § 69 par. 1; WEST GERMANY: CC § 1751.

the identity of the adopter (CC § 1747 b).

In EAST GERMANY the court may allow an adoption without parental consent, if the parent's refusal to consent to the adoption harms the child's best interests or if the parent's prior conduct indicates indifference to the child and his welfare.[834] In WEST GERMANY, parental consent may be dispensed with if there exists permanent mental incapacity on the part of the parent or, if denial of consent would involve a disproportionate disadvantage to the child, or in the case of serious and continuing neglect of parental duties, or indifference concerning the child.[835] In EAST GERMANY, the child welfare authorities bring the action to dispense with parental consent against the refusing parent,[836] whereas in WEST GERMANY, the child himself (through a representative) petitions the court to dispense with his parent's consent.[837] Naturally, if a parent is incapacitated or cannot be located, his consent is not required.[838]

In EAST GERMANY, the consent must be declared before the youth welfare authorities or attested by a notary.[839] The consent need not reveal the identity of the adopter.[840] In WEST GERMANY, the declaration of consent must be authenticated by a notary and communicated to the adopter, or child, or the appropriate court.[841] Declarations of consent to adoption are irrevocable.[842] In EAST GERMANY, consent to adoption may not be given before the birth of the child and,[843] in WEST GERMANY, the child must be at least three months of age before a valid consent may be executed.[844]

The declaration of consent to adoption does not free the natural parents from their duties *vis-à-vis* their child, especially not from their duty of support.[845] These duties terminate only upon completion of the adoption.[846]

173. In the SOVIET UNION, the law of the RSFSR requires the child's parents to consent to the child's adoption, unless they have been deprived of parental rights or determined to be wholly or partially incompetent.[847] Adoption may be ordered without parental consent if the parents have not lived with their child for more than one year and, despite warning by the guardianship authorities, have not participated in the child's upbringing or support and have not displayed parental attention and concern (FC art. 101). If a child is under guardianship, the guardian must consent. Similarly, if a child is in a state children's institution, the consent of the administration of the institution is needed.[848] (When a child is adopted by a married person singly, the consent of the adopter's spouse is required; FC art. 104). Furthermore, when a child has attained the age of ten, his own consent is required, unless, prior to the filing of the application for adoption, the child has lived in the family of the prospective adoptive parent and regards him as a parent.[849]

The required consent must be in writing.[850] Parents may grant their consent to the adoption of their child in terms of a specific person or couple or they may execute the consent in blank and leave the choice of adoptive parents to the child welfare agencies (FC art. 100 par. 3). A consent may be revoked until the adoption becomes final (FC art. 100 par. 5).

174. *Mexico, Philippines.* – In MEXICO, consent to adoption is required of the person exercising parental authority, the guardian of the person to be adopted or, if there is no parent or guardian, of the person who, for six months, has taken in the child that is to be adopted and who has treated the child as if he were his own. If there is no person who meets the standards just enumerated, consent is required of the state's attorney of the locali-

[834] FC § 70; see also FC-Commentary § 70 no. 1-3. If parental authority has been conferred on the grandparents or on the spouse of the father or mother, the same provision applies by analogy, FC-Commentary § 70 no. 1.3.

[835] CC § 1747a, as revised by Law of 14 Aug. 1973 (BGBl. I 1013).

[836] *Familienverfahrensordnung* § 34 par. 1; *cf.* also FC-Commentary § 70 no. 1.

[837] CC § 1747a (see supra n. 835); *Staudinger (-Engler)* § 1747 no. 56.

[838] EAST GERMANY: FC § 70 par. 2; WEST GERMANY: CC § 1747 par. 1, 1746 par. 2.

[839] FC § 69 par. 2. The consent must be recorded, FC-Commentary note on § 69.

[840] FC § 69 par. 3; *Schlicht* 179. In WEST GERMANY, "anonymous adoption" was developed by adoption agencies in reliance on decisions of the Supreme Court: *Staudinger (-Engler)* § 1747 no. 16 ss.

[841] CC § 1748 par. 1, 3. Consent may not be declared by proxy: *Staudinger (-Engler)* § 1747 no. 25.

[842] EAST GERMANY: FC § 69 par. 2; WEST GERMANY: CC § 1748 par. 1.

[843] FC-Commentary (ed. 3, 1970) note on § 69.

[844] CC § 1747 par. 2; *cf. Staudinger (-Engler)* § 1747 no. 30.

[845] EAST GERMANY: FC-Commentary note on § 69; WEST GERMANY: *Staudinger (-Engler)* § 1747 no. 33.

[846] EAST GERMANY: *Cf.* FC-Commentary note on § 69; WEST GERMANY: CC § 1765 par. 1.

[847] FC art. 100 par. 1 and 2.

[848] RSFSR FC art. 102. When a child is surrendered to the institution, the administration must ascertain whether the child's parents agree to the child's future adoption; FC art. 102 par. 2.

[849] FC art. 103 par. 1-3.

[850] FC art. 100 par. 4, 102 par. 1.

ty where the child resides. If the person to be adopted is more than 14 years of age, his own consent is required as well (CC art. 397). Finally, if the guardian or the state's attorney refuses to consent to an adoption without good cause, the municipal president of the locality where the incompetent resides may give his consent to the adoption, if the adoption clearly serves the moral and economic interests of the person to be adopted (CC art. 398).

As in MEXICO, a person over 14 years of age must consent to his own adoption in the PHILIPPINES. Beyond that, the PHILIPPINE Code requires the consent of the parents, the guardian or the person in charge of the person to be adopted (CC art. 340). Whereas the PHILIPPINE Code requires that consent to adoption be in writing (CC art. 340), MEXICO does not expressly specify the form consent must take.[851]

iii. *Comparative Summary*

175. *Consent of the parents.* – The adoption of legitimate children typically requires the consent of both parents (in addition to the countries here dealt with in detail, also, *e.g.*, DENMARK, GUATEMALA, SWEDEN, SWITZERLAND, SPAIN),[852] unless, as in some jurisdictions emphasizing the contractual nature of adoption, the parents represent their child in the making of the adoption contract (for instance, WEST GERMANY and, further, AUSTRIA[853]). If a parent's parental rights have been terminated under applicable provisions of law, for instance by reason of child neglect, abuse or abandonment, that parent's consent to the child's adoption typically no longer is needed. (General rule in the UNITED STATES, SOVIET UNION and, among others, DENMARK, SWEDEN).[854] Other countries require parental consent even in this situation (for instance, SWITZERLAND[855]).

In the case of the adoption of an illegitimate child, the question of the father's consent becomes relevant only when the father has been ascertained. Most systems even then continue to dispense with the father's consent. Others require his consent (ENGLAND, FRANCE, judicial interpretation of federal constitutional provisions in the UNITED STATES, as well as several state laws). Moreover, there now is serious question in the UNITED STATES whether at least a reasonable effort must be made to ascertain paternity before an adoption can become effective without the father's consent. A middle position is occupied by systems requiring that the ascertained father of a child born out of wedlock be given at least an opportunity to be heard (WEST GERMANY and, further, AUSTRIA[856]) or requiring his consent only if he has custody of the child (EAST GERMANY, a few states in the UNITED STATES).

Some systems try to assure that the mother's consent is not given in haste and without a full opportunity to consider the implications of adoption by giving no legal effect to consent executed prior to the child's birth (EAST GERMANY, states in the UNITED STATES), or by providing that a minimum period must have expired between the birth of the child and the giving of consent to his adoption, such as 72 hours (ILLINOIS), six weeks (ENGLAND and, further, SWITZERLAND[857]), three months (WEST GERMANY and, among others, DENMARK[858]) "after birth or when the mother has adequately recovered from the birth" (SWEDEN[859]).

Many systems allow consent to adoption to be given anonymously, and at least the identity of the adopter kept from the natural parent (*e.g.*, EAST and WEST GERMANY, ENGLAND, FRANCE). Other countries permit anonymous adoptions only if an officially authorized adoption agency is involved (general rule in the UNITED STATES, SOVIET UNION). Typical practice in the UNITED STATES involves a "two-way" anonymity in that neither the adopting parties nor the natural parents are identified to each other.

Different views govern whether consent to adoption, once given, may be revoked. The range is from irrevocability, absent fraud or duress (*e.g.*, WEST GERMANY, states in the UNITED STATES), to full freedom to revoke consent until the adoption is final (ENGLAND, states in the UNITED STATES, SOVIET UNION) or until a preliminary order has been entered (states in the UNITED STATES). Some jurisdictions permit revocation without important cause only for a specific period, such as six weeks (SWITZERLAND[860]) or three months (FRANCE) after the consent was originally given.

Most jurisdictions dispense with the requirement of parental consent under certain conditions

[851] CC art. 397, 398; CCProc. art. 924.

[852] DENMARK: *Adoptionslov* § 7 par. 1; GUATEMALA: CC art. 243 par. 3; SWEDEN: *Föräldrabalk* ch. 4 § 5 par. 2; SWITZERLAND: CC art. 265a par. 1; SPAIN: CC art. 173 par. 2 *lit.* c.

[853] AUSTRIA: CC § 181 par. 2.

[854] DENMARK: *Adoptionslov* § 7 par. 2; SWEDEN: *Föräldrabalk* ch. 4 § 5 par. 3.

[855] Cf. CC (see *supra* n. 782) art. 265a par. 1.

[856] AUSTRIA: CC § 181a par. 1 no. 4.

[857] CC (see *supra* n. 782) art. 265b par. 1.

[858] *Adoptionslov* § 8 par. 2.

[859] *Föräldrabalk* ch. 4 § 5 par. 2.

[860] CC (see *supra* n. 782) art. 265a par. 2.

and allow consent to adoption to be given by an appropriate court or agency. One such condition, recognized in some jurisdictions, involves situations where consent is unjustifiably withheld (*e.g.*, ENGLAND, WEST GERMANY and, further, AUSTRIA[861]). Other grounds, recognized almost universally, include abandonment or neglect of the child, lack of mental capacity on the part of the person whose consent would normally be required (ENGLAND, FRANCE, states in the UNITED STATES, EAST and WEST GERMANY and, further, SWITZERLAND[862]) and, more rarely, conviction of serious crime, alcoholism or prostitution (states in the UNITED STATES).

176. *Consent of the person to be adopted.* – Even if not of the age of majority, the child proposed to be adopted must consent to his own adoption after having reached a certain age. These ages usually range between 10 and 15 years (states in the UNITED STATES), 10 years (SOVIET UNION), 12 years (DENMARK, SWEDEN),[863] 14 years (EAST and WEST GERMANY, MEXICO, PHILIPPINES and, among others, SPAIN[864]) or 15 years (FRANCE and, further, BELGIUM[865]). If the child already lives with the proposed adoptive family and already views the intending adopters as his parents, the child's consent may be excused (SOVIET UNION, also DENMARK[866]).

D. EFFECT OF ADOPTION

i. *Principal Approaches*

177. Strong cross currents govern the effect adoption may produce. Some systems see blood ties as so important that they cannot conceive of them being cut fully. They leave the adopted child in a relationship to both his biological and adoptive families and, one might say, view adoption as a glorified form of foster care. Other systems feel that adoption should create a social parent-child relationship that resembles a natural parent-child relationship as closely as possible. This requires the adopted child to be integrated fully into the adopter's family which means, in turn, that all ties must be cut between the child and his biological family. Several systems have sidestepped the problem. They simply provide for two forms of adoption. One form is complete and cuts all relationship between the child and his natural family and the other form does not. This approach goes back to ROMAN law (*adoptio plena vs. adoptio minus plena*) and, after a prolonged absence, is now again embodied in FRENCH law.

The modern trend is away from the foster care approach. The full integration view is gaining acceptance. In many systems, however, the transition is not yet complete. Even where the adopted child is the full legal equivalent of the legitimate child of his adopters, he may yet have a right to inherit from his natural parents. This is true in some COMMON LAW and some CIVIL LAW jurisdictions. The typical CIVIL LAW country provides the child a compulsory share, and that can mean that the adopted child has a right to two compulsory shares, one from his natural and one from his adoptive parents. Similarly, inheritance from the adopted child sometimes remains channeled to the natural family, perhaps on the theory that the adopter should not gain by his adoption. Such a prohibition may be absolute or may concern only assets that have come to the child from his natural family.

Summing up, variations between legal systems principally concern the question of the effect of adoption on the child's legal ties with his natural family, the question of the adopter's rights (especially inheritance) *vis-à-vis* the child, and whether the effect of adoption extends to the adopter's greater family. Differences also may be based on whether the adopters are strangers or relatives of the child. Despite many variations, it safely may be said that the adopted child obtains the status of a legitimate child *vis-à-vis* the adopter nearly everywhere. He usually obtains the adopter's name, goes under the adopter's parental authority and has a full right of support and inheritance. Incest prohibitions typically remain in effect between the adopted child and his natural family, and new incest prohibitions may be imposed on the adopted child in respect of his adoptive family.

An important limitation on the fullness of the adoptive relationship is set by the possibility of revocation. If it is possible to terminate an adoptive relationship where a natural relationship would be immune, provisions that speak of the adopted child having the same legal rights as a legitimate child obviously do not give the whole answer. Revocation will be discussed fully in a later division (*infra* E).

861 AUSTRIA: CC § 181 par. 3.

862 SWITZERLAND: CC (see *supra* n. 782) art. 265c.

863 DENMARK: *Adoptionslov* § 6 par. 1; SWEDEN: *Föräldrabalk* ch. 4 § 5 par. 1.

864 CC art. 173 par. 2 *lit.* b.

865 CC art. 348 par. 3.

866 *Adoptionslov* § 6 par. 1.

ii. *Illustrations*

178. In AMERICA, adopted children inherit from their adoptive parents,[867] although a few states deny an adopted child the rights to take property that was taken by his adoptive parents as "heirs of the body".[868] A distinction, now rare,[869] sometimes is made between inheriting *from* adoptive parents and[870] inheriting *through* them.[871] Many statutes expressly provide that an adopted child no longer inherits from his natural family,[872] but a number of states preserve such rights.[873] Practically all AMERICAN states let adoptive parents inherit from their adopted child to the exclusion of the natural family,[874] although a few states do not allow the adoptive parents to inherit property the child got from his natural family.[875]

With these limited exceptions, adoption ends all of the natural parents' rights and obligations *vis-à-vis* their child in the vast majority of states.[876] Most statutes simply state that the adopted child shall be treated as a legitimate child of the adopters[877] and a few statutes specify rights and obligations in detail.[878] Everywhere, the obligation to support the child and the right to custody pass to the adoptive parents.

A few AMERICAN statutes governing the construction of wills, trusts and similar instruments provide expressly that terms such as "child" shall include adopted children unless a contrary intent appears,[879] and at least one state treats an adopted child as an after-born child for purposes of wills.[880] In the absence of a specific statute, cases have been inconsistent and often have denied an inheritance to the adopted child. Most states provide for the change of the adopted person's surname to that of the adopters.[881] Typically, statutes also provide for the issuance of a new birth certificate upon entry of the final adoption order and the sealing of the old certificate.[882]

179. In ENGLAND, adoption transforms the adopted child into a legitimate child of the adopter and all relations with the biological family cease.[883] Since 1949, even the inheritance relationship is limited to the adoptive family, whereas the 1926 Act had continued the adopted child's inheritance relationship with his natural family.[884] An interesting feature is that the ENGLISH Adoption Act makes special provision for the maintenance of a register of adopted children. While any person is entitled to search that register,[885] a search will not reveal the identity of the adopted person's natural parents. All records connecting the original birth registration and the adoption registration are closed to general search.[886]

180. FRANCE, interestingly, distinguishes between full and limited adoption. Full adoption integrates the child as a full member into the adopter's family and the effects of adoption extend to the adoptive parent's relatives.[887] The child takes the adopter's surname and may be given a new first name (CC art. 357). If the adopted child is an alien, a FRENCH adopter confers FRENCH nationality on him.[888] Full adoption destroys all ties between the child and his biological family, with the exception of incest prohibitions on marriage (CC art. 356). But even this vestige of relationship is obscured by the practice of amending an adopted child's birth certificate so as to hide the identity of the natural parents.[889]

Limited adoption has less drastic effects. The adopted person remains partially connected with his biological family. The child retains an inheritance relationship as well as a duty to render support to his natural parents, should they be in need.[890] Reciprocally, the natural parents of the "simply" adopted child retain a subsidiary duty of support (CC art. 367 par. 2). Still, the primary legal relationship of the "simply" adopted child is with his adoptive parents who acquire full parental authority (CC art. 365 par. 2) and owe the child support (CC art. 367 par. 1). With respect to inheritance, the "simply" adopted child is in the same position as a legitimate child of the

867 For AMERICAN sources, see *Clark* 665-666; *Leavy* 72.

868 MAINE Rev.Stat.Ann. tit. 9 § 535 (1964).

869 *Clark* 660.

870 See, *e.g.*, CONNECTICUT Gen.Stat.Ann. § 45-65 (1960).

871 See, *e.g.*, ALABAMA Code tit. 27 § 4 (1940).

872 See, *e.g.*, CONNECTICUT Gen.Stat.Ann. § 45-65 (1960).

873 ARKANSAS Stat.Ann. § 56-109 (1971).

874 *Ibidem.*

875 See, *e.g.*, GEORGIA Code Ann. § 74-414 (1964).

876 See, *e.g.*, ALABAMA Code tit. 27 § 5 (1940).

877 ARIZONA Rev.Stat.Ann. § 8-117 (1956).

878 See, *e.g.*, MISSOURI Ann.Stat. § 453.090 (1969).

879 See, *e.g.*, CONNECTICUT Gen.Stat.Ann. § 45-65a (1960).

880 DELAWARE Code Ann. tit. 13 § 920 (1970).

881 See, *e.g.*, ALABAMA Code tit. 27 § 4 (1958).

882 *Ibidem.*

883 Adoption Act, 1958, s. 13(1), (2).

884 *Bromley* 466-467.

885 Adoption Act, 1958, s. 20.

886 Adoption Act, 1958, s. 20(4)(5), 21.

887 CC art. 358; *cf. Ferid* 1351.

888 *Code de la nationalité* (Code Concerning Citizenship) of 19 Oct. 1945 (JO 20 Oct. 1945 p. 6700) art. 35.

889 *Cf. Ferid* 1352.

890 CC art. 364 par. 1, 367 par. 2.

adoptive parents (CC art. 368). However, if the "simply" adopted child leaves no descendants, property stemming from the adopter goes back to the adopter, property stemming from the natural family goes back there, and the remainder is shared equally between the two families (CC art. 368-1). In the case of limited adoption, the child may or may not take the adoptive person's surname or simply add that name to his, although the court may order that the adopter's name be given to the child (CC art. 363). Finally, limited adoption does not confer FRENCH nationality.[891]

Neither limited nor full adoption removes the (incest) marriage prohibitions between the adopted child and his natural family.[892] In addition, new marriage prohibitions become applicable in respect of the child's new family. These prohibitions are less broad in the case of limited adoption than in the case of full adoption and certain restrictions may even be dispensed with by the President, if serious reasons exist (CC art. 366).

181. In EAST and WEST GERMANY, the adopted child acquires the legal status of a legitimate child of the adopter, irrespective of whether the child is legitimate or illegitimate or whether the adopter is married or unmarried.[893] This includes full support and inheritance rights for the child.[894] WEST GERMANY, however, allows the contract of adoption to deny the child a right to inherit from the adopter (CC § 1767 par. 1). The adopter has no right of inheritance from the adopted child, but the child may make a will in his favor after the age of 16.[895] EAST GERMANY extends the effect of adoption to the adopter's blood relatives (FC § 72 par. 1), but WEST GERMANY does not (CC § 1763). The adopter's spouse is not considered related to the adopted child, nor is the child's spouse considered related to the adopter (CC § 1763). Finally, while the effect of adoption extends to the adopted child's unborn descendants in both GERMANIES,[896] WEST GERMANY expressly provides that a descendant living at the time the adoption contract is made is covered only if he is a party (CC § 1762). As an impediment to marriage, the effect of the adoption extends only to the adopter and the adopted person.[897] WEST GERMANY holds valid a marriage celebrated in violation of this impediment and considers the adoptive relationship terminated by operation of law (CC § 1771).

The adopted child generally acquires the surname of his adoptive parent. In EAST GERMANY, the youth welfare authorities may permit the child to retain his original name in special cases (FC § 71 par. 2). In WEST GERMANY, the child may add his former surname to his new name, unless the adoption contract provides otherwise.[898]

EAST GERMAN law terminates all legal ties between adopted child and biological parents.[899] WEST GERMANY, on the other hand, views the adopted child as the member of two families, with the adoptive relationship having primacy.[900] This means that the natural parents – even the illegitimate father – remain secondarily liable for support (CC § 1766) and the child retains full reciprocal inheritance rights with respect to his biological family (CC § 1764). In WEST and EAST GERMANY, the adopter obtains full parental authority over the minor adopted child and the natural parents (or the mother if the child is illegitimate) lose their parental authority over the child including any right of visitation or contact.[901]

182. In SOVIET law, the adopted child and his descendants have full, reciprocal rights and duties, equal to those of relatives by blood, with respect to the adoptive parents and their relatives.[902] Consistently with this position, the adopted child loses all rights and is relieved of all obligations with respect to his natural parents and their relatives.[903] Only a pension or an allowance from state or social organizations that may be due the child through his natural parents may continue.[904]

If a child is adopted by only one person, the child's rights and duties may be preserved at the

891 *Code de la nationalité* (*supra* n. 888) art. 36. Naturalization, however, is available more readily, art. 55, 64 no. 6.

892 CC art. 364 par. 2, 356.

893 EAST GERMANY: FC § 66. WEST GERMANY: CC § 1757; *Staudinger (-Engler)* § 1757 no. 1.

894 EAST GERMANY: FC-Commentary § 66 no. 2. WEST GERMANY: CC § 1757 par. 1, 1766.

895 CC § 1759, 2229; *Staudinger (-Engler)* § 1759 no. 3.

896 EAST GERMANY: *Cf.* FC § 72 par. 1. WEST GERMANY: *Cf.* CC § 1762 par. 1.

897 EAST GERMANY: FC § 8 no. 3, 72 par. 2. WEST GERMANY: *Ehegesetz* § 7, CC § 1771.

898 CC § 1758 par. 4; see also *Staudinger (-Engler)* § 1758 no. 26.

899 FC § 73 par. 1. This includes the adoptee's relationship with his sisters and brothers: FC-Commentary (ed. 3, 1970) § 73 no. I. Of course, if a spouse adopts the other spouse's child (common in the case of an illegitimate child of one of the spouses), the relationship between the child and the other spouse and his relatives subsists, FC § 73 par. 2.

900 CC § 1764; *Staudinger (-Engler)* § 1757 no. 2 ss.

901 EAST GERMANY: FC § 66, 72, 73. WEST GERMANY: CC § 1765.

902 RSFSR FC art. 108 par. 1.

903 RSFSR FC art. 109.

904 RSFSR FC art. 109.

request (and in respect) of the natural mother, if the adopter is a man, or at the request (and in respect) of the natural father if the adoptive parent is a woman.[905] Moreover, if one of the child's natural parents has died and if the adopter does not object, the parents of the deceased (*i.e.*, the grandfather and grandmother of the child) may request that the child's rights and duties be preserved with respect to the relatives of the deceased parent.[906]

On the adopter's request, the adopted child may be given the surname of the adoptive parent and a patronymic based on the latter's first name. The adopted child's first name also may be changed at the request of the adopter. If the adopted child has attained the age of ten, any change in his name requires his consent.[907] The adoption order must specify any change in name.[908] On their request, the adoptive parents may be recorded in the official birth records as the parents of their adopted child.[909] Again, if the adopted child is more than ten years of age, his consent is required.[910]

The secrecy of adoption is protected by law even to the extent that the birthplace of the adopted child may be changed on the birth certificate. In exceptional cases, the date of the child's birth may be changed by up to six months.[911] Marriage between adoptive parents and children is prohibited.[912]

183. In MEXICO and the PHILIPPINES, adoption produces a reciprocal parent-child relationship between adopter and adopted, but in both countries, the child's relationship with his biological family continues, with the exception of the natural parents' parental authority which is transferred to the adopter.[913] The adopted child obtains the adopter's name and becomes his heir.[914] Reciprocally, MEXICO allows the adopter to inherit from his adopted child along with the child's natural parents[915] whereas the PHILIPPINE Code specifically denies inheritance to the adopter and holds that the natural parents alone may take (CC art. 342). In the PHILIPPINES it is quite clear, and it would appear to be so in MEXICO as well, that the adopted child has the right to two compulsory shares, one stemming from his natural parents and one in the estate of his adopted parent,[916] while the PHILIPPINE Code provides expressly that *inter vivos* gifts to adopted children will be charged against the compulsory share.[917] On the other hand, although purporting to treat the adopted child "as if he were a legitimate child of the adopter" (CC art. 341 par. 1), the PHILIPPINE Code nevertheless relegates him to the right of succession of an acknowledged natural child when he competes with the adopter's legitimate parents or other ascendants (CC art. 343). This has the effect of not excluding the ascendants as heirs, which would result if a legitimate biological child would compete with them. In competition with the legitimate biological child, however, the adopted child is treated as the former's equal.[918] In both countries, the legal effect of adoption extends to the adopter and adopted persons only. Accordingly, an adopted child does not represent his deceased adoptive parents in inheritance situations.[919]

Both countries agree that the adoptive relationship goes beyond the immediate parties in terms of marriage impediments. MEXICO provides specifically that marriage may not be contracted between adopter and the adopted person or his descendants, so long as the adoptive relationship continues in effect.[920] The PHILIPPINES express a similar prohibition, going even further, when they hold "void from the beginning" a marriage contracted "between the adopting father or mother and the adopted, between the former and the surviving spouse of the latter", or "between the legitimate children of the adopter and the adopted" (CC art. 82).

iii. *Comparative Summary*

184. *The effect of various forms of adoption.* – The effect of adoption generally varies with the purpose of adoption perceived by the legislator. "Full adoption" involves complete integration of the adopted child into the adopters' family, with attainment of status equivalent to that of a legitimate child of the adopters. All legal ties with

905 RSFSR FC art. 108 par. 3.

906 RSFSR FC art. 108 par. 4.

907 RSFSR FC art. 105 par. 2. If the child has lived in the family of the adopter prior to submission of the application for adoption and regards him as his parent, the child's consent is not required, FC art. 105 par. 2, 103 par. 3.

908 RSFSR FC art. 105.

909 This must be specified in the adoption order, RSFSR FC art. 106 par. 1, 3.

910 RSFSR FC art. 106 par. 2.

911 RSFSR FC art. 110 par. 2.

912 Fundamentals of Family Law art. 10 par. 3.

913 MEXICO: CC art. 395, 396, 403. PHILIPPINES: CC art. 341.

914 MEXICO: CC art. 395 (as amended 1970), 396. PHILIPPINES: CC art. 341, 365.

915 CC art. 395, 403.

916 *Padilla* 313.

917 CC art. 344, 1061.

918 CC art. 341 no. 3, 979 par. 2.

919 MEXICO: CC art. 402; PHILIPPINES: CC art. 341 par. 3.

920 CC art. 402, 157.

the natural family are terminated (ENGLAND, many states in the UNITED STATES, FRANCE, EAST GERMANY, SOVIET UNION and, among many others not discussed in detail above, DENMARK, SWITZERLAND, the NETHERLANDS and ITALY).[921]

"Limited" adoption, on the other hand, is offered by many systems and maintains (some) legal tie to the natural family (FRANCE, MEXICO, PHILIPPINES, WEST GERMANY, also AUSTRIA and ITALY).[922] In these systems, the adopted person thus has, in some respects, two families, but the adoptive relationship typically takes precedence. For instance, "incomplete" adoption may mean that a support obligation is retained by the natural parents but is subsidiary to that of the adoptive parents, or that inheritance from the child passes primarily to the adoptive parents, with exceptions made, for instance, regarding funds the child received from his natural family which would go back there. It also may mean that the child remains fully the heir of his natural parents and, in addition, has the same status as to his adoptive parents.

Not all jurisdictions have opted for one form of adoption to the exclusion of all others, although most have. FRANCE and many jurisdictions that base their law on FRENCH origins (such as ITALY, SPAIN, ARGENTINA, BOLIVIA), permit the adopter to choose the form of adoption most suited to the situation.

Certain ground rules apply to all forms of adoption. For instance, the incest prohibition applicable to the child and his natural parents remains in effect universally, whether the adoption is of the full (FRANCE, WEST GERMANY, UNITED STATES, also, for instance, ARGENTINA, BOLIVIA, SWITZERLAND)[923] or limited (for instance, ENGLAND, FRANCE, WEST GERMANY) variety.

185. *Parental authority and support obligations.* – Regardless of the form of adoption, the adopters typically acquire parental authority concerning the child along with a duty of support (UNITED STATES, ENGLAND, EAST and WEST GERMANY, FRANCE, MEXICO, PHILIPPINES, and, among many others, ARGENTINA and SPAIN).[924] Other legal consequences, such as the child's surname or inheritance rights, depend more often on the form of the adoption.

185a. *Name of adopted child.* – In many jurisdictions, the child acquires the surname of the adopter(s) (UNITED STATES, as well as many others, such as AUSTRIA, DENMARK, JAPAN, NETHERLANDS, SWEDEN).[925] The same rule applies to full adoption in countries which permit choice between the two forms of adoption (FRANCE, and, among others, ARGENTINA, SPAIN).[926] In several countries the child may retain his original surname after adoption (for instance, EAST GERMANY) or combine his old surname with the surname of the adopter(s) (WEST GERMANY). Some countries, such as DENMARK and SWEDEN, permit both options.[927]

In the case of limited adoption, similar alternatives apply. For instance, FRANCE (CC art. 180 par. 2) and other countries permit the retention of the original name, the acquisition of the name of the adopter(s) or the combination of both names. Some jurisdictions, such as ARGENTINA,[928] permit a choice between the first two alternatives only.

186. *Adoption and inheritance.* – The adopted person typically acquires inheritance rights relating to the adopter(s) and often the extended adoptive family (*e.g.*, ENGLAND, UNITED STATES, EAST and WEST GERMANY, as well as many other countries, such as DENMARK, NORWAY).[929] WEST GERMANY permits inheritance rights to be excluded by the contract of adoption. Comparison of inheritance rights, of course, is complicated by the recognition of the *légitime* in the typical CIVIL LAW country and its traditional absence in the COMMON LAW.

The adopted person typically loses his right to inherit from his natural family (ENGLAND, many states of the UNITED STATES, and, among many others, NORWAY[930]). Where the adopted person's legal relationship to his natural family remains more or less intact, rights of inheritance usually remain in effect (WEST GERMANY, FRANCE (limited adoption), and, among others, AUSTRIA, GUATEMALA).[931] In some states of the UNITED STATES, an otherwise fully complete adoption may leave the

921 DENMARK: *Adoptionslov* § 16 par. 1; SWITZERLAND: CC art. 267; NETHERLANDS: New CC art. 229; ITALY: CC art. 314-26 par. 2.

922 AUSTRIA: CC § 182a; ITALY: CC art. 300 par. 1.

923 ARGENTINA: *Ley de adopción* art. 14; BOLIVIA: FC art. 242; SWITZERLAND: CC art. 100 no. 3.

924 ARGENTINA: *Ley de adopción* art. 14, 22; SPAIN: CC art. 176 par. 4.

925 AUSTRIA: CC § 183 par. 1; DENMARK: *Lov om personnavne* § 3 sent. 1; JAPAN: CC art. 810; NETHERLANDS: New CC art. 5 par. 1; SWEDEN: *Namnlag* § 3 par. 1.

926 ARGENTINA: *Ley de adopción* art. 17; SPAIN: CC art. 178 par. 4.

927 DENMARK: *Lov om personnavne* § 3 sent. 3; SWEDEN: *Namnlag* § 3 par. 1 und 5.

928 *Ley de adopción* art. 23.

929 DENMARK: *Adoptionslov* § 16 par. 1; NORWAY: *Lov om adoption* § 14 par. 1.

930 *Lov om adoption* § 14 par. 2.

931 AUSTRIA: CC § 182b par. 1; GUATEMALA: CC art. 237.

adopted person intestate succession rights relating to his natural family.

While adoptive parents are permitted to inherit from their adopted child in numerous countries, (most states in the UNITED STATES, ENGLAND, MEXICO, FRANCE (full adoption), and others, such as DENMARK[932]), there are countries which limit or exclude the adoptive parents' right to inherit from their adopted child (PHILIPPINES, WEST GERMANY and, among others, GUATEMALA, ITALY).[933]

E. REVOCATION OF ADOPTION

i. *Principal Approaches*

187. If revocation of adoption is to be permitted, all other provisions of law relating to the fullness of the adopted child's rights *vis-à-vis* his adoptive parents must be read with that in mind. Once again reflecting different concepts of adoption, some systems allow and others flatly forbid revocation. For example, in systems which adhere to the contract view of adoption and even in some that do not, revocation (or rescission) may be possible by mutual consent, and court action may or may not be needed. If, on the other hand, adoption is viewed as final, parental authority can be terminated only in accordance with the law applicable to natural parents. Between these extremes, many permit revocation on a variety of grounds.

Several situations should be distinguished: It is one thing to allow an adoption to be revoked if the best interests of the child are served thereby and quite another to allow revocation for the convenience of the adoptive parents or at the instance of third parties (such as the adoption agency that handled the placement) or the natural parents. When the interests of the child are at stake, adoption may be subject to revocation more readily than a natural parent's rights could be cut off. When the interests of the adoptive parents are involved, grounds range from mistake or fraud to very bad behavior on the part of the adopted child.

The effect of revocation typically is to restore the child to his original biological family.

ii. *Illustrations*

188. Only a few AMERICAN[934] states provide specifically for the revocation or annulment of an adoption order. In these states, common grounds for revocation include the fact that the child is feeble-minded, epileptic, insane or has developed venereal disease as a result of conditions existing at the time of the adoption which were unknown to the adoptive parents.[935] In two states revocation is (or was) allowed on racial grounds.[936] In at least one state an adoption may be annulled if the parents divorce within two years of the final order and the adoption involved a minor child.[937] In another, it may be annulled for wilfull desertion or ill behavior.[938]

Most states that provide for revocation allow only the adoptive parents to petition for revocation. A few states provide for revocation by the child or an interested person acting on the child's behalf,[939] on grounds such as failure to fulfill support obligations to the child.[940] NEW YORK details grounds upon which an "abrogation" on behalf of the child may be sought. These grounds include cruelty, abuse, inability or refusal to support, maintain or educate the child, attempt to change, or make a change in, or failure to safeguard the religion of the child.[941] Further, NEW YORK provides for "abrogation" upon mutual consent of the parties if this is in their best interests.[942]

Generally, a petition for revocation must be filed within a specified period from the adoption de-

[932] *Adoptionslov* § 16 par. 1.

[933] GUATEMALA: CC art. 236 par. 1; ITALY: CC art. 304 par. 1 (limited adoption).

[934] For AMERICAN sources, see *Clark* 666-671; *Leavy* 70.

[935] See, *e.g.*, ALABAMA Code tit. 27 § 4; ARKANSAS Stat.Ann. § 56-110; GEORGIA Code Ann. § 74-416; IOWA Code Ann. § 600.7; MINNESOTA Stat.Ann. § 259.30; MISSOURI Ann.Stat. § 453.130.

[936] See KENTUCKY Rev.Stat.Ann. § 199.540 (if the child reveals definite traits of "ethnological ancestry different from those of the adoptive parents" and the parents had no prior knowledge or information of such fact); MISSOURI Ann.Stat. § 453.130 (if the child "shall prove to be a member of a race, the members of which are prohibited by the laws of this state from marriage with members of the race to which the parents by adoption belong").

[937] ARKANSAS Stat.Ann. § 56-110.

[938] NEW YORK Domestic Relations Law § 118-6 (applies only to children placed through an agency).

[939] ARKANSAS Stat.Ann. § 56-110; GEORGIA Code Ann. § 74-416; MAINE Rev.Stat.Ann. tit. 9 § 538; NEW YORK Domestic Relations Law § 118-a.

[940] ARKANSAS Stat.Ann. § 56-110; GEORGIA Code Ann. § 74-416; MAINE Rev.Stat.Ann. tit. 9 § 538.

[941] NEW YORK Domestic Relations Law § 118a.

[942] NEW YORK Domestic Relations Law § 118.

cree[943] or the ground upon which the petition is based must have occurred within a given period after the decree.[944]

189. ENGLAND specifically allows revocation of an adoption in only one instance. This involves the case of an illegitimate child who was adopted by his father or mother alone and whose parents subsequently marry. Revocation is allowed to provide the child the benefit of full legitimate status *vis-à-vis* his parents. In all other cases, attack on adoption appears possible by way of appeal only.[945] In short, ENGLISH law views finality of adoption as an overriding social value.

190. The FRENCH Civil Code of 1804 made adoption irrevocable. Today full adoption remains irrevocable (CC art. 359). Limited adoption, on the other hand, may now be revoked by a court decision for "serious reasons" on application of close blood relatives of the child or if the latter is 16 years old (CC art. 370). The trial court determines whether "serious reasons" exist (CC art. 370 par. 1) and its discretion is so broad that it may not be overridden on appeal.[946] "Serious reasons" may encompass the behavior of the adopter as well as that of the adopted person. An order revoking adoption has no retroactive effect.[947] The possibility of attack on either form of adoption by third parties is limited so strictly that it is without practical importance.[948]

191. *East and West Germany.* – Since EAST GERMANY accomplishes adoption by administrative decision, whereas WEST GERMANY views adoption as a contract, different routes lead to dissolution of adoption.[949] Still, both countries allow revocation of an adoption by the appropriate court if the child's development is jeopardized.[950] In EAST GERMANY, the adopter must have culpably and gravely violated his parental duties (FC § 75 par. 1). In WEST GERMANY, the question whether the child's welfare requires revocation is judged by objective criteria and fault must not be proved.[951] In EAST GERMANY, a joint adoption by spouses may be revoked with effect as to both spouses, if revocation is indicated as to one of them (FC § 75 par. 2). WEST GERMANY is similar, but also permits revocation between the adopted person and one spouse only.[952]

Further, EAST GERMAN law allows judicial revocation of an adoption if, within five years after adoption, it appears that the child suffers from a grave and incurable disease which renders a true parent-child relationship impossible, or if an adopted child who is more than 14 years old, seriously attacks the adopter, his spouse or his children.[953] After the adopted person has attained majority, a state notary may rescind the adoption in exceptional circumstances on the request of the adopter and the adopted person (FC § 77 par. 1). If the child was adopted by a couple and one spouse has died, the surviving spouse's request, coupled with that of the adopted person, is sufficient (FC § 77 par. 2).

In WEST GERMANY, the adoption may be rescinded by contract between the adopter and the adopted person and any descendants of the adopted person who are covered by the adoption.[954] The contract terminates the adoptive relationship prospectively,[955] and must conform to similar

943 ALABAMA Code tit. 27 § 4 (5 years); GEORGIA Code Ann. § 74-416 (7 years, but no limit if parents fail to perform obligations and adoptee is at least 17); KENTUCKY Rev.Stat.Ann. § 199.540 (5 years on social grounds, otherwise 2 years); MISSOURI Ann.Stat. § 453.130 (5 years).

944 ARKANSAS Stat.Ann. § 56-110 (grounds must develop within 5 years of final decree, in case of a revocation on behalf of the parents); IOWA Code Ann. § 600.7 (grounds must develop within 5 years of final order); MINNESOTA Stat.Ann. § 259.30.

945 *Bromley* 257-258.

946 Cass.civ. 12 Jan. 1966, D.1966, 236.

947 CC art. 370-2. The order revoking adoption must be noted in the birth certificate (CC art. 370-1 par. 2).

948 *Cf. Ferid* 1352.

949 In WEST GERMANY, the general rules of contract law apply to the rescission of an adoption (see *Staudinger (-Engler)* § 1768 no. 14). An adoption is void by operation of law, if the adopter's or adoptee's declaration or one of the required declarations of consent are void (*nichtig*) by reason of CC § 105, 116, 117, 138. Further, the adoption contract may be voided if the adopter's or adoptee's declaration or one of the declarations of consent involved a mistake, fraud or threat, see CC § 119-124.

950 EAST GERMANY: FC § 75 par. 1. The Youth Welfare Authorities must bring the action against the adopter, *Familienverfahrensordnung* § 34 par. 2. WEST GERMANY: CC § 1770a; *Staudinger (-Engler)* § 1770a no. 5.

951 An incurable disease which renders the adopter incapable of educating the child may be reason for revocation, *Staudinger (-Engler)* § 1770a no. 8.

952 CC § 1770a; *cf. Staudinger (-Engler)* § 1770a no. 15.

953 FC § 76. See, especially, FC-Commentary § 76 no. 2, 3. The action must be brought against the adopted child within one year after knowledge of the relevant facts is obtained. The court must provide the Youth Welfare Authorities an opportunity to comment: FC § 76 par. 2; *Familienverfahrensordnung* § 34 par. 2; *cf.* FC-Commentary § 76 no. 2.

954 CC § 1768 par. 1, 2. This is also true if the adoptee has died (CC § 1769).

955 *Staudinger (-Engler)* § 1768 no. 6.

formal restrictions and conditions as apply to the adoption itself (CC § 1770). If there is a joint adoption or if one spouse has adopted the other spouse's child, both spouses need be parties to the contract of rescission with the child.[956] An adoption terminates automatically when the adopter (though illegally) marries his adopted child.[957] EAST GERMANY also allows revocation of an adoption that took place without a parent's consent if that parent was incapable of giving his consent at the time of adoption and now has regained his capacity.[958] Before entering judgment, the court must consult the Youth Welfare Authorities.[959] In both countries, the court must consider whether a rescission of the adoption would interfere with the adopted child's welfare.[960]

Revocation terminates all relationships created by the adoption[961] and the legal relationship between the adopted person and his parents is re-established. The adopted person even takes back his original name,[962] unless the adoption was revoked only with respect to one of two spouses.[963] Nevertheless, parental authority over a minor child does not automatically revert to the natural parents,[964] and a child more than 14 years of age must be heard before his natural parents can regain parental authority.[965]

192. SOVIET law distinguishes between annulment and revocation of an adoption. In either case a judicial proceeding must be brought against the adoptive parents.[966] Any person whose rights were violated by the adoption may demand that it be declared invalid, as may the guardianship authorities and the procurator, if they believe that there are grounds for revocation.[967] If the natural parents do not know who adopted their child, the demand is served on the guardianship authorities where the adoption decree was issued.[968] The guardianship authorities will inform the adopter who may participate in the consideration of the case in court.[969]

State and social organizations as well as private citizens who regard an adoption as subject to revocation are under a duty to inform the guardianship authorities or the procurator who will decide whether to bring an action.[970] An adoption may be declared invalid on the grounds that it was based on falsified documents, that the adopter is a person who has been deprived of parental rights or has been legally declared wholly or partially incompetent, or that the adoption was fictitious.[971] An adoption may be revoked if the adoption took place without consents required by law and revocation is in the best interests of the child.[972] If the adopted child has attained the age of majority at the time of a demand for revocation of the adoption, revocation may be granted only if there is mutual agreement by the parents, the adopter and the adopted child.[973]

Annulment or revocation of an adoption produce different consequences. Annulment invalidates the adoption *ab initio*,[974] whereas revocation takes effect at the time it is decreed.[975] In both cases, the child's legal relationship with his biological family is restored[976] and the termination of adoption terminates all rights and duties between the adoptive parent and his relatives and the adopted child.[977] Nevertheless, in a case of revocation, the former adopter may continue to be liable for the support of the child.[978]

When an adoption is annulled or revoked, the court determines on the basis of the child's best interests, whether the child is to be restored to the custody of his biological parents or given into the custody of the guardianship authorities.[979] On revocation, the court also decides whether the

[956] CC § 1768 par. 3; *cf. Staudinger (-Engler)* § 1768 no. 7.

[957] *Ehegesetz* § 7; CC § 1771.

[958] *Cf.* FC § 74 par. 1, 70 par. 2; *Schlicht* 181. This case is covered in WEST GERMANY by CC § 1770b, see *Palandt (-Lauterbach)* § 1770b no. 2.

[959] EAST GERMANY: FC § 74 par. 2. In addition, a child more than 14 years of age must be heard by the court (FC § 53; FC-Commentary § 74 no. 2). WEST GERMANY: *Jugendwohlfahrtsgesetz* (Youth Welfare Law) of 6 Aug. 1970 (BGBl. I 1197) § 48a par. 1 no. 10.

[960] The court must investigate whether the natural parents fulfilled their parental duties prior to the adoption. Further, the court will consider how long the adoptive relationship had continued. EAST GERMANY: FC-Commentary § 74 no. 2. WEST GERMANY: *Staudinger (-Engler)* § 1770b no. 10.

[961] EAST GERMANY FC § 78; WEST GERMANY: CC § 1768, 1772.

[962] EAST GERMANY: FC § 78 par. 1, 2; WEST GERMANY: CC § 1772.

[963] WEST GERMANY: CC § 1772.

[964] EAST GERMANY: FC § 78 par. 3; WEST GERMANY: *cf.* CC § 1765 par. 2.

[965] EAST GERMANY: FC § 53; WEST GERMANY: CC § 1765 par. 2.

[966] RSFSR FC art. 3.

[967] RSFSR FC art. 112 par. 2, 115 par. 1, 113.

[968] RSFSR FC art. 114 par. 3.

[969] RSFSR FC art. 114 par. 4.

[970] RSFSR FC art. 115 par. 2.

[971] RSFSR FC art. 112 par. 1.

[972] RSFSR FC art. 113 par. 1.

[973] RSFSR FC art. 116.

[974] RSFSR FC art. 112 par. 3.

[975] RSFSR FC art. 113 par. 2.

[976] RSFSR FC art. 112 par. 2, 4.

[977] RSFSR FC art. 117 par. 1, 2.

[978] RSFSR FC art. 117 par. 1.

[979] RSFSR FC art. 112 par. 5, 117 par. 3.

child is to retain any names, including first names or surname, he may have acquired through the adoption. If the child has attained the age of ten, his wishes are taken into account.[980]

193. *Mexico, Philippines.* – In MEXICO, the adopted person, if a minor at the time of adoption, may contest his own adoption within one year after reaching majority. If he was otherwise without legal capacity at the time of adoption, he may contest his adoption within one year of regaining legal capacity (CC art. 394). While the MEXICAN Civil Code does not specify grounds for revocation, the PHILIPPINE Code allows rescission of an adoption on the grounds on which parental authority may be terminated (CC art. 347). The PHILIPPINE Code, on the other hand, sets a five year period of limitation reckoned from the time the cause giving rise to the rescission occurred.[981]

In MEXICO, an adoption may be revoked by mutual agreement of the adopter and the adopted person. (If the adopted person is a minor, the consent of the persons who consented to the adoption is necessary.) The adopter also may revoke adoption unilaterally by a showing of the adopted person's "ingratitude" (CC art. 405) which is defined as including the adopted person's criminal act (with a penalty of more than one year's imprisonment) against the person, honor or property of the adopter, the latter's spouse, his descendants or ascendants. "Ingratitude" may also be found if the adopted person has formally accused the adopter of a serious crime, even if the accusation was true, unless the crime was committed against the adopted person, his spouse, his descendants or ascendants. Finally, "ingratitude" may consist of the adopted person's refusal to support his impoverished adopter (CC art. 406).

In the PHILIPPINES, the adopter may petition the court for rescission or revocation of an adoption if the adopted person has made an attempt on the life of the adopter, when the adopted minor has abandoned the home of the adopter for more than three years or when the adopted person has definitely repudiated the adoption by other acts.[982]

In MEXICO, given the appropriate facts, the judge is bound to revoke the adoption, if he has convinced himself that the revocation occurred voluntarily or that revocation is in the best moral and economic interests of the adopted person (CC art. 407). The judge's decision invalidates the adoption and restores the status *quo ante* (CC art. 408). In the case of revocation for "ingratitude", moreover, the adoption is voided as of the time of the act in question, although the formal judgment is rendered later (CC art. 409). As in the case of the adoption itself, judgments relating to the revocation of an adoption must be communicated to the civil register of the locality in which the adoption was certified, so that the certification may be invalidated (CC art. 410).

iii. *Comparative Summary*

194. *Revocation and dissolution.* – While the artificially created adoptive family relationship may seem to offer a more acceptable target for dissolution than does the natural family relationship, many jurisdictions have concluded that no distinction should be made. Accordingly, some countries exclude the revocation of adoption altogether (FRANCE (full adoption), and, among many others, ARGENTINA, BOLIVIA, PORTUGAL)[983] or permit revocation only within narrowly defined limitations (ENGLAND, many states in the UNITED STATES).

Some jurisdictions distinguish between revocation and dissolution of adoption, with legal consequences resembling those of annulment of marriage *ex nunc* or *ex tunc*. Thus, an adoption which suffered from severe defects at the outset, material fraud, legal ineligibility to adopt, absence of consent, for instance, often may be revoked or annulled with retroactive effect, whereas some jurisdictions permit circumstances developing after an adoption has been completed to effect a dissolution *ex nunc*, typically through a judicial or administrative proceeding (*e.g.*, SOVIET UNION, and, among others, ARGENTINA, AUSTRIA).[984] Still other jurisdictions deny retroactive effect to the dissolution of adoption (FRANCE (limited adoption), ITALY, and compare the NETHERLANDS).[985]

Generally speaking, the treatment of revocation or dissolution of adoption is closely related to the function the legislator has assigned to adoption. Thus, where adoption is intended to mirror the natural family relationship closely, revocation or dissolution is made difficult or impossible, whereas revocation or dissolution is more readily available if the legislator has set a more limited role for adoption.

195. *Grounds for revocation.* – Grounds for revocation of adoption vary widely. Some juris-

[980] RSFSR FC art. 117 par. 3.

[981] *Nolledo* s. 5 (rule 100) par. 2.

[982] CC art. 348; *Moran* III sec. 1 (rule 100).

[983] ARGENTINA: *Ley de adopción* art. 18, 28; BOLIVIA: FC art. 228, 240; PORTUGAL: CC art. 1986 par. 1 and art. 2002 par. 1.

[984] ARGENTINA: *Ley de adopción* art. 28 par. 2, 30; AUSTRIA: CC § 184-185.

[985] ITALY: CC art. 309; NETHERLANDS: New CC art. 232 par. 3.

dictions employ general phrases relating to the "best interest" of the child or refer to "important reasons" (*e.g.*, WEST GERMANY, FRANCE, similarly, NETHERLANDS[986]). More commonly, however, grounds for dissolution are defined with precision.

Bases for revocation or dissolution of adoption may relate to the adoptive parents as well as to the adopted child (*e.g.*, FRANCE, WEST GERMANY, SOVIET UNION). Some jurisdictions, on the other hand, grant the right to revoke or demand dissolution to either the adoptive parents (states in the UNITED STATES) or, conversely, to the adopted child (for instance, the NETHERLANDS).[987]

Grounds relating to the adoptive child usually include insanity, idiocy, or may reach to serious faults of the child (a few states in the UNITED STATES). Other jurisdictions, on the other hand, do not permit an adoption to be revoked for such reasons (DENMARK[988]) or only for a limited period after the adoption (*e.g.*, EAST GERMANY: five years) or only if other, severely restrictive conditions are fulfilled (NORWAY[989]). Many systems take the position that adoptive parents, like natural parents, must adjust themselves to developments relating to their child that do not wholly conform to their expectations and thus make revocation or dissolution very difficult or impossible. This approach differs drastically from that of several LATIN jurisdictions which consider "gross ingratitude" a sufficient ground for the revocation of adoption (MEXICO) or refer to the grounds for disinheritance in allowing an adoption to be revoked (*e.g.*, BOLIVIA, PORTUGAL, SPAIN).[990] The NETHERLANDS occupies an interesting intermediate position and permits an adoption to be revoked only between the second and third year after the adoptive child has reached the age of majority.[991]

Grounds relating to the adoptive parents include serious offenses directed against the child (*e.g.*, DENMARK, NORWAY),[992] a serious violation of parental duties (*e.g.*, EAST GERMANY, FRANCE, and, among others, PORTUGAL[993]) or the grounds which determine loss of parental authority generally (PHILIPPINES), or failure to fulfill the support obligation relating to the adopted child (states in the UNITED STATES, also ARGENTINA[994]). The death of the adoptive parents may be a basis for dissolving an adoption, at least where dissolution is in the child's best interest (for instance, DENMARK, NORWAY).[995] ENGLAND, finally, may permit an adoption to be revoked if this will clear the way to legitimation of the child by marriage between the child's mother and father. Most everywhere, of course, the regular remedies covering the termination or curtailment of parental rights are applicable to adoptive parents as well as to the natural parents.

In some countries, an agreement between the adoptive parents and the adopted person may revoke the adoptive relationship (*e.g.*, MEXICO, WEST GERMANY). However, revocation by agreement may be reserved to adopted persons who have reached the age of majority (*e.g.*, EAST GERMANY, and, among other countries, ARGENTINA, GUATEMALA, NORWAY)[996] or if a minor child is involved, may be permitted only under special circumstances (DENMARK).[997]

196. *Consequences of revocation.* – Generally, the revocation or dissolution of adoption terminates the adoptive relationship in all respects (*e.g.*, EAST and WEST GERMANY, FRANCE, MEXICO, SOVIET UNION), although some countries may permit the retention of some incidents of the adoption even after dissolution. These incidents may include the surname the child acquired by adoption or his right of support (for instance, DENMARK, NORWAY),[998] or prohibitions on marriage that resulted from the adoptive relationship (*e.g.*, ARGENTINA[999]).

Typically, revocation or dissolution of the adoption revives the legal relationship between the child and his natural family (e.g., EAST and WEST GERMANY, SOVIET UNION, but also AUSTRIA, NETHERLANDS),[1000] or the court may restore the original relationship by specific order, if that seems appropriate (DENMARK, NORWAY).[1001]

986 New CC art. 231 par. 2 (obvious interest of the child).

987 New CC art. 231 par. 1.

988 *Cf. Adoptionslov* § 18, 19.

989 *Lov om adoption* § 23 par. 1.

990 BOLIVIA: FC art. 227 par. 1; PORTUGAL: CC art. 2000, 2166; SPAIN: CC art. 177 par. 3 no. 1.

991 New CC art. 233 par. 2.

992 DENMARK: *Adoptionslov* § 19 par. 1; NORWAY: *Lov om adoption* § 22 par. 1.

993 CC art. 2001 *lit.* a.

994 *Ley de adopción* art. 28 *lit.* a.

995 DENMARK: *Adoptionslov* § 18 par. 3; NORWAY: *Lov om adoption* § 21 par. 2.

996 ARGENTINA: *Ley de adopción* art. 28 par. 1 *lit.* b; GUATEMALA: CC art. 246 no. 1; NORWAY: *Lov om adoption* § 21 par. 1.

997 DENMARK: *Adoptionslov* § 18 par. 1 and 2.

998 DENMARK: *Adoptionslov* § 23 par. 1; *Lov om personnavne* § 10. NORWAY: *Lov om adoption* § 27 par. 1.

999 ARGENTINA: *Ley de adopción* art. 28 par. 2.

1000 AUSTRIA: CC § 185 par. 2; NETHERLANDS: New CC art. 232 par. 2.

1001 DENMARK: *Adoptionslov* § 23 par. 3. However, if the adoption was revoked by agreement with the natural parents, the restoration of the child's legal relationship to his natural parents is automatic (*Adoptionslov* § 23 par. 2). NORWAY: *Lov om adoption* § 27 par. 2.

VI. ARTIFICIAL INSEMINATION

197. *General.* – The relationship created by the modern practice of artificial insemination stands somewhere in between legitimate, illegitimate and adoptive kinship relations. Recent AMERICAN estimates of the incidence of children born in consequence of artificial insemination run from 1000 to 20000 children per year.[1002] Whatever the true figure, there clearly are enough children to take this matter out of the genre of science fiction and to raise realistic questions. The most important question goes to the legal status *vis-à-vis* the married mother's husband of a child conceived by artificial insemination with semen donated by a third party. Another question may be asked as to that child's status *vis-à-vis* the donor of the semen.

198. *United States.* – The world's legal systems have been surprisingly slow to respond. In AMERICA,[1003] for example, in the situation where a married woman had conceived a child with the consent of her husband by artificial insemination from a donor other than her husband, judicial treatment has ranged from a holding that the resultant child is the husband's legitimate child[1004] to the extreme of branding the child a bastard and the mother an adulteress.[1005] In many such cases, of course, the presumption of legitimacy applicable to children born in wedlock has helped the child to obtain legitimate status *vis-à-vis* his mother's husband. However, liability of the donor for support or even full legal responsibility as a parent remains at least a technical possibility.

Statutory treatment of the question has been scant.[1006] A 1967 OKLAHOMA statute sensibly provides that a child born to a married woman as a consequence of heterologous artificial insemination is legitimate as to the husband (and of course the mother), if the insemination was performed by an authorized medical practitioner with the written consent of husband and wife.[1007] A similar provision is contained in the new Uniform Parentage Act § 5.

199. *France, West Germany.* – Neither the FRENCH nor the GERMAN Codes cover the question of artificial insemination. A few years ago, the FRENCH Code Reform Commission proposed legislation to the effect that the mother's husband may not dispute the legitimacy of a child conceived by artificial insemination if he had given his written consent.[1008] The proposal was not enacted. Similarly, WEST GERMANY has failed to make specific provision for artificial insemination. As in FRANCE, the rules which presume the legitimacy of a child born to a married woman apply.[1009] This leaves open the possibility that a child conceived by artificial insemination with semen donated by someone not the mother's husband may be bastardized, even if the husband consented to the insemination.[1010] Indeed, there would seem to be no obstacle to the imposition of support liability on the donor, if his identity could be ascertained in a paternity action![1011]

(Completed in July 1975)

1002 *Wadlington,* Artificial Insemination – The Danger of a Poorly Kept Secret: 64 N.W.U.L.Rev. 777, 785 (1970).

1003 See generally *Clark* 157–58, 329; *Smith,* Through a Test Tube Darkly– Artificial Insemination and the Law: 67 Mich.L.Rev. 127 (1968); *Wadlington (supra* n. 1002) 777.

1004 *People v. Sorensen,* 68 Cal.2d 280, 66 Cal.Rptr. 7, 437 P.2d 495 (1968), involved a child who had been conceived through artificial insemination pursuant to an agreement between the husband and wife. In a nonsupport action, the mother's husband was held to be the "lawful father" of the child.

1005 *Doornbos v. Doornbos,* 23 U.S.L.W. 2308 (Super. Ct. Cook Co. 1954). The appeal was dismissed, but the appellate court held that the declaratory judgment was not binding on the child since it had not been represented in the proceedings, *Doornbos v. Doornbos,* 12 Ill. App.2d 473, 139 N.E.2d 844 (1 Dist. 1956). *Cf., Gursky v. Gursky,* 39 Misc.2d 1083, 242 N.Y.S.2d 406 (S.Ct. Kings Co. 1963); *Strnad v. Strnad,* 190 Misc. 786, 78 N.Y.S. 2d 390 (S.Ct.N.Y. Co. 1948). A new case summarizing legal developments in this area is *Matter of Adoption of Anonymous,* 72 Misc.2d 99, 345 N.Y.S. 2d 430 (Sur.Ct. Kings Co. 1973).

1006 CALIFORNIA PC § 270 (West Supp. 1968), dealing with failure to provide support, provides: "The husband of a woman who bears a child as a result of artificial insemination shall be considered the father of that child for the purposes of this section, if he consented in writing to the artificial insemination." CALIFORNIA CC § 196b (West Supp. 1968) provides: "The husband of a woman who bears a child as a result of artificial insemination shall be liable for support of the child in the same manner as if he were the natural father, if he consented in writing to the artificial insemination". A model statute on artificial insemination is proposed in Comment, 9 Vill.L.Rev. 77, 90–93 (1963).

1007 OKLAHOMA Stat.Ann. tit. 10 § 551–553 (1971). Similarly, GEORGIA Code Ann. § 74-9904, 74-101.1 (1973).

1008 *Gebler,* Le droit français de la filiation et la vérité (Nancy 1970) 153.

1009 CC § 1591 ss.; *Dölle* II 45; *Gernhuber* 506–507; *Palandt (-Lauterbach)* § 1591 no. 4.

1010 *Dölle* I 37; *cf., Gernhuber* 507.

1011 WEST GERMANY CC § 1593.

LIST OF PRINCIPAL WORKS

(1)

1. COMPARATIVE LAW: *Aksoy*, Das Erbrecht der ausserehelichen Kinder in rechtsvergleichender und kritischer Darstellung (2 vol.) (Thesis, Zürich 1954); *Bergmann and Ferid*, Internationales Ehe- und Kindschaftsrecht (ed. 4 Frankfurt 1969 ss.); *Bernhard*, Überblick über die Gestaltung des Unehelichenrechts in den osteuropäischen Ländern mit Hinweisen auf das sowjetzonale Recht: FamRZ 1962, 225-231; *García Cantero*, La situation juridique des enfants nés hors mariage. General Report for the IXth Congress of the International Academy of Comparative Law (section II A 4); *Ionasco, A.*, L'évolution de la législation sur la filiation naturelle: Rapports Généraux au VIIe Congrès International de Droit Comparé 1966 (Stockholm 1968) 142-156; *Krause*, Illegitimacy – Law and Social Policy (Indianapolis and New York 1971); *Rexroth*, Uneheliche Kinder: Rvgl. HWB VI (1938) 633-676; *Saario*, Study of Discrimination Against Persons Born out of Wedlock (New York 1967); *Schmidt-Hidding*, Die Stellung des unehelichen Kindes in den romanischen Rechtsordnungen Europas (Bielefeld 1967); *Wahl*, Adoption: Rvgl. HWB II (1929) 43-51; *Zweigert and Kötz*, Einführung in die Rechtsvergleichung I (Grundlagen) (Tübingen 1971).

2. CHILE: *Gesche Müller*, Investigación de la paternidad ilegitima (Concepción 1967).

3. CZECHOSLOVAKIA: *Plank*, Einige Bemerkungen zur Problematik der Feststellung der Vaterschaft: Stud. Jur.Pécs 65 (1968) 40.

4. DENMARK: *Bitsch*, Lov om børns retsstilling (Copenhagen 1969).

5. FRANCE: *Carbonnier*, Droit civil I (ed. 7 Paris 1967); *Ferid*, Das Französische Zivilrecht II (Frankfurt and Berlin 1971); *Madlener*, Das französische Unehelichenrecht (Bielefeld 1969); *Marty and Raynaud*, Droit civil I 2 (Les Personnes) (ed. 2 Paris 1967); *Mazeaud, H.L. and J.*, Leçons de droit civil I (ed. 3 Paris 1963) – cited Leçons; *Mazeaud, H., J. and L. (-de Juglart)*, Leçons de droit civil I 3 (ed. 4 Paris 1970-1971) – cited Leçons; *Mazeaud and Tunc*, Traité théorique et pratique de la responsabilité civile délictuelle et contractuelle (ed. 5 Paris 1957); *Planiol and Ripert*, Treatise on the Civil Law I 1 (Baton Rouge 1959); *Savatier*, L'évolution de la condition juridique des enfants naturels en droit français: Le statut juridique de l'enfant naturel (Bibliothèque de la Faculté de Droit de l'Université catholique de Louvain no. 1) (Brussels 1965) 37.

6. GERMANY: *Bechthold*, Die Neuregelung des Unehelichenrechts in beiden Teilen Deutschlands: ROW 1968, 1; *Werner*, The Unmarried Mother in German Literature (New York 1917).

a. EAST GERMANY: *Benjamin*, Das Familiengesetzbuch – Grundgesetz der Familie: NJ 1966, 1; *Halgasch*, Das Eltern-Kind-Verhältnis nach dem Familiengesetzbuch der DDR, insbesondere die Rechtsstellung des ausserhalb der Ehe geborenen Kindes: Stud.Jur.Pécs 65 (1968) 73; *Ministerium der Justiz* (ed.), Das Familienrecht der DDR – Lehrkommentar (Berlin 1966), cited FC-Commentary; *Schlicht*, Das Familien- und Familienverfahrensrecht der DDR (Tübingen and Basle 1970); *Schrodt*, Das Erbrecht des ausserhalb der Ehe geborenen Kindes: NJ 1966, 299.

b. WEST GERMANY: *Beitzke, Hosemann, Dahr and Schade*, Vaterschaftsgutachten für die gerichtliche Praxis (ed. 2 Göttingen 1965), cited *Beitzke a.o.*; *Dölle*, Familienrecht (2 vol.) (Karlsruhe 1964-1965); *Gernhuber*, Lehrbuch des Familienrechts (ed. 2 Munich 1971); *Jansen and Knöpfel*, Das neue Unehelichengesetz (Frankfurt and Berlin 1967); *Lutter*, Das Erbrecht des nichtehelichen Kindes (ed. 2 Frankfurt 1972); *Palandt*, Kommentar zum BGB (ed. 26 Munich and Berlin 1967); *Ponsold*, Lehrbuch der gerichtlichen Medizin (ed. 3 Stuttgart 1967); *Siehr*, Auswirkungen des Nichtehelichengesetzes auf das Internationale Privat- und Verfahrensrecht (Bielefeld 1972); *Staudinger (-Engler)*, Kommentar zum Bürgerlichen Gesetzbuch IV (ed. 10/11 Berlin 1967).

7. MEXICO: *De Pina*, Elementos de derecho civil mexicano I (ed. 5 Mexico 1968); *Rojina Villegas*, Compendio de derecho civil I (Mexico 1964).

8. NORWAY: *Arnholm*, Laerebok i Familierett (ed. 3 Oslo 1958); *Idsøe*, Vilkarene for idømmelse av farskap: Lov og Rett 1964, 321; *Lundevall*, Anvendelse av sannsynlighetsberegninger ved blodtypebestemmelser i farskapssaker: NRt. 1961, 123.

9. PEOPLE'S REPUBLIC OF CHINA: *Meijer*, Marriage Law and Policy in the Chinese People's Republic (Hong Kong 1971).

10. PHILIPPINES: *Moran*, Comments on the Rules of Court (6 vol.) (Manila 1963); *Nolledo*, Rules of Court Annotated (rev.ed. Manila 1968); *Padilla*, Civil Law. Civil Code I (ed. 3 Manila 1953); *Paras*, Civil Code of the Philippines Annotated I (ed. 6 Manila 1969).

11. POLAND: *Czachórski*, Einige Betrachtungen zum Unterhalt für Kinder geschiedener Eltern und unehelicher Kinder nach dem polnischen Recht: Stud.Jur. Pécs 65 (1968) 45; *Gwiazdomorski*, Die Anerkennung der unehelichen Vaterschaft: Stud.Jur.Pécs 65 (1968) 82; *Lasok*, Polish Family Law (New York and Leyden 1968).

12. SWEDEN: *Lind*, Faderskap och arvsrätt (Stockholm 1970).

13. UNION OF SOVIET SOCIALIST REPUBLICS: *Bilinsky*, Zu den "Grundlagen der Gesetzgebung der UdSSR und der Unionsrepubliken über Ehe und Familie": JbOstR 9 (1968) I, 181-208; *Geiger*, The Family in Soviet Russia (Cambridge, Mass. 1968); *Geilke*, Unifizierung und Reform der sowjetischen Familiengesetzgebung: WGO 10 (1968) 142; *Gorkin*, Concern for the Soviet Family: Sov.L.G. 7 (1968/69) no. 3, 29-35; *Korkisch*, Ehe- und Familienrecht der UdSSR: OER 1972, 2; *Kourilsky*, La loi de 1968 et l'évolution du droit soviétique de la famille: Annuaire de l'URSS 1969, 251; *Stone*, The New Fundamental Principles of Soviet Family Law and Their Social Background: 18 I.C.L.Q. 392-423 (1969); *Waehler*, Neues sowjetisches Familienrecht: FamRZ 1968, 557.

14. UNITED KINGDOM: *Bromley*, Family Law (ed. 3

London 1966); *Hall*, The Law of Adoption (London 1928); *Halsbury* (- *Whiteside*), Laws of England III (ed. 3 London 1953) *s.v.* Bastardy and Legitimation – cited Bastardy; *Hooper*, The Law of Illegitimacy (London 1911); *Nicolas*, A Treatise on the Law of Adulterine Bastardy (London 1836).

15. UNITED STATES OF AMERICA: *Clark*, The Law of Domestic Relations in the United States (St.Paul, Minn. 1968); *Leavy*, The Law of Adoption (ed. 2 New York 1954); *Madden*, Illustrative Cases on Persons and Domestic Relations (ed. 2 St.Paul, Minn. 1931); *Sussman*, Blood Grouping Tests (Springfield, Ill. 1968).

(2)

LIST OF STATUTORY MATERIAL

ALBANIA: *Kodit Familjes* (Family Code) no. 4020 of 23 June 1965 (G.Z. no. 7/1965; German transl.: *Bergmann and Ferid, s.v.* Albanien 13) – cited FC.

ARGENTINA: *Ley de adopción* (Adoption Act) no. 19134 of 21 July 1971 (ADLA XXXI-B, 1408; German transl.: *Bergmann and Ferid, s.v.* Argentinien 42); *Ley del nombre* (Law Concerning Names) no. 18248 of 10 June 1969 (ADLA XXIX-B, 1420; German transl.: *Bergmann and Ferid, s.v.* Argentinien 46).

AUSTRIA: *Bundesgesetz über die Neuordnung der Rechtsstellung des unehelichen Kindes* (Law Reforming the Legal Status of Illegitimate Children) of 30 Oct. 1970 (BGBl. no. 342/1970); *Ehegesetz* (Marriage Act) of 6 July 1938 (RGBl. I 807).

BULGARIA: *Semeen Kodeks* (Family Code) of 15 March 1968 (D.V. no. 23 of 22 March 1968; German transl.: *Bergmann and Ferid, s.v.* Bulgarien 30) – cited FC; *Zakon no. 691 za Licata i Semejstvoto* (Law of Persons and Family) of 23 July 1949 (D.V. no. 182 of 9 Aug. 1949; German transl.: *Bergmann and Ferid, s.v.* Bulgarien 24).

CHILE: *Ley no. 7613 establece disposiciones sobre la adopción* (Adoption Act) of 11 Oct. 1943 (DO 21 Oct. 1943; German transl.: *Bergmann and Ferid, s.v.* Chile 44).

CHINA: Marriage Law of the People's Republic of China of 13 April 1950 (Engl. transl.: *Meijer*, Marriage Law and Policy in the Chinese People's Republic (Hong Kong 1971) 300–302); Marriage Law of the Chinese Soviet Republic of 8 April 1934 (Engl. transl.: *ibidem* 283–284).

CZECHOSLOVAKIA: *Zákon o rodině* (Family Code) of 4 Dec. 1963 (Sb. 1963 no. 94; German transl.: *Bergmann and Ferid, s.v.* Tschechoslowakei 25) – cited FC.

DENMARK: *Adoptionslov* (Adoption Act) no. 279 of 7 June 1972 (Dansk Lovsamling 1972, 207; German transl.: *Bergmann and Ferid, s.v. Dänemark* 41); *Lov no. 140 om personnavne* (Law Concerning Names) of 17 May 1961 (Dansk Lovsamling 1961, 105; German transl.: *Bergmann and Ferid, s.v.* Dänemark 44); *Lov no. 200 om børns retsstilling* (Law on the Legal Position of Children) of 18 May 1960 (Dansk Lovsamling 1960, 181; German transl.: *Bergmann and Ferid, s.v.* Dänemark 31) – cited *Lov no. 200.*

FRANCE: *Loi no. 72-3 sur la filiation* (Law on Parentage) of 3 Jan. 1972 (JO 5 Jan. p. 145; German transl.: *Bergmann and Ferid, s.v.* Frankreich 53); *Loi sur la liberté de la presse* (Law on Freedom of the Press) of 29 July 1881 (D.P.1881.4.65).

GERMANY (EAST): *Richtlinie no. 23 des Plenums des Obersten Gerichts der Deutschen Demokratischen Republik zur Feststellung und Anfechtung der Vaterschaft* (Directive of the Plenum of the Supreme Court Concerning Ascertainment and Avoidance of Paternity) of 22 March 1967 (GBl. II 177) – cited Directive no. 23; *Gesetz über das Personenstandswesen (Personenstandsgesetz)* (Law on Personal Status) of 16 Nov. 1956, as revised 13 Oct. 1966 (GBl. I 87); *Familienverfahrensordnung* (Family Court Procedure) of 17 Feb. 1966 (GBl. II 171); *Familiengesetzbuch* (Family Code) of 20 Dec. 1965 (GBl. 1966 I 1) – cited FC; *Einführungsgesetz zum Familiengesetzbuch* (Law Introducing the Family Code) of 20 Dec. 1965 (GBl. 1966 I 19) – cited *Einführungsgesetz; Verordnung über die Annahme an Kindes Statt* (Decreee Concerning Adoption) of 29 Nov. 1956 (GBl. I 1326).

GERMANY (WEST): *Gesetz über die rechtliche Stellung der nichtehelichen Kinder* (Act on the Legal Position of Illegitimate Children) of 19 Aug. 1969 (BGBl. I 1243) – cited *Nichtehelichengesetz; Personenstandsgesetz* (Law on Personal Status) of 3 Nov. 1937, as revised 8 Aug. 1957 (BGBl. I 1125); *Ehegesetz* (Marriage Act) of 20 Feb. 1946 (KRABl. 77, amended 294); *Gesetz zur Erleichterung der Annahme an Kindes Statt* (Law Facilitating Adoption) of 8 Aug. 1950 (BGBl. 356).

IRELAND: Adoption Act, 1952 (no. 25 of 1952); Legitimacy Act, 1931 (no. 13 of 1931); Illegitimate Children (Affiliation Orders) Act, 1930 (no. 17 of 1930).

ISRAEL: Adoption Act, 5720-1960 (14 LSI 93).

IVORY COAST: *Loi no. 64-375 sur mariage* (Law on Marriage) of 7 Oct. 1964 (JO no. 59 p. 1440; German transl.: *Bergmann and Ferid, s.v.* Elfenbeinküste 19).

NORWAY: *Lov om arv* (Law Concerning Inheritance) of 3 March 1972 no. 5 (Norges Lover 1685-1973 (Oslo 1974) 2515); *Lov om folketrygd* (Law Concerning Insurance) of 17 June 1966 no. 12 (Norges Lover 1685-1973 (Oslo 1974) 2288); *Lov om personnamn* (Law Concerning Names) of 29 May 1964 no. 1 (Norges Lover 1685-1973 (Oslo 1974) 2144; German transl.: *Bergmann and Ferid, s.v.* Norwegen 31); *Lov om gransking av arvemerke til bruk i barnefarsak* (Law Concerning Investigation of Heritable Traits in Paternity Disputes) of 21 Dec. 1956 no. 8 (Norges Lover 1685-1973 (Oslo 1974) 1759); *Lov om born i ekteskap* (Law Concerning Legitimate Children) of 21 Dec. 1956 no. 9 (Norges Lover 1685-1973 (Oslo 1974) 1759; German transl.: *Bergmann and Ferid, s.v.* Norwegen 19) – cited *Lov no. 9; Lov om born utanom ekteskap* (Law Concerning Illegitimate Children) of 21 Dec. 1956 no. 10 (Norges Lover 1685-1973 (Oslo 1974) 1764; German transl.: *Bergmann and Ferid, s.v.* Norwegen 23) – cited *Lov no. 10; Lov om syketrygd* (Law Concerning Health Insurance) of 2 March 1956 no. 2 (Norges Lover 1682-1969 (Oslo 1970) 1864); *Lov om vergemaal for umyndige* (Law Concerning Guardianship for Minors) of 22 April 1927 no. 3 (Norges Lover 1685-1973) (Oslo 1974) 951) – cited *Lov no. 3; Lov om adoption* (Adoption Act) of 2 April 1917, as revised (Norges Lover 1685-1973 (Oslo 1974) 758); *Lov angaaende odels- og aasetesretten* (Law Concerning Rights of *odel* and *aasete*) of 26 June 1821 (Norges Lover 1685-1973 (Oslo 1974) 36).

POLAND: *Kodeks rodzinny i opiekuńczy* (Family and Guardianship Code) of 25 Feb. 1964 (Dz.U. 1964 no. 9 pos. 59; German transl.: *Bergmann and Ferid, s.v.* Polen 20) – cited FC.

RUMANIA: *Codul Familiei* (Family Code) of 29 Dec. 1953 (B.O. no. 1/1954; German transl.: *Bergmann and Ferid, s.v.* Rumänien 5).

SWEDEN: *Namnlag* (Law Concerning Names) of 11 Oct. 1963 (Sveriges Rikes Lag 1975, B 1073; German transl.: *Bergmann and Ferid, s.v.* Schweden 41); *Föräldrabalk* (Parents Act) of 10 June 1949, as amended by Law of 17 Dec. 1970 (Sveriges Rikes Lag 1975, 46; German transl.: *Bergmann and Ferid, s.v.* Schweden 30); *Giftermålsbalk* (Marriage Act) of 11 June 1920, as revised (Sveriges Rikes Lag 1975, 5; German transl.: *Bergmann and Ferid, s.v.* Schweden 14).

UNION OF SOVIET SOCIALIST REPUBLICS: *Postanovlenie plenuma no. 10 ot 4 dekabri͡a 1969 g. o praktike primenenii͡a sudami Osnov zakonodatelstva Soi͡uza SSR i soi͡uznykh respublik o brake i seme* (Resolution no. 10 of the Plenum of the Supreme Court of the USSR on the Practical Application by Courts of the Fundamentals on Marriage and Family of 4 Dec. 1969) (Sbornik Postanovleniĭ Plenuma Verkhovnogo Suda SSSR 1924–1973 (Moscow 1974) 182) – cited Resolution no. 10; *Kodeks o brake i seme RSFSR* (Code on Marriage and the Family of the RSFSR) of 30 July 1969 (VVS RSFSR 1969 no. 32 pos. 1086; German transl.: *Bergmann and Ferid, s.v.* UdSSR-RSFSR 56) – cited RSFSR FC; *Osnovy zakonodatelstva Soi͡uza SSR i soi͡uznykh respublik o brake i seme* (Fundamentals of Legislation of the USSR and the Union Republics on Marriage and Family) of 27 June 1968 (VVS SSSR 1968 no. 27 pos. 241; English transl.: 18 I.C.L.Q. 410 (1969); German transl.: *Bergmann and Ferid, s.v.* UdSSR 38) – cited Fundamentals on Family Law; *Zakon SSSR ob utverzhdenii Osnov Zakonodatelstva Soi͡uza SSR i soi͡uznykh respublik o brake i seme* (Law ratifying the Fundamentals of Legislation of the USSR and the Union Republics on Marriage and Family) of 27 June 1968 (VVS SSSR 1968 no. 27 pos. 241) – cited Ratification Law; *O pori͡adke primenenii͡a Ukaza Prezidiuma Verkhovnogo Soveta SSSR ot 8 ii͡uli͡a 1944 g. v. otnoshenii deteĭ, roditeli kotorykh ne sostoi͡at mezhdu soboĭ v zaregistrirovannom brake* (Decree of the Presidium of the Supreme Soviet of the USSR Concerning the Application of the Law of 8 July 1944 to Children Whose Parents do not Live in Registered Marriages) of 14 March 1945 (VVS RSFSR 1945 no. 15 pos. 2); *Ukaz Prezidiuma verkhovnogo Soveta SSSR ot 8 ii͡uli͡a 1944 g. ob uvelichenii gosudarstvennoĭ pomoshchi beremennym zhenshchinam, mnogodetnym i odinokim materi͡am* (Decree of the Presidium of the Supreme Soviet of the USSR Concerning Increased Government Aid to Pregnant Women, Women With Many Children and Unmarried Women) of 8 July 1944 (VVS SSSR 1944 no. 37 pos. 1); *Kodeks zakonov o brake, seme i opeke* (Code on Marriage, Family and Guardianship) of 19 Nov. 1926 (Sob.uzak. RSFSR 1926 no. 82 pos.612) – cited RSFSR Family Code 1926; *Kodeks zakonov ob aktakh grazhdanskogo sostoi͡anii͡a, brachnom, semeĭnom i opekunskom prave* (Code on Acts of Personal Status, Marriage, Family and Guardianship Law) of 16 Oct. 1918 (Sob.uzak. RSFSR 1918 I no. 76–77 pos. 818) – cited RSFSR Family Code 1918.

UNITED KINGDOM: Matrimonial Causes Act 1973, c. 18; Family Law Reform Act 1969, c. 46; Maintenance Orders Act 1968, c. 36; Ministry of Social Security Act 1966, c. 20; Matrimonial Causes Act 1965, c. 72; Matrimonial Proceedings Act, 1960 (Eliz. 2, c. 48); Legitimacy Act, 1959 (7 & 8 Eliz. 2, c. 73); Adoption Act, 1958 (7 & 8 Eliz. 2, c. 5); Maintenance Orders Act, 1958 (6 & 7 Eliz. 2, c. 39); Affiliation Proceedings Act, 1957 (5 & 6 Eliz. 2, c. 55); Magistrates' Courts Act, 1952 (15 & 16 Geo. 6 and 1 Eliz. 2, c. 55); Maintenance Orders Act, 1950 (14 Geo. 6, c. 37); National Assistance Act, 1948 (11 & 12 Geo. 6, c. 29); Education Act, 1944 (7 & 8 Geo. 6, c. 31); Inheritance (Family Provision) Act, 1938 (1 & 2 Geo. 6, c. 45); Legitimacy Act, 1926 (16 & 17 Geo. 5, c. 60); Adoption of Children Act, 1926 (16 & 17 Geo. 5, c. 29).

UNITED STATES OF AMERICA: Social Services Amendments of Jan. 4, 1975 (P.L. 93-647) (88 Stat. 2351, 42 U.S.C. § 651) part B; Uniform Parentage Act, 9 U.L.A. (Cumulative Annual Pocket Part 1975, 182); Uniform Reciprocal Enforcement of Support Act, 1968, 9 U.L.A. 805; 1958 Act, 9 U.L.A. 885; Uniform Probate Code, 8 U.L.A. 287.

YUGOSLAVIA: *Osnovi zakon o odnosima roditelja i djece* (Fundamental Law on the Relations Between Parents and Children) of 1 Feb. 1947 (Sl.l.Y. no. 104/1947 pos. 761) as amended by Law of 1 March 1965 (Sl.l.Y. no. 10/1965 pos. 156; German transl.: *Bergmann and Ferid, s.v.* Jugoslawien 41); *Osnovi zakon o braku* (Fundamental Law on Marriage) of 3 April 1946 (Sl.l.Y. no. 29/1946 pos. 182) as revised by Law of 28 April (Sl.l.Y. no. 28/1965 pos. 486).

DETAILED TABLE OF CONTENTS

Volume IV

PERSONS AND FAMILY

Aleck Chloros · *Chief Editor*

PROVISIONAL TABLE OF CONTENTS

Bei Fragen zur Produktsicherheit wenden Sie sich bitte an:
If you have any questions regarding product safety,
please contact:

Walter de Gruyter GmbH
Genthiner Straße 13
10785 Berlin
productsafety@degruyterbrill.com